INSTITUTIONAL CONSTRUCTIVISM IN SOCIAL SCIENCES AND LAW

This book proposes a new institutional constructivist model, for social scientific and legal enquiries, based on the interrelations within the social and political world and the application of change in EU laws and politics. Much of the research conducted in social sciences and law examines the diverse activities of individuals and collectivities and the role of institutions in the social and political world. Although there exist many vantage points from which one can gain entry into understanding how agents in the world act, interact, shape and bear the world, socio-legal scientific epistemology has found monism and dualism to be convincing models.

This book argues that current models do not capture the complexity of our micro-worlds, macro-worlds and meso-worlds. Nor can they account for the forms and patterns of socio-legal change. Mind, time and change are brought together in an attempt to contribute to socio-legal epistemology and to enhance its toolkit.

DORA KOSTAKOPOULOU is Professor of European Union Law, European Integration and Public Policy at the University of Warwick.

INSTITUTIONAL CONSTRUCTIVISM IN SOCIAL SCIENCES AND LAW

Frames of Mind, Patterns of Change

DORA KOSTAKOPOULOU
University of Warwick

CAMBRIDGE
UNIVERSITY PRESS

CAMBRIDGE
UNIVERSITY PRESS

University Printing House, Cambridge CB2 8BS, United Kingdom

One Liberty Plaza, 20th Floor, New York, NY 10006, USA

477 Williamstown Road, Port Melbourne, VIC 3207, Australia

314–321, 3rd Floor, Plot 3, Splendor Forum, Jasola District Centre, New Delhi – 110025, India

79 Anson Road, #06-04/06, Singapore 079906

Cambridge University Press is part of the University of Cambridge.

It furthers the University's mission by disseminating knowledge in the pursuit of education, learning, and research at the highest international levels of excellence.

www.cambridge.org
Information on this title: www.cambridge.org/9781108470544
DOI: 10.1017/9781108556804

First published 2018

Printed and bound in Great Britain by Clays Ltd, Elcograf S.p.A.

A catalogue record for this publication is available from the British Library.

ISBN 978-1-108-47054-4 Hardback

To Euclid

CONTENTS

FIGURES

TABLE

ACKNOWLEDGEMENTS

The ideas on which this book is based were developed during my British Academy Thanks Offering to Britain Fellowship, which I held at Manchester University. Sir Martin Harris, then Vice-Chancellor, and Professor Andrew Sanders, then Head of Manchester Law School, made it possible for me to accept the Fellowship and to have the opportunity to develop my thoughts. The first paper on institutional constructivism appeared in the *Modern Law Review* in 2005 and is reproduced in this book without major revisions. Subsequent work has advanced, but has not essentially changed, my views. I am grateful to many colleagues in the European Union and the United States who listened to various presentations I have made or read my papers and commented on them. There is hardly a page in this book that has not benefited from their criticism. Mrs Finola O'Sullivan at Cambridge University Press has also given me invaluable assistance and advice. In addition, I would like to thank the editors, and publishers, of the *Modern Law Review, European Law Review* and the *Cambridge Yearbook of European Legal Studies* for their permission to use previously published material. Finally, Miles Davis and Freddie Hubbard kept me excellent company for years and my family has been a source of support and inspiration. I dedicate this book to Euclid who likes philosophy.

An Introduction on Schemata: Constructing Theories or Explanation

In *Republic*, Plato asked an interesting question: 'Where the starting point is something one does not know, and the conclusion and the intervening steps are fabricated out of things one does not know, how on earth can this sort of entailment ever become knowledge?'[1] For Plato, that was a paradox. His preferred solution was the replacement of the unknown starting point with a presumed known; a standpoint that precludes any further questioning. If such a standpoint existed, then knowledge could be attained. What Plato essentially proposed was an axiomatic approach. Axioms are believed to be true propositions and therefore can serve as foundations. On axiomatic premises, knowers or knowledge-seekers can visualise, interpret, explain and understand. This is not only because axiomatic premises appear to be correct, but because they are accepted as correct. Once the structure of an axiomatic system is laid out, further propositions can arise which are then put to tests, be they empirical or logical or otherwise, with a view to discovering whether they are true or false.

Sciences, including physics and mathematics, still follow the axiomatic approach. Social sciences, however, rely on a different approach. They predominantly work with schemata, not axioms.[2] Schemata, namely schemes, frames, configurations or systems of arrangements, are imaginary constructs. We need conceptual frames and frameworks in order to make our worlds intelligible. The term 'our worlds' refers to us, our associates, social relations, political relations and practices and physical environments – in short of all those things around us and all those relations affecting us. We need frames[3] and frameworks, i.e., organised sets of propositions, in order

[1] Republic, VII, 533c.

[2] It is interesting that Husserl refused the idea of the existence of 'a mathematics of phenomena'; E. Husserl, 'Die Frage nach dem Ursprung der Geometrie als intentional – historisches Problem', I *Revue internationale de philosophie*, 1939, p. 210.

[3] Goffman defined frames as 'the principles of organisation which govern social events and the actor's subjective involvement in them'; Erving Goffman, *Frame Analysis: An Essay on the Organisation of Experience* (New York: Harper and Row, 1974), p. 10.

to categorise the sensations we receive, to make sense of our experiences, to respond to stimuli, to act, to dream and to imagine. Conceptual formulations allow us to name things, find patterns and links, and to invest them with significance. Patterns often become paradigms and paradigms become theoretical frameworks by gaining broadness and generalisability.

The role, and significance, of schemata in social sciences is thus undeniable. More importantly, working with schemata and rearranging conceptualisations have some distinct advantages. They require neither a starting point, nor an axiomatic cornerstone, nor a telos – that is, an end. All that is required is that a schema fits the world, be this social, personal, political or otherwise. Once a fitting and viable schema is in operation, ordinary human beings and researchers can join in the quest for knowledge in 'the middle of a game'.[4] The viable schema thus becomes a reliable one.

We are immersed in social realities[5] and are surrounded by collective representations which become intelligible through schemata. We grow in social communities having their stock of knowledge and their own interpretative logics and we participate in the interpretation, construction and reconstruction of these realities until we die. In this respect, the concepts, theories, frames and assumptions we use must accommodate our perceptions and experiences, make sense and guide our actions. For this reason, they tend to be adaptable and revisable. If they become irrelevant,[6] we tend to shake them off. They do not any longer appeal to us because they cannot serve us.

The same applies with respect to schemata used in social scientific research. They need to be relevant, useful, endowed with explanatory power and, according to empiricists, with predictive scope as well. In this way, they are reliable. If they are not, they are substituted by, or blended with, other conceptualisations. In fact, there exists a groundless and reflexive circularity in social scientific thinking and schematism. For like Alfred Tennyson's Ulysses, social scientists are always wondering, discovering

[4] Hodes explicitly stated that the main aim of scientific inquiry is to understand what is going on; Robert Hodes, 'Aims and Methods of Scientific Research', Occasional Paper No. 9 (New York: American Institute of Marxist Studies, 1968), pp. 11–14.

[5] According to Hoover, 'the scientific way of thought is one of the number of strategies by which we try to cope with a vital reality: the uncertainty of life', Kenneth R. Hoover, *The Elements of Social Scientific Thinking*, 5th edn (New York: St Martin's Press, 1992), p. 5.

[6] Compare here Arthur L. Stinchcombe, *Constructing Social Theories* (New York: Harcourt, Brace and World, Inc., 1968); Alfred Schutz, 'Concept and Theory Formation in the Social Sciences' in M. Natanson (ed.), *Philosophy of the Social Sciences* (New York: Random House, 1963).

and yearning for more knowledge.[7] They seek 'to follow knowledge like a sinking star / Beyond the utmost bound of human thought'.[8]

Tennyson was only twenty-one years old when he wrote this poem. Perhaps surprisingly for his age, he felt demoralised, sad, almost worn out. Yet he summoned all his inner courage in order to rise above adversity by writing a masterpiece in which he has Ulysses remarking that 'all experience is an arch wherethro'/Gleams that untravell'd world ...'[9] Seeing the arch from afar, individuals know that they may yet journey to unknown places. If Tennyson's Ulysses were invited to ponder over Plato's question mentioned at the outset, I imagine he would probably remark that 'this is precisely the point of seeking knowledge'.[10] And as knowledge 'piles on' knowledge, human beings develop more sophisticated schemata and conceptual reasoning in order to eliminate fallacies. By so doing, they satisfy their 'yearning' for answers and thus their desire to know how they ought to live.

Everything we do is governed by schemata; by frames, concepts, frameworks, systems of thought, ideological templates and so on. Observing the world, measuring, making connections, understanding, behaving in a certain way, all are frame-loaded operations. For example, we cannot observe properly if we do not invent the concept of perception. And perception is influenced by ideas.[11] Similarly, we cannot measure if we do not have the concept of length and the proclivity to make comparisons in length, that is, to ascertain whether the distance between x and y is shorter or longer. In addition, we cannot make connections without the influence of a priori classifications of things, an understanding of sameness and difference, and we cannot reach an understanding of relations without invoking certain valuations as to how relations within a certain context ought to be or by using conventional labels for their functionality or disfunctionality.

[7] Alfred Lord Tennyson, Ulysses, available at www.poetryfoundation.org/poem/174659, accessed 30 June 2015.

[8] Ibid.

[9] Ibid.

[10] John Locke had made a very honest observation in his *Essay Concerning Human Understanding*: 'it is ambition enough to be employed as an under-labourer in clearing the ground a little, and removing some of the rubbish that lies in the way to knowledge'; The Epistle to the Reader in *The Works of John Locke*, Vol. 1 [An Essay Concerning Human Understanding, Part 1] [1689].

[11] The British philosopher of Science William Whewell (1794–1866) had observed this. See his book entitled *The Philosophy of the Inductive Sciences* (London: Routledge/Thoemmes Press, 1996 [1840]). For a discussion of his work, see Jonathon W. Moses and Torbjorn L. Knutsen, *Ways of Knowing: Competing Methodologies in Social and Political Research*, 2nd edn (Houndmills Basingstoke: Palgrave Macmillan, 2012), ch. 8.

This has its disadvantages too; quite often, habits of thought, certain beliefs or hidden assumptions may 'contribute both to the way in which a question is construed and, also, to the way certain answers to it are judged'.[12] In other words, like arts and humanities, social sciences are anchored on creative thinking. Only minds perceive, explain, connect, understand, test, reflect, critique and imagine. Minds dare to make those important leaps of thought.

Socio-political life also requires schemata. People stand in mutual reception (and in opposition) and thus need to make judgments about their actions, reactions and relations. In order to make judgments, and, more importantly, to make significant judgements, that is, judgments that have effects and are life-changing, there must be frames, standards that are set and approaches that can be developed. There also exist reversions, misconceptions, changed courses of action and, generally speaking, circumstances calling for a fresh approach, a new direction and a new frame of mind. Political organisations, on the other hand, need legitimising narratives and ideas to inspire politics and policy-making.

Plato's paradox about knowledge mentioned at the start of this introduction, Tennyson's arch of knowledge, conceptual advancements and paradigm shifts in social science[13] and ordinary processes of human cognition and behaviour are possible because we 'journey' in time and through time. Ulysses' sea is time itself, and journeying is only possible within a motion-ridden world that brings about change to, and in, us.[14] However reasonable our adjustments to it might be and however secure we might feel in the realities we construct, we cannot foreclose shifts in our conceptions and different realisations. We need to leave room for revelations that our angles are incorrect, for reformism and for transformation. Transformations, be they in society, social sciences or ourselves, essentially commence as re-orientations. Things suddenly look different. From this standpoint, new

[12] Gabriel Stolzenberg, 'Can an Inquiry into the Foundations of Mathematics Tell Us Anything Interesting about the Mind?' in Paul Watzlawick (ed.), *The Invented Reality: How Do We Know What We Believe We Know?* (New York: W. W. Norton and Company, 1984), pp. 257–308, 259. See also Imre Lakatos, *Proofs and Refutations: The Logic of Mathematical Discovery* (Cambridge: Cambridge University Press, 1979). Compare, Karl Popper, *Objective Knowledge: An Evolutionary Approach* (Oxford: Oxford University Press, 1972).

[13] T. Kuhn, *The Structure of Scientific Revolutions*, 3rd edn (Chicago, IL: Chicago University Press, 1996); *The Essential Tension* (Chicago, IL: Chicago University Press, 1977).

[14] As Shelley poignantly observed in his poem entitled 'Mutability': 'Man's yesterday may ne'er be like his morrow; Nought may endure but Mutability'; Percy Bysshe Shelley, *Poems* (London: Carlton Classics, 1924), p. 60.

explorations are possible, new meanings can be discovered and the fine-structure of a relation to which things can be added is revealed.

In this volume, I bring mind, time[15] and change together with a view to making a contribution to social epistemology and to enhancing its toolkit. My interest in social epistemology, that is, in how knowledge is acquired in social sciences, is unravelled through the themes of conceptual frames and patterns of change and their application in the field of EU law and politics. I essentially raise three questions, as follows. (1) If our inquiries started from the premise that the world, i.e., both micro- and macro-realities, is unbelievably complex, what kind of methodological models would we develop (– this is the issue of sufficient complexity)? Much of social epistemology has been based on either monistic paradigms or on dualisms, be they explicit or implicit. Yet, on closer inspection of both, we realise that monism and dualism have more in common than is generally believed (– this is discussed in detail in the subsequent Chapter 1). (2) If this were conceded, how could we move beyond monism and dualism in social sciences? What variables could one envisage and how would we conceive of their relations (– this is the issue of the choice of variables)? In the subsequent discussion, I argue that beyond the cause and effect epistemological principle, the empiricist tendency to explain wholes by parts,[16] one-link theories, the principle of constraints that has characterised scientific evolutionism and the dualism of dialectics, lies connectionalism; a philosophy of relations among variables and processual thinking. (3) Finally, since the realities to be known are continuously changing, how should social scientists conceive of, theorise and understand change (– this is the issue of imagery)? What are its modalities and patterns? And what might the accommodation of continuous change within an indeterministic matrix require? These questions are explored in Chapter 3 and the subsequent discussion.

The answers to these questions are far from simple. They require both mappings and multivariable models. As regards the former, in this book I use constructivism as my 'arch'. By discussing the many contributions of constructivism in social sciences, I show how these perspectives have

[15] Social scientific thinking would benefit from a more sustained attention to time and space. Notable theorists of the latter include Henri Bergson, George Herbert Mead, Martin Heidegger, Marcel Proust, Paul Ricoeur, Edward Soja, Robert Ashley, Paul Pierson, Michael Lockwood, Christopher Ray, Martin Friedman and Reinhart Koselleck. But space and time are relatively under-researched in law.

[16] Pragmatist philosophers and, in particular, William James noted this at the turn of the twentieth century.

enabled us to construct realities and move to more complex discussions and from there to continue our quest for understanding the balance among being, knowing, acting and reflecting. In terms of models, I develop a *Connexio Rerum* model and show the productive quality of turning things into relations and of highlighting connections within moving ensembles. The subsequent chapters reveal how I draw the proposed map of knowing, gather things together and envision various connections.

I do not wish to claim that the subsequent discussion will provide a perfect map for scholarly exploration. Nor do I believe that other approaches are necessarily deficient in providing lenses through which to understand and explore the world.[17] But I do believe that this volume will furnish a useful and reliable map[18] for social scientific explorations in law and in other disciplines, such as political science, sociology and European studies.

Because this is a book on methodology, normative theorising does not receive a visible and sustained exposure. Unlike my previous work, the subsequent discussion does not address the question of alternative social realities, does not suggest new democratic practices and does not embark upon the redesign of institutions. I am more concerned about drawing maps for knowledge acquisition and the understanding of realities, institutions and events that enable a new gaze on them and on our relation to them. Certainly, questions of doxa, power, privilege and prejudice cannot be disentangled from the socio-legal context. Nor are social scientists and the work they produce separate from it. Methodological principles, models and concerns, on the other hand, rely on the freedom to explore and experiment, on democratic critique and the desire to improve the conditions of our lives and society, in general. In writing this book, I take all the above for granted and steer the discussion explicitly and in a more concerted manner within the confines of the epistemological domain, knowing that

[17] Generally speaking, it is true that researchers are interested in justifying their chosen methodology and illustrating its superiority. Readers, on the other hand, always entertain doubts. They tend to ask questions, such as: Why is this better than others? Does it help produce more accurate results? Does it help us tell more interesting stories? Does it provide better explanations? How does it compare to other methods? What are the noticeable differences between (a) and (b)? What are the limitations? What are their strengths? Do they provide suitable adjustments to changeable situations? Do they lead to more reliable data?

[18] I follow, here, Quine's argument that the test of a good system of logic is the extent to which it functions as a way for scientists to 'see the world'. And although I do not share the criteria he lists as the determining factors in comparing systems, I agree with him that the litmus test is how well it works; V. W. Quine, *Philosophy of Logic* (Englewood Cliffs, NJ: Prentice-Hall, 1970).

the latter cannot be kept separate from 'conviction and critique',[19] and that methodological change is more often than not linked with socio-political visions and transformation.[20]

The Arch of Social Epistemology and the Glimpse of a Post-Disciplinary World

If the role of social science is to make a difference to the way we live and how we are governed,[21] the role of social epistemology has been to aid social scientists in this endeavour by devising premises, concepts and explanatory models. And in the same way that theorists' diagnoses of social phenomena diverge, there exists dissent in social epistemology as to which method, which theory and which variable(s) might be the most fruitful and reliable in scientific inquiries. Social sciences entail fields with fuzzy boundaries, contested thinking and contested methodologies.

This does not mean that testable propositions are scarce. Nor does it imply that judgement, reflexive criticism and reason cannot serve to highlight those methods of social knowledge which are insightful and promising. Once the very first seeds of a theory are planted, scholars tend to build an arch from which they can travel.[22] Initially, this is an imperceptible process. But as thematic applications of the theory increase, one can discern the spur towards innovation, dynamism and inspiring engagements. This continues until the limitations of a theory become apparent. When this happens, its adherents obtain cold feet. For example, in his *Essays on Truth and Reality* (1914), Bradley defended what has been termed the coherence theory of truth, which is the assumption of the existence of an internal consistency between one's perception of an object and the object itself.[23] In the theory of language this gave rise to the semantic theory of truth, which was wonderfully articulated by Carnap, Tarski and the work of the logical

[19] I borrow this from Paul Ricoeur, *Critique and Conviction* (Cambridge: Polity Press, 1998).

[20] Pierre Bourdieu's work exemplifies this. His 'thinking tools' had a broader socio-political purpose, namely, to unravel truth and to 'liberate' individuals and society from the hegemonic social forces. See, *inter alia*, *Science of Science and Reflexivity*, trans. R. Nice (Cambridge: Polity, 2004); *Interventions 1961–2001* (Marseilles: Agone, 2002); *Acts of Resistance: Against the New Myths of Our Time*, trans. R. Nice (Cambridge: Polity, 1998).

[21] Steven Seidman, *Contested Knowledge: Social Theory Today* (Oxford: Blackwell, 2008), p. xi.

[22] Thomas S. Kuhn's notion of a paradigm or 'a disciplinary matrix' captures the same idea. Kuhn defined paradigms as 'the entire constellation of beliefs, values, techniques and so on shared by the members of a given community'; *The Structure of Scientific Revolutions*, 2nd edn (Chicago, IL: University of Chicago Press, 1970 [1962]), p. 173.

[23] Oxford: Clarendon Press, 1914.

positivists in the 1930s. Carnap's publication of *Introduction to Semantics* in 1942 crystallised the semantic theory of truth.[24] A few decades later, Paul Feyerabend criticised the theory of truth espoused by Carnap.[25] The assumed correspondence of observation sentences with sensations in the world led Feyerabend to call into question the idea that the meaning of sentences is stable and invariant because it reflects an empirical content. Accordingly, he defended the possibility of the existence of rival, yet incommensurable, theories and argued that the positivist paradigm cannot really explain why the scientific community makes certain theory choices.

In the philosophy of language, the Swiss linguist, Ferdinand de Saussure (1857–1913), had shown that the relation between a word and its content in the world is arbitrary.[26] Language was seen to be a system of signs mediated by relations of difference between the signifier and the signified. Signs do not correspond to the essential properties of things/objects. As Saussure noted, 'any subject in order to be discussed must have a reasonable basis'.[27] As Hawkes observes,

> there exists no necessary 'fitness' in the link between the sound-image, or signifier 'tree', the concept, or signified that it involves, and the actual physical tree growing in the earth. In other words, the word 'tree' has no 'natural' or 'tree-like' qualities, and there is no appeal open to a 'reality' beyond the structure of the language in order to underwrite it.[28]

Influenced by the Saussure's conception of language, just after World War II, Levi-Strauss, the French anthropologist, made structural linguistics the premise of social thinking.[29] Russian and Eastern European linguists such as Todorov and Jakobson, as well as French poststructuralists, explored further the productive power of language in creating meanings as well as in justifying and thus legitimising the status quo.[30] Notions

[24] Cambridge: Harvard University Press, 1942.

[25] Paul Feyerabend, *Against Method: Outline of an Anarchistic Theory of Knowledge* (London: New Left Books, 1975).

[26] Ferdinand de Saussure, *Course in General Linguistics* (Glasgow: Fontana/Collins, 1977 [1916]).

[27] Ferdinand de Saussure, *Cours de Linguistique Generale*, trans. Wade Baskin, (New York, 1959), p. 73, cited in Terence Hawkes, *Structuralism and Semiotics* (London: Methuen and Co., 1977), p. 27.

[28] Ibid., p. 27.

[29] Claude Levi-Strauss, *Structural Anthropology* (Harmondsworth: Penguin Books, 1972).

[30] On this, see Claude Levi-Strauss, *The Savage Mind* (London: Weidenfeld and Nicolson, 1966). For the application of poststructuralism and postmodernism in research design, see Carol Grbich, *New Approaches in Social Research* (London: Sage, 2004).

such as language games, floating signifiers, discursive configurations and deconstruction smashed the glass ceiling of neutrality in social scientific research and revealed the power dynamics underpinning the production of knowledge. Interruption, the rebellion against logocentrims, the subversion of hierarchical binary oppositions, the empowerment of marginalised voices all featured centrally in the works of Foucault, Derrida, Lyotard, Baudrillard, Poulantzas, Culler, Fanon and Said.[31] The linguistic turn in social epistemology was immensely fruitful. Steiner[32] commented on the creative capacities of language by stating that: 'every act of speech has a potential of invention, a capacity to initiate, sketch, or construct "anti-matter". In fact, this poiesis or dialectic of counter-statement is even more complex, because the "reality" which we oppose or set aside is itself very largely a linguistic product'. Chomsky's contributions highlighted the correlation between the structure of the human mind and the structure of language,[33] while Derrida further accentuated the creative function of language; he commented on actuality and coined the term artifactuality in order to highlight the fact that reality is made and communicated through fictional devices.[34] In some respects, this work echoed Gaston Bachelard's ideas expressed in his *New Scientific Spirit*.[35] In this book, Bachelard showed that a new instrument, the telescope, could change how people perceived the world. By creating an epistemological rupture, it would thus give rise to a new scientific world view. For Bachelard, the telescope became part of a phenomenotechnique, and in the light of the discussion here, a Tennyson's arch. But even before Bachelard, in 1725 the Italian Jurist Giambattista Vico had published his thoughts on the ability of human beings to construct myths and social institutions – essentially the world around them. In his book which was entitled *The New Science*, Vico referred to the existence of a 'mental language' which enables human

[31] Frantz Fanon, *The Wretched of the Earth* (New York: Grove Press, 1968); Edward Said, *Culture and Imperialism* (New York: Vintage, 1994); *Orientalism* (New York: Vintage, 1978), Homi Bhabha, *The Location of Culture* (New York: Routledge, 1994); Jonathan Culler, *Structuralist Poetics* (Abingdon: Routledge and Kegan Paul, 1975).

[32] George Steiner, *After Babel: Aspects of Language and Translation* (London: Oxford University Press, 1975), p. 228.

[33] Noam Chomsky, *Syntactic Structures* (The Hague: Mouton, 1957); *Language and the Mind* (New York and London: Harcourt Brace, 1968).

[34] 'The Deconstruction of Actuality: An Interview with Jacques Derrida', 68 *Radical Philosophy*, 1994, pp. 28–41, at p. 28.

[35] Boston, MA: Beacon Press, 1985, trans. A. Goldhammer.

beings to create structures, meanings and things – a sapienza poetica (poetic wisdom).[36]

Writing in the early twentieth century, Dilthey (1833–1911) and Mannheim (1893–1947) travelled in a somewhat different direction. Dilthey believed that there exists a distinctive world view characterising each historical epoch and suggested a method that would allow researchers to make sense of different epochs in history.[37] Both Dilthey and Mannheim were thus interested in drawing a typology of worldview.[38] Their sensitivity to the social and cultural context and an awareness of how differences of context may impact upon the construction of meaning and thus of understanding have been at the heart of the hermeneutic turn. Fact-finding and statistical correlations, which are presumed to de-subjectivise research and to turn researchers into dispassionate observers of social phenomena, were sidelined in order to leave room for the intrusion of the researcher into their subject matter so that they could 'live into' an evolving social situation and discover the mind set of social actors. An 'interpretive understanding' (verstehen) celebrated a quasi-subjective approach to social reality. Phenomenology, existentialism and hermeneutics thus inverted the assumption that researchers discover truths and facts about social phenomena by remaining detached and externalised. They highlighted the need for the 'qualitative relatedness' of the researcher with the persons, the facts and the recorded data. By so doing, they reignited the call towards dynamic social research in the 1930s.[39] Dilthey's student, Martin Heidegger, and Heidegger's student, Has-Georg Gadamer, developed the philosophical perspective of hermeneutics.

Gadamer, who has been the most notable exponent of hermeneutics,[40] premised his theory on the dialogic communication and the reciprocal

[36] Harmondsworth: Penguin Classics, 1999.

[37] See Don Martindale, *The Nature and Types of Sociological Theory* (Boston, MA: The Riverside Press, 1960), ch. 1.

[38] Ibid., pp. 414–18.

[39] John J. Hader and Eduard C. Lindeman, *Dynamic Social Research* (London: Kegan Paul, Trench, Trubner and Co. Ltd, 1933), p. 111.

[40] See his *Truth and Method* (London: Sheed and Ward, 1975). John Dewey had laid down a foundation for hermeneutics; see his *The Quest for Certainty* and in particular his chapter on the 'Naturalisation of Intelligence'. Gadamer's hermeneutics must be distinguished from Bhaskar's 'hermeneutic moment' which essentially refers to his belief that social actors' conceptual schemes and understandings are only a part of social reality. There exist real things in the world independent of our knowledge of them (ontological realism) and it is the blending of the latter with the awareness that human knowledge about them is historically and socially shaped that led to what he called transcendental realism; R. Bhaskar, *A Realist Theory of Science*, 2nd edn (Sussex: Harvester Press, 1978). Compare also Anthony

processes of questioning and learning from one another and moving back and forth between the general and the particular. Habermas, on the other hand, posited an ideal speech communication that would enable parties to reach consensus on truth claims.[41] The foregoing discussion shows the richness of social epistemology and social sciences, in general. Irrespective of whether policy makers are willing to utilise their insights, social science research and the quest for epistemological innovation are very relevant to all key aspects of life and to the socio-political world.

Bearing in mind that most social scientific disciplines are not very old, this is a significant achievement. Sociology itself emerged as a discipline in the US universities in the 1920s.[42] Political science followed sociology. In fact, the pluralisation of academic disciplines in social sciences is a phenomenon associated with the post-1945 era. It was at that time that area studies also emerged as a new institutional categorisation. Indeed, in 1958 Peter Winch wrote 'that social sciences are in their infancy has come to be a platitude amongst writers of textbooks on the subjects'.[43] While the institutionalisation of social science disciplines facilitated new explorations, brought about the flourishing of non-western perspectives and enabled the production of cutting edge research, it also led to the emergence of silos.[44] In establishing themselves, disciplines had to erect boundaries and often led insular lives. In other words, the pursuit of distinctiveness in processes of disciplinary institutionalisation hindered cross-fertilisation. They developed their own languages, canons and themes of inquiry without looking further afield. Exchanging insights between anthropology, sociology, law, political theory, political science and international relations unfortunately still remains the exception rather than the norm. But this does not preclude the possibility of a rapprochement in the future.

Believing in the artificiality of the separation of disciplines and the fruitfulness of finding synergies among them, this book has a post-disciplinary orientation. On the one hand, it might be argued that its subject matter

Giddens's 'double hermeneutic' approach (1982); A. Giddens, 'Hermeneutics and Social Theory' in *Profiles and Critiques in Social Theory* (Berkeley, CA: University of California Press), pp. 1–17. This is discussed in the subsequent chapter.

41 Jurgen Habermas, *The Theory of Communicative Action, vol. 2: Lifeworld and System: A Critique of Functionalist Reason* (Boston, MA: Beacon Press, 1987).

42 See Peter Wagner, *A History and Theory of Social Sciences* (London: Sage, 2001).

43 Peter Winch, *The Idea of a Social Science and Its Relation to Philosophy* (London: Routledge and Kegan Paul, 1958), pp. 1–24.

44 For an excellent historical account, see the Report of the Gulbenkian Commission on the Restructuring of the Social Sciences, *Open the Social Sciences* (Stanford, CA: Stanford University Press, 1996), ch. 2.

demands this. Any epistemological quest has to escape narrow disciplinary confines if it wishes to have more general applicability. In addition, concerns about what to look at when we seek explanations and how to combine micro perspectives with more macro orientations do not bear the tag of a specific discipline. Similarly, striving to see underlying patterns, constraints and possibilities, and questioning standard assumptions about monism and dualism are exercises that appeal to more than one discipline.

While all this is true, I must also confess that I intentionally sought to integrate multidisciplinary perspectives in seeking to address questions that concern social scientists. In so doing, I did not see myself as a trespasser or an infiltrator, despite the fact that my own discipline is law. Having said that, I was also very conscious of the fact that carrying out my ambitious plan could only make my own human limitations more pronounced. It is very difficult to include everything and everybody in a discussion and, if I have omitted theorists or drawn the parameters of my research too narrowly, or too widely, in the opinion of readers, I hope I will be forgiven.

Narrowing the gap among the social scientific disciplines and between social sciences and humanities could facilitate the development of new explanatory models and the generation of more sophisticated understandings. I sincerely hope that social research develops a post-disciplinary face in the future. It would be very nice if political theorists, for example, felt uneasy about leaving out Dewey or Mead or Mary Douglas from their reading lists in the same way that sociologists in the future might feel uncomfortable about the omission of J. S. Mill, Bentham and John Locke from theirs. In 1996, the members of the Gulbenkian Commission in the US articulated this wonderfully:

> To be historical is after all not the exclusive purview of persons called historians. It is an obligation of all social scientists. To be sociological is not the exclusive purview of persons called sociologists. It is an obligation of all social scientists. Economic issues are not the exclusive purview of economists. Economic questions are central to any and all social scientific analyses.[45]

To put it differently, a dialogue across disciplines and a willingness to transcend the disciplinary 'skin' of research foci might well be the key to attaining a better understanding of socio-political life and developing more

[45] Ibid., p. 98. The members of the Gulbenkian Commission were: Immanuel Wallerstein (chair), Calestous Juma, Evelyn For Keller, Jurgen Kocka, Domenique Lecourt, V. Y. Mudkimbe, Kinhide Miushakoji, Ilya Prigogine, Peter J. Taylor and Michel-Rolph Trouillot.

rigorous social scientific models, methods and theories. I hope this book contributes towards this direction.

I am not alone in making the plea for a post-disciplinary world. More than one hundred years ago, Cooley (1909), an American sociologist, highlighted the need for the transcendence of disciplinary divides.[46] Cooley felt that sharp demarcations among disciplines were artificial. He and others would not be persuaded by 'pure theories' of law or political science or philosophy or by 'correct' – in the sense of getting one's own discipline's approval – epistemologies. Merleau-Ponty also complained in 1951 that philosophy and sociology had long lived separate lives and that the time was ripe for a form of union.[47] Much later, Mancur Olson noted that 'any effort to compartmentalise the substantive domains of discipline is inevitably artificial and arbitrary'.[48] The above-mentioned scholars felt that compartmentalisation had exclusionary effects. Talking across disciplines and utilising insights from one another can thus bring about interesting exegeses and a lively sense of possibility.

Let me conclude the introduction by adding a proviso about the scope of the subsequent discussion. This is not a book about social science and democracy. Nor does it focus on the public face of social research and the processes of the social production of knowledge. Karl Mannheim's *Ideology and Utopia*, published in 1936 called effectively into question the presumption that knowledge is a neutral enterprise uncoloured by the interests of its producers.[49] His research aligned knowledge production with public policy making and showed how propositions in social science benefit certain groups in society. Of course, Marx had already done so, but Marxism did not postulate a normative sociology of knowledge. Since the publication of Mannheim's book, much has been written about experts' power and the implications of the influence they exert over democratic decision-making. Social movements and civic society activism, on the other hand, have also convincingly shown that the value neutrality of scientific knowledge has been a myth propagated by elites. Understanding, including systematic academic understanding, is always a matter of

[46] Charles Horton Cooley, *Social Organisation: A Study of the Larger Mind* (New York: Schocken Books, 1909).

[47] Maurice Merleau-Ponty, 'Le Philosophie et la Sociologie', X *Cashiers internationaux de sociologie* (1951), pp. 53–69.

[48] Mancur Olson 'Toward a Unified View of Economics and Other Social Sciences', in James E. Alt and Kenneth A. Shepsle (eds.), *Perspectives on Positive Political Economy* (New York: Cambridge University Press, 1990).

[49] New York: Harcourt Brace, 1936.

translation and translation is socially, spatially and temporally situated, as Steiner has argued.[50] Otherwise put, 'knowledge about the social world is always knowledge-in-context; it is socially situated and has social consequences'.[51] I share these observations. But I should add that an examination of the political facets of knowledge production and dissemination is beyond the scope of this book. Foucault's observations about the systems of control implicated in the production of discourse and knowledge remain valid.[52] Since these questions do not fall within the ambit of the subsequent chapters, readers would have to look elsewhere for a detailed discussion on the positivist and post-positivist faces of social science, its socio-political relevance[53] and on the intertwining of knowledge and political power.[54]

[50] Steiner, *After Babel*; Compare also P. Freire, *Pedagogy of Hope* (New York: Continuum, 1998); W. Connolly, *The Terms of Political Discourse*, 2nd edn (Princeton, NJ: Princeton University Press, 1983); Willard Van Orman Quine, *From a Logical Point of View* (Cambridge, MA: Harvard University Press, 1953); *Word and Object* (Cambridge, MA: MIT Press, 1960).

[51] Moses and Knutsen, *Ways of Knowing*, p. 201.

[52] M. Foucault, *The Archaeology of Knowledge and the Discourse on Language* (New York: Pantheon, 1972).

[53] On the latter, see G. Delanty, *Social Science: Beyond Constructivism and Realism* (Buckingham: Open University Press, 1997). The demise of positivism in social science reinvigorated interest in interpretation, understanding and the importance of language and hermeneutics; Steve Fuller, *Social Epistemology* (Bloomington and Indianapolis: Indiana University Press, 1988); Craig Calhoun, *Critical Social Theory* (Oxford Basil Blackwell, 1995); John A. Hughes and Wesley S. Sharrock, *The Philosophy of Social Research* (Harlow: Longman, 1990); A. S. Stouffer, *Social Research to Test Ideas: Selected Writings* (New York: Free Press, 1962); A. Ryan, *The Philosophy of the Social Sciences* (London: Macmillan, 1970); M. Hollis, *The Philosophy of Social Science* (Cambridge: Cambridge University Press, 1994).

[54] Sheila Jasanoff, *States of Knowledge: The Co-production of Science and Social Order* (London: Routledge, 2006).

Part I

Theory, Perspectives and *Connexio Rerum*

1

On the Methodology of Social Sciences: The Case for *Connexio Rerum*

1.1 Introduction

Why do we value knowledge? If happiness is the secret to a successful life, one might argue that we value knowledge because it provides us with information that enables us to lead happier lives. While the contribution of either wealth or love or friendship to our level of happiness is easily ascertainable, when it comes to knowledge and its relation to happiness, we tend to be rather circumspect. This is because attaining knowledge requires effort, struggle, and, more often than not, loneliness. Yet, notwithstanding all of the above, we seek knowledge because we believe it is a worthwhile good. Knowledge makes us more 'at home' in both the world surrounding us and the world within. It increases our understanding of these outer and inner worlds and invests things with meaning. Hegel eloquently observed that 'the aim of knowledge is to divest the world of its strangeness, and to make us feel at home in it'.[1]

The paths to knowledge and greater understanding vary, as noted in the introduction. No one can claim that there exists one true epistemology. And generally speaking, epistemologies do not normally have a very long life span; their adherents are likely to 'defect' after a certain period of time. Falsehood, fatigue and repetition often lead people to 'switch off' from what was previously believed to be the correct way of making sense of reality. A cursory look at history shows that some widely acknowledged truths have turned out to be erroneous. Without a doubt, science is a social institution.[2] Additionally, different philosophical traditions, political ideologies and scientific disciplinary orthodoxies prescribe different epistemologies. Although it is difficult to identify the best mental map for

[1] Georg Wilhelm Friedrich Hegel, *The Smaller Logic*, para. 194 Z.

[2] Harry M. Collins, *Changing Order: Replication and Induction in Scientific Practice* (London: Sage Publications, 1985); Mary Hesse, 'Changing Concepts and Stable Order', 16 *Social Studies of Science* (1986), pp. 714–26.

making the unknown knowable,[3] it is nevertheless the case that the human mind is attracted to simple and singular explanations. Its innate curiosity is accompanied by a simultaneous aversion to complexity. Complexity requires mental effort and reflection. Singularity or duality, on the other hand, is easy. One or two constituent variables, as opposed to many interacting ones, attract: our investigations seem more manageable, and our findings tend to be more convincing, if we simplify.[4]

Simplicity in social science research manifests itself in either monism or dualism. Rationalists cherish oneness. Empiricists cherish it too. And when it becomes difficult to explain things on the basis of oneness, duality prevails. It is the interrelation – be this co-action, interaction or the opposition between A and B (or not-A) – that apparently explains reality. Dualism appears to be epistemologically privileged. But by placing A against B (or against not-A), like boxers in a ring, we cannot but view them as external to each other. We believe that their exteriority allows us to measure their interaction in time *t* and to determine causality. We thus measure punches and reactions and believe that we can account for that crucial knock-out punch. In this way, we could claim that A is the important, or the primary, cause and that all consequences flow from it. But what if these two variables, and some others, did not stand in a position of exteriority to one another, affecting each other from the outside, but instead were inside each other? What if these two different things, forces, parts, dimensions are dimensions of the same thing? And further, what if we are accustomed to assume their separation because we wish to project a reality onto the world that is both comprehensive and comprehendible by us? How would we react, if we discovered that every phenomenon is a nexus of relations? Could we then make a convincing argument that the time has come to abandon both oneness (monism), and dualism and to embrace, instead, ensembles and connectionalism?

Answering the foregoing questions is the subject matter of this chapter. Unlike natural scientists, social scientists have been attracted to worlds of few dimensions; monism (Section 1.2) and dualism (Section 1.3). Accordingly, the whole is carved into parts in order to fit a particular lens, and the multi-dimensional reality is reduced to a one- or two-dimensional one. But nothing is one-dimensional and nothing is the cause of everything.

3 Feyerabend, *Against Method*; *Science in a Free Society* (London: Verso, 1978); *Farewell to Reason* (London: Verso, 1987); Kuhn, *The Structure of Scientific Revolutions*.

4 Compare here Mach's insightful observation that 'the fundamental conception of the nature of science [is the] economy of thought; E. Mach, *The Conservation of Energy* (La Salle, IL: Open Court, 1911), p. 91.

Structure, agency, institutions and discourse all intersect and interact in specific locations at a given time. Understanding their interactions even when one of them is phenomenally non-existent and developing a formula for what I call the *connexio rerum* are the foci of Section 1.4. I argue there that the worlds around us, and our role as both observers and participants in them, are shaped by multiple and co-implicated lines of influence which require an ensemble-like epistemology. The final section of the chapter contains the concluding remarks.

1.2 The World of One Dimension

Monism is a simple but also audacious social scientific approach. It is simple because it seeks, and propounds, a single, unitary basis for all socio-political phenomena. It is audacious because, in spite of the overwhelming evidence that realities are complex, it contends that all events, developments, institutions, relations, social orders and so on arise, and become effective, owing to the decisive role of one principle or cause. The latter can be seen, studied and measured because it exists and accounts for everything. Identifying the cause therefore does not only help to explain social events, relations and phenomena, but also allows us to observe patterns and regularities in all of the above as well as to predict their future recurrences.

If we examine causation more closely, we discern that, by its nature, it presupposes a one-sided influence of one phenomenon on another: A is the cause of B. In other words, it starts from the premise that there exist two different phenomena, whereby A is 'the starter' exerting a one-directional effect on B. By definition, B cannot be related to A, for that would make it the cause of A. This premise guides both scientific research designs and the ensuing research findings. In sum, in monism we find the following propositions:

(i) A and B are different. A is not B;
(ii) A and B are separate phenomena. A is not related to B;
(iii) A causes B.

In addition to the presumption that A 'creates', or 'produces', B, the monistic reasoning works best if time (t) is bracketed. For it may well be that in time t-1, A and B were related or were affecting each other and it is only by slicing time differently or by focusing on one moment or period of time that we could see the effect of A over B and not the effect of B over A. Furthermore, if the effect of B over A cannot be seen now, this does not necessarily mean that it is, and has been, inexistent. While we might wish to entertain such a possibility, monistic reasoning does not permit it, simply because it would turn the cause into just another variable. And more importantly, it would turn it into variable that is correlated with other variables. And if this were the case, 'the starter' would be a 'false starter'.

Furthermore, while it might be easier to apply this premise to the natural world, it becomes more difficult to apply it to the time-bounded and interconnected world of social science. For the latter's main units of analyses, i.e., individuals, institutions, groups, systems, structures, relations, discourses, symbols and so on, are not only time and space specific but they are also interconnected. It would be a mistake to compartmentalise socio-political life, since social phenomena stand in relations of mutual dependence. In addition, neither social phenomena nor human behaviour are always predictable.

While the above contentions are generally accepted today, when we begin to excavate the past we discover a different reality. Beliefs in the existence, and the will, of God dominated the Middle Ages. The divine was perceived to be the First Cause of everything. Natural law brought the divine into the earthly domain. But as the power and hegemony of ecclesiastical elites waned, confidence in human reasoning increased, thereby leading to scientific discoveries and the development of natural science. Galileo Galilei (1564–1642) sought to establish laws through systematic experimentation and is seen to be the father of modern science.[5] Social science developed by mirroring these discoveries and borrowing ideas from natural science. For a considerable period of time it was thus assumed that the social space was very much analogous to physical space. What was needed was to discover nature's own laws and language.[6]

Accordingly, since the natural world was governed by the Newtonian laws of gravitation and inertia, then the same laws presumably applied to the social world and could account for the development and decay of societies as well as for individuals' life journeys. Indeed, in the seventeenth century, Edhard Weigel's ambition was to develop a universal quantitative science called 'Mathesis universae'.[7] The basic rationale underlying Weigel's quest was his belief in Pantometrica, that is, in the measurability of everything, social and natural phenomena alike. Quantities and causal relations

[5] See Bertrand Russell, *The Scientific Outlook* (New York: W. W. Norton, 1931), ch. 1.

[6] The phrase 'nature's own language' is borrowed from Richard Rorty, 'Method, Social Science and Social Hope', XI(4) *Canadian Journal of Philosophy* (1981), pp. 569–88.

[7] It was published in 1669.

thus were responsible for everything that happened in the physical, social and moral landscapes. Weigel's conception of moral quantities captured social dignity, power, prestige, crime, services and economic value. A similar reasoning is found in W. Perry's *Several Essays in Political Arithmetics* (1699)[8] and George Berkeley's (1685–1753) account of 'social physics'. Like physics, social physics was governed by the postulates of moral attraction and social stability.[9]

Social physics and social dynamics preoccupied Saint-Simon (1760–1825) and Fourier. The new science of social physics promised to study scientifically the collective development of humankind and to formulate laws concerning the progress of civilisation akin to the laws of gravitation.[10] Both Saint-Simon and Fourier brought into the social world Newton's law of gravitation in the form of the existence of a constant struggle of centrifugal and centripetal forces in society as well as in the natural world. Struggle or competition and their gradation, namely war, in turn influenced a whole body of sociological and political thinking in the eighteenth and nineteenth centuries, and all schools of thought consistently pursued their monistic explanations. The school of struggle sociology (or conflict sociology) was formally established by Gumplowicz (1838–1909). His theory of group enmity influenced the formation of ideas such as class struggle, group selection, Lebensraum[11] imperialist ideology and the struggle of civilisations.

Ludwig Gumplowicz, and his followers, made struggle and rivalry for power among groups antagonistic to each other the main explanatory variable of institutions, political life and the state. Individuals were completely subsumed by groups; as he wrote: 'we contend that the real elements of a social process are not separate individuals but social groups'.[12] Group antagonism resulted in a continuous struggle, culminating in the victory of one of them and, thus, in the suppression of the others.

[8] It was published in 1690.

[9] See his Essay on *The Principles of Moral Attraction*, available online at http://opensiuc.lib.siu.edu/cgi/viewcontent.cgi?article=3599&context=ocj, accessed 30 March 2016.

[10] See Hayek's chapter on 'Social Physics: Saint-Simon and Comte'; Friedrich A. Hayek, *The Counter-Revolution of Science: Studies on the Abuse of Reason* (New York: The Free Press of Glencoe, Collier-Macmillan limited, 1955), pp. 129–42.

[11] See Mark Bassin, 'Imperialism and the Nation-State in Friedrich Ratzel's Political Geography', 11 *Progress in Human Geography* (1987), pp. 473–95.

[12] Ludwig Gumplowicz, *Outlines of Sociology*, tr. by Moore (Philadelphia, PA: American Academy of Political and Social Science, 1899), pp. 76–82. He was the most influential conflict theorist of his time. For contemporary work on warfare and nationalism, see Paul Kahn, *Out of Eden: Adam, Eve and the Problem of Evil* (Princeton, NJ: Princeton University Press, 2006).

It was believed that states owe their existence to such struggles; in fact, states were viewed to be unions of the victorious and the subjugated groups. Co-operation in society was replaced by enmity and rivalry. Social life became nothing more than the by-product of struggles and the idea of 'humanity', which characterised Enlightenment, disappeared. The 'conflict reasoning' became prevalent in the second part of the nineteenth century; everything in society could be interpreted through the lens of conflict or struggle or competition or war. In other words, conflict was not only a primary datum but also socio-politically and economically productive. Gumplowicz utilised the conservative thinking of J. Bodin (1530–96), T. Hobbes (1588–1679) and A. Ferguson (1723–1816) – with the latter expressing similar views in his essay entitled 'An Essay on the History of Civil Society' published in 1767, as well as Darwin's theory of evolution. In turn, he influenced both A. W. Smart in the United States and Marx and Engels in Europe. Among his most important works were *Rasse und Staat* (1875), *Philosophisches Staatrecht* (1877) and *Der Rassenkampf* (1833), and all three books extolled group membership and group activity.

Gumplowicz's thinking also inspired Ratzenhofer (1842–1904), who wrote on race and space and popularised the contention that the driving factor of the state and its evolution is not the individual, but the social group. The only status that matters for individuals is that of group membership. The latter implies adherence to the commands of the group engaging in an endless quest for power and supremacy. The causal priority given to the group *qua* group was later given to war. War became the driving force of all social, political and economic phenomena in conservative circles, while the struggle of opposed economic classes became the 'primary cause' in Marxism.

According to Marxism, everything, including social dynamics and change, can be explained on the basis of economic relations. Economics is thus sealed off from the wider society and is denied its correlations with other phenomena. The economic mode of production determines the social, political, cultural and symbolic processes existing in a polity. This is the base upon which the socio-political superstructure is built. Class struggle becomes the key force compelling the transformation of the economic system of production and exerts one-sided influence to all social phenomena. The relevant formula has been described by Sorokin[13] as: A and Non-A = f(Econ).

[13] Pitirim Sorokin, *Contemporary Sociological Theories* (New York: Harper and Row, 1928), p. 534.

If one pauses to reflect on this formula, one realises that it implies a metaphysical determinism. God, the heavenly first cause, is supplanted by economic relations as the *causa efficiens* of most social phenomena. Indeed, the similarities between the Marxist conception of the economic base and the medieval conception of the omnipotent and omnicompetent God are striking; the causa impacts on, determines, creates and sustains all other relations. Its power is one-directional; there is little room for correlations, interdependence, probabilities, accidents or uncertainty. The outcome or result is pre-given considering the nature of the (capitalist) mode of production. Althousser sought to address some of the shortcomings of the Marxist monistic approach by stressing the relative importance of ideology and the types of state apparatuses,[14] but the economic base still overdetermined the superstructure, including the various ideological manifestations. Gramsci's conception of hegemony sought to do the same.[15] As a result, anthropologists such as Malinowski commented on the intertwining of economic relations with religion and magic in the societies they studied.[16] Durkheim and Weber also illustrated the religious origin of modern capitalism.[17] Post-Marxist approaches sought to highlight the distinctiveness of a number of social phenomena and to pinpoint their weak or stronger correlation and mutual dependence with economic relations.[18] By so doing, they exposed the fallacy of lifting one factor from the rich tapestry of socio-political life, namely, the economic one, and making it the primary and overriding activator of a causal chain of phenomena and relations.

An early critic of economistic monism was Vifredo Pareto in the early twentieth century. He believed that it was simplistic to believe that A causes B which in turn gives rise to C, for A + B + C may be implicated in the production of a certain phenomenon or structure. Nor is it simply a case of producing a more nuanced account of the cause, such as A1, B1 and C1. Social life has many facets and therefore one ought to take into

[14] Louis Althusser, *On the Reproduction of Capitalism: Ideology and Ideological State Apparatuses*, trans. and ed. G. M. Goshgarian (London: Verso, 2014).

[15] Antonio Gramsci, *Selections from the Prison Notebooks* (London: Lawrence and Wishart, 1971).

[16] Bronislaw Kasper Malinowski, *Myth in Primitive Psychology* (London: Norton, 1926).

[17] Emile Durkheim, *The Elementary Forms of the Religious Life* (New York: Macmillan, 1915); Max Weber, *The Protestant Ethic and the Spirit of Capitalism* (New York: Scribner's, 1930).

[18] Ernesto Laclau and Chantal Moufee, *Hegemony and Socilalist Strategy* (London: Verso, 1986); Ernesto Laclau, *Reflections on the Revolution of Our Times* (London: Verso, 1990).

account the variables involved and their functions. Pareto[19] advocated a shift of approach away from causational determinism to studying the functional correlations among interdependent variables. Cause and effect were thus substituted by 'variable' and 'function'. Mathematics provided ample scope for the study of correlations, including partial correlations, and thus prompted the spurt of quantitative measurements of uniformities in social relations.[20] While Pareto's observation was correct, he nevertheless did not manage to break away from monism completely, because his thinking was influenced by another monistic paradigm, or to use Pepper's terminology, another world hypothesis, namely, organicism. He saw society as a living system comprising units standing in complex mutual relationships. In his *Treatise in Sociology* he proceeded to study the social system(s) from the standpoints of a number of factors, such as (i) economic factors, (ii) social mobility and elite circulation, (iii) ideas and ideologies, (iv) the heterogeneity of human beings and social groups and (v) the main drives of human actions.[21] The latter are instincts or dispositions, which he called 'residues'. Pareto's methodological contribution was that he sought to develop a theory of factors.

Among these factors, residues, i.e., drives or reflexes, and derivations, i.e., speech reactions or ideologies, play an important role in Pareto's theoretical schema.[22] Instincts, which are nothing else than the manifestation of the natural law of physical gravitation, are natural. But they can easily become social instincts. By shifting the focus on the individual's bio-organic make up, Pareto struck a chord with the instictivist school which was growing at that time and which sought to account for human action and social phenomena on the basis of biological drives and satisfaction. Human psychology was fashionable in the early twentieth century and both the behaviouralist strand of the Psychological School,[23] which focused on conditioned and unconditioned reflexes, and introspectivism made human desires, interests, emotions and wishes the primary explanatory devices. The economistic formula was thus replaced by a simple transition from instinct to desire and then to action. This meant that a whole

[19] See also E. Barone, 'L'opera di V.Pareto e il progresso della scienza', 1924 *Giornale d. Economisti*, pp. 22–4.

[20] Vilfredo Pareto, *The Mind and Society* (New York: Harkourt, Brace, 1935). J. R. Commons in the United States who pioneered institutional economics also commented that the early nineteenth century economists patterned their research on the sciences of physics and chemistry; *The Economics of Collective Action* (New York: Macmillan, 1950), p. 36.

[21] In Vilfredo Pareto, *The Mind and Society*, n. 20.

[22] On this, see Sorokin, Contemporary Sociological Theories, pp. 42 et seq.

[23] Floyd H. Allport, *Social Psychology* (Boston, MA: Chocolate Muffins, 1924).

social life and process from A to Z could be explained on the basis of an single-variable which was physical/psychological. Other intervening variables and circumstances were usually bracketed and the other facets of social phenomena were disregarded.

The same applied with respect to the anthropomorphic, bio-organismic conceptions of society influenced by Darwin's theory of evolution. Spencer, for instance, believed that society was a living organism subject to growth, evolution, adaptation and decay.[24] Evolution became the master signifier that could account for the state, society and its constituent units. The 'societal body' thus was seen to represent a unity that could only function in a harmonious way if there existed homogeneity, integration and centralised control. If something did not fit the principle of evolution, it was either bracketed or rejected. The state, too, was seen to be a complex organism and both Coker and Ratzel in the early twentieth century commented on its morphological resemblance to biological phenomena. Ratzel even identified its soul, or what he termed its *Seele*.[25]

In brief, monism, that is, the attribution of a primary cause to all social phenomena, be this God or the divine, the rational or Spirit, the individual, the instinctual, the aggregate (group), the bio-organic or the conflictual, is a simple and effective paradigm. But it is also destined to be called into question. As soon as one problematises its fundamental premise, which is to say the presumed primacy and self-sufficiency of the cause, monism crumbles. This can be most successfully achieved by showing the correlation and mutual interdependence of the antecedent cause with other historical and socio-political variables. This is not a difficult exercise because the primary cause does not only condition, but is also conditioned by all those socio-political phenomena that it brackets. In addition, since the latter are the product of social life, the assumed primary cause might well be time and space sensitive and coloured by the prevailing climate of opinion and ideology.

24 Herbert Spencer, *The Principles of Sociology* (New York: D. Appleton and Co., 1910), Vol. I. Part II; R. Worms, *Les principes biologiques de l'evolution sociale* (Paris: D. Appleton and Co., 1910).

25 Friedrich Ratzel, *Der Staat und sein Boden geographisch betrachtet* (Leipzig: Bei S. Hirzel, 1896); W. F. Coker, 'Organismic theories of the state. Nineteenth-century interpretations of the state as organism or as person', Studies in History, Economics, and Public Law, 38, No. 2 (New York: Longmans, Green and Co., 1910), pp. 41–2. Another perspective, called the energistic perspective, was influenced by thermodynamics and made human energy and its transformation into motion the main explanation of social phenomena. N. L. Sim, who wrote *Society and its Surplus* (1914) and T. N. Carver, who wrote *The Economy of Human Energy* (1924) espoused it.

1.3 The World of Two Dimensions

If monism cannot provide an adequate explanation of social phenomena, dualism might be a more convincing alternative. Dualism in social sciences is common; there have been several manifestations of it which, in turn, either grounded or sustained schools of thought such as dialectics, contractarianism, syncretism, contextualism and purposive thinking, among others. One could devote long sections to discussing the most common dualisms, such as the mind vs. the body; or the Apollonian belief in reason vs. the Dionysian reality of passion; the matter of materialists vs. the spirit or the ideas of idealists; the Cartesian thinking substance vs. the extended substance; individual vs. society; structure vs. agency; structure vs. discourse; determinism vs. processualism; fixed structures vs. change and so on. While dualist imageries are diverse, all are based on an assumed opposition or antagonism between the two entities in the relation.

This is understandable. If dualist thinking did not entail the presumption that two things or entities are different from each other and against one another, it would collapse into monism. It is therefore important for all dualistic thinking to:

(a) Posit two separate entities;
(b) Assume that these are independent and asymmetrical;
(c) Assume that one opposes the other and, by so doing, precludes its realisation;
(d) Postulate that the final act of bringing the two independent parts together has productive power.

The basic premise is one of an assumed self-sufficiency – and a separate existence – of the part, which results in giving it a quality that is irreducibly one's own, that is, unaffected by any interaction with another part. Because of the irreducible difference of the parts contending with one another to varying degrees, the act of bringing them together and making them parts of the same totality is an important and productive move. One notices the circularity here in that the explanandum is already contained in the explanans. For if one supposes that the original asymmetry of the parts is not tight, then the final step – the synthesis of the differences – becomes unnecessary. This is because the two entities were dimensions of the same reality in the first place. They were complementary parts of the same thing.

Dialectics, too, suffers from the same circularity. Every given something has something to oppose it and, following its negation, it survives in a higher synthesis of the oppositionalities. Instead of adhering to the

Aristotelian logic of identity (and substance), exemplified by A is A, Hegel begins with A's difference or antithesis; that is, A is not-A. Negation is thus a necessary part of the constitution of the identity of something and there is no identity without the important role-playing by difference(s) that prevents an identity from realisation. The dialectical movement from thesis to antithesis and to synthesis (the coincidentia oppositorum) led Hegel to argue that objects emerge into full consciousness as independent realities only through their opposites.[26] Yet, if the original premise were A is A in some aspects, just other to B with respect to other aspects and similar to B in other aspects, the dialectical moment cannot unfold. In addition, the dialectical moment could not proceed if one brought simultaneity, instead of just sequence (i.e., step 1: thesis, step 2: antithesis, step 3: synthesis), into the relation. For example, the presumed asymmetry between body and mind cannot be sustained if one commences one's inquiry with the reality of the embodied mind or the spiritual body. After all, both body and mind are instances of the same individuality. Descartes insisted on the separation of material and mental substances.[27] As Whitehead observed in 1938, the latter are external to the former and 'neither type requires the other type for the completion of its essence'.[28] Similarly, the opposition between the individual and society collapses if one views the individual as a socius on the one hand, and society as the aggregation of individuals and groups on the other. In brief, the simultaneous embrace of A and not-A would disrupt the unfolding of the dialectical logic.

Functionalism and structural functionalism are built on dualist thinking since the social system consists of interrelated individuals having various relations which in turn serve certain functions.[29] Everything serves the perpetuation of the living system and has a function. But function is the trigger of a reverse causation process, which often leads to a monistic source. Contextualism, too, works best in a world of two dimensions: A is A because of the context within which it is situated. A in a different context would result in an altered A; in fact A would not be A in such a scenario. It is not A that changes the context, but the context, which could be socio-economic, environmental, political, sociological, institutional and so on, that is responsible for A or accounts for A's emergence and development.

[26] Compare, William James, *A Pluralistic Universe: Hibbert Lectures at Manchester College on the Present Situation in Philosophy* (London: Longmans, Green and Co., 1909).

[27] Rene Descartes, *Les passions de l'âme*. It was published in 1649.

[28] Alfred North Whitehead, *Modes of Thought* (New York: The Free Press, 1968), p. 149.

[29] Talcott Parsons, *The Social System* (Glencoe, IL: The Free Press, 1951).

This enables the drawing of typologies and correlations, such as A = f (B) or, in the case of indirect conditioning, C = f (B) and therefore A = f (C).

Interestingly, the most commonly discussed dualism in social sciences has been the individual versus society or, following the rise of structuralism, structure versus agency. Durkheim's sociological thinking placed society in a position of exteriority: society stands outside of (and above) the societal members and exerts a one-directional impact on them. The latter is primarily a constraining one. It is manifested in the imposition of commands, guidelines and constraints via established rules and regulations, be they legal or moral. As Durkheim put it, 'society sees farther and better, than individuals'.[30] The social reality is thus different from the individual reality or the reality of individual minds. Collective consciousness is outside of, and above, individual consciousness. Evidently, the exteriority of the social reality, which became explicit in his book entitled *Regles de la methode sociologique*,[31] is fictitious. Society does not exist, and cannot exist, without its members, for it is the members' actions, interactions, relations and inter-relations that create and sustain society. The same applies to all institutions, small and large. Imagine, for example, a church without a congregation and a priest. It would be reduced to an empty and decaying religious infrastructure.

American sociologists in the early twentieth century, such as Cooley, departed from Durkheim's analysis and pinpointed the close alignment between the individual and the social. They argued that the 'we' is not more ontologically potent than the 'I' and that the 'I' is not more ontologically potent than the 'we', since both 'I' and 'we' emerge in interaction and as a result of their interaction.[32] As Cooley put it, 'a separate individual is an abstraction unknown to experience, and so likewise is society when regarded as something apart from individuals'[33] and 'I think, then, that the antithesis, society versus the individual, is false and hollow whenever used as a general or philosophical statement of human relations'.[34] Past interactions among societal members have left their imprint in crystallised and

[30] Durkheim, *The Elementary Forms of the Religious Life*.

[31] Paris: F. Alcan, 1895. It was translated as *The Rules of Sociological Method* and was published by Chicago University Press in 1938.

[32] See Werner Stark, *The Fundamental Forms of Social Thought* (London: Routledge and Kegan Paul, 1962).

[33] Charles Horton Cooley, *Human Nature and the Social Order* (New York: Charles Scribner's Sons, 1902), p. 36.

[34] Ibid., pp. 41–2.

sedimented rules, structures, institutions and practices that make society what it is.

French sociologists, too, criticised Durkheim's sociological realism. Tarde, in particular, was highly critical; he commented: 'it is difficult to understand how, after excluding the individuals, we can have a society as a remnant. If the students and the professors are excluded from a university, I do not think there remains in it anything but the name. Durkheim apparently tries to return us to the realism of the Middle Ages'.[35]

Giddens's structuration theory was initially conceived of as laying the foundations for a post-Durkheimian theory of suicide and reflected his concern of reconciling the structural properties of systems with dynamic social action. His notion of the duality of structure shows that 'structures are both the medium and outcome of the reproduction of social practices',[36] since agents reproduce institutionalised practices in their daily lives. Of course, they may decide not to do so. Giddens knows that there is no guarantee and that all 'reproduction is contingent and historical'.[37]

Another related dualism, which the development of contractarianism – associated with the work of Hobbes, Locke, Rousseau and Kant – sought to overcome, is that of rulers versus the ruled. With the rise of the modern state and the bourgeoisie, the conception of society as unus corpus mysticum[38] could no longer ensure the perpetuation of both ecclesiastical rule and monarchy. The social contract idea in theory furnished a justification for the origin of the modern state and for the legitimate exercise of power over the people. It inspired the drawing of constitutional charters in practice which limited the power of rulers and ensured that they ruled with due regard to the rights, and interests, of the people.[39] Political societies were thought to have been built on social contracts designed to safeguard individuals' pre-existing moral rights. The conflict between the powerful few and the multitude was thus subsumed under an equilibrium model which placed the social pact at the apex of the political order. The stability of the

35 G. Tarde, *La Logique Sociale* (Paris: Felix Alcan, 1895), pp. 1ff.

36 Anthony Giddens, *Current Problems in Social Theory: Action, Structure and Contradiction in Social Analysis* (London: Macmillan, 1979), p. 5.

37 Anthony Giddens, *A Contemporary Critique of Historical Materialism: Volume 1: Power, Property and the State* (London: Macmillan, 1981), p. 27. See also *New Rules of Sociological Method* (London: Hutchinson and Co., 1976).

38 The term was used by Richard Hooker (1554–1600).

39 For the distinction between civil and constitutional contractarianisms, see David Boucher and Paul Kelly (eds.), *The Social Contract: From Hobbes to Rawls* (London: Routledge, 1994); D. D. Raphael, *Problems of Political Philosophy* (Basingstoke: Macmillan Press, 1970), pp. 78–114.

social system was thus ensured in so far as the governing elites respected the (fundamental) rights of the ruled and were guided by the general will and not by sectoral interests. Social utilitarianism is an offspring of contractarianism. Social life, institutions and political relations all have a purpose and individual conduct must be coordinate with the wider purposes of the state and social life. These must thus ensure the greatest happiness of the greatest number. Often the interests of atomistic individuals might be frustrated, but their sacrifices are justified because the state and/or other public institutions provide services for all. Conversely, if the state fails to promote the common good, it loses its right to command the obedience of the population.

To suggest that dualist thinking is in conflict with such epistemologies and the logic of monism would not surprise readers. But this discussion has also shown that dualism can only convince if its basic premise and the sequential unfolding of the logic are not put into question. For if one acknowledges that A and B (or not-A) may be simultaneously co-present, then one would have to concede both the artificiality of, and the existence of inherent contradictions in, the world of two dimensions.

1.4 *Connexio Rerum*

In the foregoing section I argued that, in all its manifestations, the world of two dimensions is premised on the existence of two constituents that are different from each other and are only externally related to one another. It is the irreducible difference between the two that underpins dualities or pairs of opposites. Division can only be overcome by inserting the oppositional constituents within a higher totality, be this the higher rationality of a synthesis in logic or an imaginary contract which contains all the 'oughts' pertaining to human and official conduct, such as a constitution, or the moment of creating an optimum equilibrium between two opposites.

In brief, unlike monism, dualism insists that the world must be broken and then bridged. And like monism, it ends up preaching the possibility of a final unity. In the nineteenth century, William James made the astute observation that 'the absolute of monism is replaced by the ultimatum of dualism.'[40] In dialectics too, duality needs to be transformed into a trinity (thesis, antithesis and synthesis), which then collapses into a unity or oneness. In contextualism, on the other hand, equilibrium is attained by

[40] William James, *Pragmatism and the Meaning of Truth* (Cambridge: Harvard University Press, 1978), p. 78.

ensuring the flow of movement back and forth between the thing or the event and its context.

What is clearly missing from both monism (the universe-based view) and dualism (the biverse-based view) is the possibility of the existence of a multiverse, that is, of more than two variables which stand not only alongside each other, but are also inside each other. These are: (i) agency, (ii) institutions and (iii) discourse, and all are situated in a given space–time (ST). Interestingly, neither monism nor dualism embraces time and space. In fact, they are presumed to be atemporal and aspatial. Their projected representation of reality is assumed to be the real representation at all times and in all locations.[41]

If I were to draw a formula capturing what I am proposing here, it would look like this:

$$K = f(A + D + I - GIT)^{ST}$$

As mentioned above, A refers to agency, D refers to discourse while I denotes institutions. GIT is Godel's incompleteness theorem.[42] Its inclusion owes much to the fact that I wish to leave room for 'the uncanny' – the unpredictable, and often unimaginable, happenings that subvert the intentions of actors. GIT thus captures events, unpredictable implications of actions, accidents, crises and so on on the one hand, as well as the possibility of incorrect theorising on the other. Essentially, it is a compromise between our endless quest for understanding and our limitations as human thinkers and observers. Its presence in the formula serves to draw attention to the impossibility of absolute certainty and of intellectual exactness. And all the above variables are situated in ST. I will illustrate this in the subsequent chapter, which discusses the dependence of A, D and I on space and time, and the advantages of examining the inter-relations of the variables, as opposed to looking at single variables. It would suffice to mention here that time is conceptualised as both temporal duration (Chronos) and the 'right time' or the time of 'here and now' (Kairos). Both dimensions of time are important since it is often the case that the circumstances of time

[41] Pierre Bourdieu has gone a step further to argue that scientific practice is so 'detemporalised' that it tends to exclude even the idea of what it excludes. 'Because science is possible only in relation to time which is opposed to that of science, it tends to ignore time and, in doing so, to reify practices'; *Outline of a Theory of Practice* (Cambridge: Cambridge University Press, 1977), p. 9.

[42] Solomon Feferman et al. (eds.), *Kurt Godel: Collected Works*, Vol. 1 (New York: Oxford University Press, 1986).

or the environment (Kairos) explain why something can happen or unfold only at a particular point in time and not at 'any time'.[43]

All variables, as will be shown in more detail in Chapter 2, form an integrated circuit. Agency is shaped, but not determined, by structures and is generative of institutions and discourses which in turn legitimise, but can also de-legitimise, structures and institutions. In this process, agents transform themselves, construct new meanings, redesign institutions and crystallise discursive practices. So instead of focusing on isolated variables or pairs of variables, we reach an understanding that draws things together and projects reality as a relational affair unfolding in ST.[44] The latter setting is important since there is no guarantee that the same co-mingling of variables would have produced the same outcome at a different point in time and in a different location. The co-action of agency, institutions and discourse could have yielded a different phenomenon or a different reality – an allotopia – at a given point in time. This means that the interrelations among the variables have their own suis generic reality and that any necessities we perceive are the crystallised contingencies of the interaction of a given structure, a specific agency and a certain discourse in an ST.

Paying attention to the interrelations of variables is important because they do not affect each other ab-extra, but ab-intra. As the foregoing discussion has noted, individuals taken out of structures or society is an unrealistic abstraction. Similarly, institutional structures are not entities superimposed on individuals; in fact, if they are emptied of individuals, they become just fossilised entities (see Chapter 3). Agency is in structure and structure is in agency since things do not only happen to human beings, but they also happen by them. As noted above, structures shape and are shaped by agency's actions and discourses socialise and imprint

[43] For an excellent account of the distinction between Chronos and Kairos, or time and qualitative time, see John E. Smith, 'Time and Qualitative Time', 40(1) *Review of Metaphysics* (1986), pp. 3–16. Smith discusses the qualitative character of time on page 4. See also his article entitled 'Time, Times and the "Right Time"', 53 *The Monist* (1996), pp. 1–13.

[44] Institutions are formed, evolve and are reformed within wider structural environments and settings. In the subsequent chapters, I will discuss the importance of time for institutional outcomes and for agents' actions and practices. T. S. Eliot captured the interplay between time and discourse wonderfully in his poem 'The Rock', Chorus VII: 'A moment in time but time was made through that moment: for without the meaning there is no time, and that moment of time gave the meaning'; T. S. Eliot, *The Complete Poems and Plays* (London: Faber and Faber limited, 1969), p. 160. P. DiMaggio and W. W. Powell referred to 'cultural scripts' which are diffused in organisational environments, but they did not examine in detail how easily the latter can change with time owing to agents' actions and practices; *The New Institutionalism in Organizational Analysis* (Chicago, IL: University of Chicago Press, 1991).

ideas and beliefs on people's minds, but they are also produced by them and change in time. Accordingly, there is no primacy or overriding presence of one of them, because each cannot exist without the other. They are simultaneously emergent, co-implicated and interacting.

Similarly, although we are embedded within structures and institutions,[45] we tend to view them as monolithic and soulless entities. In both our ordinary conversations and our reflections we often view them as representations of a 'world without time'. And 'a world without time' is, inevitably, a 'world without actors'. Institutions are thus part of this world, but they are not part of our world. Otherwise put, they have objective facticity, but do not have subjective relationality. But in reality, 'their world' is 'our world'. We are instrumental in reproducing and stabilising institutional realities, as Giddens's structuration theory has so eloquently revealed.[46] We are also capable of triggering changes to them and even destroying them.

The merger of objective and subjective realities, of the factitious and the noumenon, applies to the relation between institutions, agency and discourse. The Cartesian subject (I cogito) does not stand outside the world and its constituents. Agents take part in them and make them real. For 'the real' for agents is not the object (res) (circumambient phenomenology). The object by itself exists without our perception of it. But to know it, to reach it (make it real), we must perceive it, reflect on it and understand it. The observer and the observed are thus commingled; we look into the world through our percepts and conceptions of it. The intrinsic relation among the variables mentioned above means that there is nothing that includes or supersedes everything but all stand in a simultaneous mutual reception and interact in procuring an explanandum.

In this respect, it would be very difficult indeed to understand institutions without situating them within their historical, social and structural settings and without giving them a 'human face'. Actors within them generate outputs, forms and practices which, in turn, change the operation of institutions and the institutional logic or culture. Consequently, these can then impact on the larger structural field and on the relationship among

[45] I adhere to a broad definition of institutions, encompassing formal as well as informal practices, rules, norms, procedures and organisations facilitating human cooperation and coordinated action. See Asbjorn Sonne Norgaard, 'Rediscovering Reasonable Rationality in Institutional Analysis', 29 *European Journal of Political Research* (1996), pp. 31–57, 29; K. Armstrong and S. Bulmer, *The Governance of the Single Market* (Manchester: Manchester University Press, 1998), p. 56.

[46] Giddens, *New Rules of Sociological Method: A Positive Critique of Interpretative Sociologies*. For an excellent analysis, see Ira J. Cohen, *Structuration Theory: Anthony Giddens and the Constitution of Social Life* (London: Macmillan, 1989).

organisations and actors. Gradually, new collective meanings emerge which become paradigms that then guide actors and activities.

In light of the above, it may be observed that realities are complex,[47] multidimensional and interlaced. But interlacing and conjunction do not necessarily imply that the variables cannot be separated so as to make it possible for the observer to identify the 'heavier' presence of one over the others at a given point in time. We can perceive them as separate but we cannot divide them or disregard their intermingling. True, we often obtain what might be termed the summit view, thereby being unable to see what goes on below the summit. But this should not preclude an awareness of complexity, that is, the interactions among agency, discourse and institutions, which can neither be reduced to a cause of all causes (monism) or A/not A (dualism).

Connexio rerum thus depicts an unbroken world of conjunctions and interactions among elements that are co-implicated but can also be distinguished from each other.[48] Basing social scientific inquiry on the *connexio rerum*, therefore, uncovers a world of relations, mutual entanglement and synergy. It is a polycentric epistemology. As the variables are dependent on one another and live in one another, none of them can be lifted out of their relations and given an over-inflated importance. As such, they form a dynamic, integrated system which leads to the production of a given phenomenon or outcome.

1.5 Conclusion

The cognitional value of social sciences is significant. Without their input, we would have been unable to navigate the socio-political world around us and to make sense of our life journeys. Knowing 'our' worlds, both outer and inner, is part of the ordinary process of living. The problem facing us is that the quest for knowledge and for ways of understanding[49] the world and our place in it is full of assumptions. Some of them are visibly

47 For the notion of multiple realities see the works of William James and Alfred Schutz.

48 Compare also Whitehead, Modes of Thought, pp. 231–2; William James, 'Lecture IV: One and the Many' in *Pragmatism and the Meaning of Truth* (Cambridge, MA: Harvard University Press, 1978), p. 77.

49 I am using the term 'understanding' because I do not believe that understanding and explanation are opposites. Rorty was correct to argue that 'the idea of explanation and understanding are opposed ways of doing social science is as misguided as the notion that microscopic and macroscopic descriptions of organisms are opposed ways of doing biology', in Michael T. Gibbons ed. *Interpreting Politics* (Oxford: Basil Blackwell, 1987), p. 247. Compare also Fuller, *Social Epistemology*.

contingent and incorrect. Other assumptions are more concealed and often get elevated to the status of norms or values. As such, they escape justification and critical scrutiny despite the fact that they surface, and resurface, in social scientific outputs and official discourses. Perhaps this is to an extent unavoidable. Once assumptions become points of departure and thus the centre of mental frames, they tend to gain immunity from rigorous critical scrutiny. They cannot be tampered with. In addition, as Myrdal stated once 'chaos does not organise itself into cosmos. We need viewpoints and they presume valuations. A "disinterested social science" is, from this viewpoint, pure nonsense. It never existed and it will never exist. We can strive to make our thinking rational in spite of this, but only by facing the valuations, not by evading them'.[50] Eight years later, Karl Popper made a similar observation: he remarked that historians select and order the facts of history.[51] Examining the underlying assumptions of social scientific research, which do not seem to need justification because they serve as premises for syllogisms, and defending the need to embrace complexity and connectionalism have been the main aims of this chapter.

The socio-political world around us is neither singular nor simple. Nor does it stand in a position of exteriority to us, affecting us from the outside. We inhabit this world and make it what it is. For this reason, we never cease striving to understand it, notwithstanding our human limitations and its unpredictability and opaqueness. Paying a simultaneous attention to the cyclical and flowing movement among actors, institutions and discourses in spatialised time is quite promising. Since nothing exists separately, embracing the *connexio rerum*, looking for relations rather than things or factors, makes visible the intellectual blindspots and furthers the quest for knowledge and understanding.[52]

My argument here should not be seen as a personal quest for an all-embracing epistemology. That would be an intellectual hubris. Nor is it a quest for a unified vision of the social world. That would certainly be an illusion. I have sought to show the unfruitfulness of both oneness (monism) and pairs of opposites (dualism) and to highlight the advantages of embracing multiplicity and multiformity; that is, considering things in

[50] Gunnar Myrdal, *Value in Social Theory* (London: Routledge and Kegan Paul, 1958).

[51] Karl Popper, *The Open Society and Its Enemies*, Vol. 2 (Princeton, NJ: Princenton University Press, 1962), p. 269.

[52] For the opportune distortion of knowledge, see William James, 'The Will to Believe' and 'On a Certain Blindness in Human Beings' in *On Some Life's Ideals* (New York: Longmans, 1912); Compare also Gaston Bachelard's *New Scientific Spirit* (Boston, MA: Beacon Press, 1985).

their interrelations and connections. Splits and one- or two-dimensional ways of seeing the social world do not further understanding. Nothing in life is just either/or or against one another. Rather, social phenomena unfold in manifold sites, have manifold sides and are the product of conjunctions and the co-implication of several variables. As Pepper noted in another context, 'these acts or events are all intrinsically complex, composed of interconnected activities with continuously changing patterns. They are like incidents in the plot of a novel or drama. They are literally the incidents of life.'[53] And life can be neither lived nor understood without connectionalism.

[53] Stephen Pepper, *World Hypotheses* (Berkeley, CA: University of California Press, 1992 [1942]), p. 233.

2

Constructivisms and Institutional Constructivism

2.1 Introduction

Theoretical frameworks are not singular entities; they tend to have many variants. They resemble rich tapestries containing various facets and expositions. The latter may coalesce around common themes or core premises, but can also diverge as they unfold or develop. This is perfectly understandable. The human mind has infinite creativity and imagination.[1] It draws associations often among disparate things and constructs meanings. It projects ideas that often form a life of their own by escaping specific contexts and by being amenable to new correlations. In this respect, theoretical perspectives, methodological tools and scholarly practices form paths for perceiving, interpreting, knowing reality and for constructing meaning. As noted in the introduction, the perceived world is always an interpreted world and, therefore, an intelligible world. In this chapter, I would like to 'zoom into' the world of the many dimensions discussed in the previous chapter and to develop the model of institutional constructivism. But in doing so I also need to delve further into constructivism as an epistemological perspective which enables us to 'see into the life of the world' and to use this knowledge in order to live with others and to shape the world.

As is the case with all 'isms', constructivism contains several 'constructivisms', that is, constructivist perspectives which have been advanced by artists and scholars in social sciences and humanities. Identifying the fountain and mapping the many streams that sprang from it would enable me to simultaneously situate and develop the interactional constructivist approach. Once again, my objective is not to find similarities or to criticise existing constructivisms in order to 'build' the interactional constructivist approach. On the contrary, my journey is one of mapping an intellectual

[1] On imagination, see Mary Warnock, *Imagination* (Berkeley: University of California Press, 1976).

terrain and of unravelling the beauty of human creativity in handling partial, socio-culturally mediated knowledge and weaving meaning through discourse and social practices.

The subsequent discussion involves three steps; namely, the exploration of constructivism and the tracing of its roots in the philosophical tradition of pragmatism and in art; a discussion of constructivisms, which is not intended to be exhaustive; and finally, the explication of the interactional constructivist approach I discussed Chapter 1. This discussion is, in turn, lays the path for theorising institutional change (Chapter 3) and for a more applied focus in the subsequent chapters where I discuss the fruitfulness of institutional constructivism in explaining the complex dynamics and the evolution of European Union citizenship and Brexit.

2.2 Constructivism as a Theory of Cognition, Action and Imagination

In Chapter 1 I noted that constructivism neither idealises the real nor reduces it to an objective state of things. It views reality as the merger between the objective world and subjective encounters of it; a fusion of 'I' and 'id'. This merger gives rise to the construction of meanings, the framing of world events and the weaving of representations. All the above are discursively mediated and both existentialism and poststructuralism have elaborated on the importance of language.[2] The human mind theorises – sees,[3] interprets, understands and comprehends – both the natural and social worlds by weaving complex tapestries of meaning. By so doing, human beings are not only in the world; they also inhabit it and feel at home in it.

Imagine, for example, that you stand in front of a beautifully constructed country hall which, having been abandoned by its owners, remains locked. One can only admire its splendour from the courtyard and can only imagine the internal layout of the rooms adorned with marbled fireplaces and oak carved ceilings. Contrast this with an inhabited hall with open windows and doors that allow its dwellers and visitors to circulate and to admire the beauty of its rooms from different locations, from multiple perspectives and from many vantage points. The lived reality of the second

[2] For more discussion on this, see the introduction above.

[3] The ancient Greek word 'theoria' (that is, theory) and the corresponding verb contain the verb 'oro', which means to see.

manor is richer and more complex than the singular reality of a building seen solely from the courtyard.

Imagine further that the manor's owner decides to place a canvas depicting the lake and landscaped gardens of the hall in front of an open window that overlooks the lake and the gardens. Magritte has, indeed, painted a picture depicting a canvas placed before a window that replicated the view outside the window.[4] The real landscape seen from the open window is exactly the same as the one in the coloured canvas. It is as if the internal world is connected with the external one so closely that there is no disharmony in having a painting that brings an imaginary world into existence. However, as the canvas is positioned exactly in front of the window, a dweller present in the room might not be able to gain a 'glimpse of the real' – the painting conceals the real view by representing it and thus constructing a new one. But an observer of the dweller in the room can clearly see two realities,[5] one 'out there' and another 'in here', thereby making connections and juxtapositions between them – an image that may or may not be easily graspable if the observer were the dweller.

Seeing things as they are thus requires the removal of the painted canvas from the window[6] or seeing things differently by juxtaposing and connecting one's own perceived reality with those of others, for the common reality can be perceived both in identical as well as in radically different ways.[7] In both cases, however, human beings' capacity to gaze at things that were not previously easily accessible, to reach, understand, connect and disconnect and to construct new meanings, marks their existence. This is a basic premise of constructivism.

Dewey highlighted the capacity of human beings to invent meanings that go beyond their immediate encounters and to shape practices with a view to attending to the 'lived situations of life'.[8] This is precisely what phenomenologists, such as Merleau-Ponty, meant by saying that 'because we are in the world, we are condemned to meaning'.[9] Meaning and

[4] Rene Magritte, The Human Condition (1933). The painting is in the National Gallery of Art in Washington DC.

[5] Alfred Schutz, 'On Multiple Realities', in *Collected Papers I: The Problem of Social Reality* (The Hague, Netherlands: Martinus Nijhoff, 1967).

[6] This could also be expressed as the Heideggerian moment of aletheia or unconcealment; Martin Heidegger, *Being and Time* (Oxford: Blackwell, 1967).

[7] Jerome Bruner has shown that minds have a preference for different kinds of worlds; *Actual Minds, Possible Worlds* (Cambridge, MA: Harvard University Press, 1986).

[8] John Dewey, *Art as Experience* (New York: Minton, Balch, 1934), p. 263.

[9] *Phenomenology of Perception* (London: Routledge and Kegan Paul, 1967), p. xix, cited in Maxine Green, 'A Constructivist Perspective on Teaching and Learning in the Arts', in

construction take place through the development of frames (schemata) which eventually become generalised and routinised. Frames become conceptual frameworks, theoretical frameworks, ideologies, world-creation stories, narratives of peoplehood, shared understandings and world views (Weltanschauungen) (see Introduction and Chapter 1).

As frames become routinized, reproduced and sedimented, they are imbued with objectivity. The construction of reality[10] is an affair that goes beyond the subjective construction of reality; it is intersubjective and socio-political.[11] It is also dynamic, that is, is always unfolding in time. As Gellner wonderfully noted,

> Societies exist in time. Notoriously, the ways in which various societies conceive themselves to be situated in time, differ a good deal. The way in which time and its horizons are conceived is generally connected with the way the society understands and justifies itself. A society can possess a world-creation story, in which the creation of the world and the foundation of the society itself are tied up: the cosmic and the social foundation-stones may be identical or both may be invoked to validate the moral order.[12]

Paying attention to these world-creation stories and to a socio-political order's legitimising suppositions is also a *differentia specifica* of constructivism. And, of course, those stories and suppositions can also be underpinned by preconceptions and misconceptions, perceptions and misperceptions, biases and prejudices which affect how we see the world and render it intelligible.[13]

Transcending limiting and outmoded beliefs and superstitions and the arbitrary exercise of power has also been tied up with the idea of societal progress that emerged with the advent of Enlightenment in Europe in the eighteenth century. Accordingly, even contemporary philosophers cannot conceive of the possibility of justice without a hypothetical freedom to detach oneself from the world and to strip oneself of all prejudices and private experiences. They insist that justice can only be rendered intelligible by looking at the organisation of society with a fresh perspective untainted

---

Catherine Twomey Fosnot (ed.), *Constructivism: Theory, Perspectives and Practice* (New York: Teachers College, Columbia University, 1996), p. 130.

[10] Peter Berger and Thomas Luckmann, *The Social Construction of Reality: A Treatise in the Sociology of Knowledge* (London: Penguin Books, 1971 [1966]). But compare John Searle's book entitled *The Construction of Social Reality* (New York: The Free Press, 1995).

[11] Heinz Von Foerster, 'On Constructing a Reality', in Watzlawick (ed.), *The Invented Reality*, pp. 41–61.

[12] Ernst Gellner, *Thought and Change* (London: Lowe and Brydone, 1964), p. 1.

[13] Daniel Kahneman, *Thinking Fast and Slow* (London: Penguin Books, 2011).

by fear, comfort, desire, privilege and material wealth.[14] A good and just society can thus be designed from a morally and socially neutral point of view; that is, by thinning societies' complexity. More importantly, it can be designed by either an external Law Giver, who, like Solon in ancient Athens, could graft just laws onto the system,[15] or by its members deciding to 'opt out' of it in order to pass authoritative and good judgments on it.[16]

Both individuals and societal units are therefore unavoidably immersed into journeys of perception, cognition, narrative construction and reflection. And these journeys are time specific. The arduous struggle of attaining understanding never ends, for even if we believe that we have 'cracked an enigma', our euphoria is only momentary since the process of deciphering a new reality and negotiating meaning in a new social interaction starts again. What emerges out of this incessant process is a new perspective and a new construction. 'There is no structure apart from construction', Piaget noted.[17] Gellner believed so, too: 'we cannot divest ourselves of our conceptual clothing and stand bare and receptive to the world "as it really is", for we can only perceive and categorise the world through some system of concepts, some particular setting of our sensibility'.[18] And both construction and comprehension require human beings' reflection on, and reconstruction of, existing conceptual frames and perceptual lenses. According to von Glasersfeld, once the operations by means of which we assemble the experiential world can be explored, the possibility of doing things differently and, perhaps, better presents itself.[19]

Pragmatism, symbolic interactionism and the sociology of Max Weber and Emile Durkheim nurtured constructivist thinking. Max Weber contributed to the development of the sociology of spiritual meaning, while Durkheim sought to unravel the many layers of social reality; namely, the surface reality or morphology of established collective behaviours, symbols corresponding to institutions, values, ideas and ideals and, finally,

[14] John Rawls, *A Theory of Justice* (Oxford: Oxford University Press, 1971). Compare also Stammler's conception of justice in his 'Die Lehre von dem Richtigen Rechte'.

[15] Compare Carl L. Becker, *The Heavenly City of the Eighteenth Century Philosophers* (New Haven, CT: Yale University Press, 1932).

[16] The fact that these constructions aid a specific understanding of the world and of ourselves has been pointed out by Wittgenstein and Gellner among others; Ludwig Wittgenstein, *Philosophical Investigations* (London: Blackwell, 1953), Gellner, *Thought and Change*, p. 107 et seq.

[17] Jean Piaget, *Structuralism* (New York: Basic Books, 1970), p. 140.

[18] Gellner, *Thought and Change*, p. 108.

[19] Ernst von Glasersfeld, 'An Introduction to Radical Constructivism', in Watzlawick (ed.), *The Invented Reality*, pp. 17–40, at p. 18.

states of the collective mind.[20] All these observations reveal Weber and Durkheim's refutation of the existence of a social objectivity outside discourse and mental process.

Karl Mannheim's *Ideology and Utopia*[21] and his article 'Wissensociologie' (1931) established constructivism as a framework in the philosophy of social sciences. Like Weber, Mannheim saw society as an ensemble of meaningful individual actions which take place in certain socio-economic and cultural locations. And like Marx, he recognised the importance of class-based actions. But unlike Marx, he was not willing to concede the overdetermination of structure with respect to beliefs and ideologies, thereby allowing space for 'free-floating' constructivism. Ideology was contrasted to utopia, which reflected the anti-ideology of the dominated group struggling to bring about change. In his *Diagnosis of Our Time*,[22] Mannheim thought that both ideology and utopia could be transcended by studying, and reflecting on, the historical milieu and producing a genuine qualitative knowledge of social affairs which would be 'relational', but not relativist. Intellectuals from various social strata and having different perspectives could come together to make true knowledge possible. Mannheim's work established constructivism as a theory of action, in addition to being a theory of cognition. Social change and finding effective solutions to the problems of social life constitute the second main premise of constructivism.

It is true that the individualistic or cognitive variant of constructivism has been juxtaposed with social constructivism, but, as I remarked in Chapter 1, the individual and the social cannot be treated as separable and antagonistic. For they are complementary and symbiotic. Certainly, it would be incorrect to treat the individual as an asocial, ahistorical and acultural agent capable of perceiving and articulating their perceptions. Equally, it would be incorrect to view the individual as an interpellated subject, unable to think for themselves and to reflect on the conditions of their existence and incapable of procuring changes to them. 'Thinking within', a process that includes introspective reflections, is simultaneously 'acting upon', that is, an action that yields effects in the social environment. In this respect, Bourdieu was correct to argue that the separation between theory and practice is unsustainable; theory can be a form of

[20] Max Weber, *Gesammelte Aufsatze zur Wissenschaftslehre* (Tubigen: Mohr, 1922); Emile Durkheim, *Suicide* (Tubingen: Routledge and Kegan Paul, 1952).

[21] New York: Harcourt, Brace, 1936.

[22] New York: Oxford University Press, 1944.

practice as well as impacting upon practice.[23] Accordingly, irrespective of whether one finds either Bourdieu's structuralist constructivism or Berger and Luckmann's more agent-oriented constructivism more convincing,[24] constructivist theorists in the main see theoretical innovation as closely linked to social action and social change. There is the expectation that through reflective thinking and critical social scientific knowledge a new subjectivity will be created 'in confrontation with objectified social structures'.[25] Feminist, critical race and post-colonial epistemologies have also embraced constructivism as a theory of cognition as well as of social action. Their social scientific insights and the production of knowledge are closely linked to bringing about transformation in society and to challenging structures of domination and power. De Sousa Santos, Unger, Scott, Beck, Habermas and Apel all have espoused an interventionist social science aimed at deepening and radicalising democracy.[26] Unger's book, entitled *Politics: A Work in Constructive Social Theory* (1987),[27] makes explicit the need for social reconstruction and his conception of social science as a struggle to 'reinvent society'.[28] In this way, transformative politics is placed at the heart of the constructivist project. Grounded theory or 'embedded utopianism'[29] is seen as the antidote to an adherence to a revolutionary

[23] It is true that not all constructivisms would accept this tenet; Luhmann's autopoetic constructivism differs from Bourdieu's structuralist constructivism. This is discussed later.

[24] Bourdieu retains the links with structural Marxism; he believes in the objectivity of structure and that the meanings actors will weave depend on their location in the objective structures of sociality. Agents have a habitus which impacts on how they perceive the world and what is important in it; Pierre Bourdieu, *The Logic of Practice* (Cambridge: Polity Press, 1990). Drawing on Bourdieu as well as on the New French Pragmatism of Boltanski and Latour, IR scholars have recently utilised the concept of 'practice' and advocated a shift of attention to international practices. See, for example, Emanuel Adler and Vincent Pouliot (eds.), *International Practices* (Cambridge: Cambridge University Press, 2011); Christian Bueger and Frank Gadinger, *International Practice Theory: New Perspectives* (Houndmills: Palgrave Macmillan, 2015); Christian Bueger, 'The Play of International Practice. Minimalism, Pragmatism and Critical Theory', *International Studies Quarterly* (2014), available at www.Researchgate.net, accessed on 11 March 2016; Peter Jackson, 'Pierre Bourdieu, the Cultural Turn and the Practice of International History', 34(1) *Review of International Studies* (2008), pp. 155–81.

[25] Delanty, *Social Science*, p. 115.

[26] The same applies to Bhaskar's critical realism; *A Realist Theory of Science*; *Scientific Reason and Human Emancipation* (London: Verso, 1986); *Dialectic* (London: Verso, 1993). For a good discussion of the similarities and dissimilarities between constructivism and critical realism, see Delanty, *Social Science*.

[27] Cambridge: Cambridge University Press, 1987.

[28] Delanty, *Social Science*, p. 116.

[29] Dora Kostakopoulou, *The Future Governance of Citizenship* (Cambridge: Cambridge University Press, 2008).

rupture, on the one hand, and to producing social scientific knowledge that aims to defend and perpetuate the existing material and ideological status quo, on the other.

The identification of new possibilities for social relations and for socio-political reconstruction cannot be made without recourse to imagination. Imagination reflects the potential in existing structures and inspires agents to transformative social action. Society is no longer conceived of as an integrated, mysterious whole that is untouchable, but as an ensemble of relations that can be tampered with, with a view to creating freer and more congenial environing conditions. In *The Self-Production of Society* (1977) and *Return of the Actor* (1988), Touraine sought to capture the 'rebirth of the subject' following the post-structuralist focus on the overdetermination of agency by structure.[30] Inspired by social movements, he emphasised the ability of social agents to effect social change while acknowledging their inability to determine both the scope and direction of it in a radically open and indeterminist world.

Castoriadis also focused on the ability of human beings to change social relations and to engage in creative, autonomous activity in all domains of socio-political life. He outlined the positive, creative role of imagination in creating societal institutions which nurture human beings' ability to create and determine the conditions of their existence. His analysis of Athenian democracy extoled the human self-creative spirit. The ancient Greek Anthropos (human) was characterised by an awareness of death and a desire to prattein/poiein, that is, to make, to do and to create, notwithstanding the futility of their existence.[31] Humanity is self-creation: 'humans took nothing from the gods, and no god gave them anything. This is the spirit of the fifth century, and this is the tragedy that the Athenians chose to reward'.[32] Singular human beings are thus endowed with a radical imagination which can disrupt sedimented social imaginaries and institute new significations and imaginaries. The radical imagination of human beings 'has to be tamed, channelled, regulated and brought into line with life in society, and also with what we call reality'.[33] This is achieved by socialisation and all the other mechanisms designed to instil

[30] Alain Touraine, *The Self-Production of Society* (Chicago, IL: University of Chicago Press, 1977); *Return of the Actor* (Minneapolis: University of Minnesota Press, 1988).

[31] Cornelius Castoriadis, *Figures of the Thinkable* (Stanford, CA: Stanford University Press, 2007); *Crossroads in the Labyrinth* (Cambridge, MA: MIT Press, 1984); *The Imaginary Institution of Society* (Cambridge, MA: MIT Press, 1987).

[32] Castoriadis, *Figures of the Thinkable*, p. 11.

[33] Ibid., p. 75.

conformity. But the mastery and control of individuals is bound to remain incomplete; individuals are partly 'walking fragments of the institution of society'.[34] They also thinkers and capable of autonomous creation and self-creation. These 'elemental facts – the self-creation of humanity, the self-creation of societies – are, almost always, almost everywhere, veiled; they are concealed from society by its very institution'.[35] But the radical democratic project can only unfold by using them as the necessary scaffolding for social action and change. Constructivism, in this sense, becomes the art of creation, of co-creation and of innovation.

2.3 Constructivisms: Disciplinary Perspectives

One cannot sidestep the fact that there exists a long tradition of constructivism in art. In the 1920s, Russian artists sought to refashion the relationship between human beings and their environment. They called into question the assumed relationship of harmony between the two. They also questioned the view that the world exists in order to provide a sympathetic resonance to human expressions. As an alternative, they posited the presence of the 'human constructor' and their new world. By celebrating the capacity, and the ensuing responsibility, of human beings to create their own future, they fused art and politics. A wonderful pictorial representation of this is El Lissitzky's protogram in 1924, in which he superimposed his head onto his hand. Head, for thinking and imagination, and hand, for artistic expression and action, would combine in creating art from the world of the imagination. Cognition of the world was thus linked to (social) action and imagination with a view to creating the 'New Man' who would invent the 'new society'. Constructivism became a progressive art movement for an egalitarian new society.

The artworks of Tatlin and Gabo provided illustrations of both ideas and, even though Gabo was using the term 'construction' before the 1920s, it is widely held that constructivism as a movement arose in 1920 amid leftist artists. Of course, Kazimir Malevich had already exhibited his red and black squares (thirty-nine canvasses) at the Dobychina Gallery in Petrograd, Russia, in 1915. In the Gallery's catalogue, Malevich's work was entitled 'Quadrilateral' and the exhibition consisted of floating, weightless compositions of squares. His 'suprematism' captured both the idea of total freedom and the beauty of non-hierarchical forms floating from, and

[34] Ibid., p. 92.
[35] Ibid., p. 102.

within, geometrical spaces (non-objective art). For him, the real became movement and canvasses became expressions of motion, mobility and dynamism. His red square became the symbol of change; life in its fullness, according to some commentators, and a signal for revolution, according to others. Like Malevich, Lyubov Popova (1889–1924) displayed vertical planes floating in space, coining the term 'architectonics'. The latter was defined as the 'science of architecture and the arrangement of knowledge'.

Influenced by Malevich, El Lissitzky named the abstract art he was creating 'Proun', which is a Russian acronym for 'project for the affirmation of the new' (pro unovis). Although Lenin, who died in 1924, and Stalin demanded that art should reflect the truths of socialist realism and propagate the unambiguous and the real, Lissitzky disagreed. He emphasised processes. Accordingly, a canvas would only be a momentary image of a process and not the expression of a solidified principle. In Europe, Modrian and the cubists also embraced the 'necessity of construction' which, in reality, was the expression of a desire for reconstruction. The Dutch De Stijl – a founding member of which was Modrian – and the German Bauhaus movements were deeply influenced by the constructivist ideas and the perception of art in both social and functional terms. Art, everyday life, society and politics were thus seen to be intimately connected. Gabo's 'The Realist Manifesto' embodied the belief in the independent and productive social role of art and the close alignment between artistic thought and practice in 'building up anew'.[36] Similarly, his 1937 Circle, an 'international survey of constructive art', which he co-edited, defended 'The Constructive Idea in Art' amid deteriorating political conditions, particularly in Germany.

A clear definition of constructivism was provided by the Blok group in 1924. The group was founded at Lotz, Poland, in 1922 by Wladislaw Strzeminski, and the 'Editorial' in the first issue of its magazine bearing the same title stated that 'constructivism does not aspire toward the creation of style as an immutable stereotype relying on previously invented and established forms; but it accepts the problems of construction – which can and must give way to continual changes and improvement under the impact of those newer and even more complex demands that the general development of life presents us with'.[37] The editorial ended by noting

[36] The Realist Manifesto was written in 1920 to accompany an open-air exhibition in Tverskoy Boulevard, Moscow.

[37] Cited in Stephen Bann (ed.), *The Tradition of Constructivism* (New York: Da Capo Press, 1974), p. 103.

'the inseparability of the problems of art and the problems of society'.[38] Strzeminski himself published his theory of Unism in Blok and until the end of his life he remained committed to effecting social change though art. He never saw art as something separate from, and alien to, ordinary routines and social life. In fact, the celebration of the everyday life has been one of the hallmarks for the constructivist movement.

By the late 1920s it was widely accepted that constructivism represented a creative world view which responded to the concrete needs of contemporary life, and this world view was visible in literature, poetry, and architecture as well as kinetic art.[39] The main task of constructivist artists was to change collective imaginations with a view to procuring material transformations in the social order. That was the ethos of the Circle which was co-edited by Naum Gabo. As he put it, 'life without creative effort is unthinkable, and the whole course of human culture is one continuous effort of the creative will of Man'.[40] In his letter to Herbert Read (1942), Gabo confessed that:

> This [constructive] idea means more to me. It involves the whole complex of human relation to life. It is a mode of thinking, acting, perceiving, and living. The Constructive philosophy recognises only one stream in our existence – life (you may call it creation, it is the same). Any thing or action which enhances life, propels it and adds to it something in the direction of growth, expansion and development, is Constructive. The 'how' is of secondary importance ... 'Perfection', in the Constructive sense, is not a state but a process; not an ultimate goal but a direction. We cannot achieve perfection by stabilising it – we can achieve it only by being in its stream; just as we cannot catch a train by riding in it, but once in it we can increase its speed or stop it altogether, and to be in the train is what the Constructive Idea is striving for.[41]

These ideas found fertile ground in the field of education. Maria Montessori (1870–1952) had already made her mark, and the belief that learning must be creative and autonomous, as opposed to heteronomous, that is, imputed by another person, characterised Jean Piaget's work.[42] In

[38] Ibid., p. 106.

[39] Jakob Chernikov, 'The Constitution, Study and Formation of Constructivism' in Bann (ed.), *The Tradition of Constructivism*, p. 169.

[40] Naum Gabo, 'The Constructive Idea in Art' in Bann (ed.), *The Tradition of Constructivism*, p. 212.

[41] Ibid., pp. 214–20, at p. 217.

[42] One should also mention here the sociohistorical work of Lev Vygotsky, *Mind in Society* (Harvard, MA: Harvard University Press, 1978) and Nelson Goodman's *Ways of Worldmaking* (Indianapolis, IN: Hackett, 1978).

'*Logique et connaissance scientifique*' (Logic and Scientific knowledge) published in Encyclopédie de la Pléiade (1967), he defended the merits of the constructivist epistemology, and has thus been recognised as a pioneer.[43] As the director of the International Centre for Genetic Epistemology, Piaget invited Heinz von Foerster to a symposium he organised in 1976. Von Foerster was a renowned cybernetician. At the University of Illinois he had established the Department of Biophysics and Physiology in 1957. His interest in processes of cognition was manifested in his address to the Fourth International Design Research Association conference in 1973, which was entitled 'On Constructing Reality'. In this address, which can be read in Paul Watzlawick's edited collection The Invented Reality,[44] Foerster outlined the neurophysiological foundation of human perception but was also keen to refute the claim that all reality is the mind's invention (solipsism). He drew an interesting figure (figure 20) in order to highlight 'the social construction of reality'. As he put it, 'neither I nor the other can be the center of the universe'.[45] At the conference organised by Piaget, he presented a paper which was entitled 'Objects: tokens for (Eigen-) behaviours'. This was destined to become a classic text of constructivist epistemology.

Piaget noted the importance of empowering pupils through their involvement in the exploration of ideas and experiential learning. The merits of this approach had been defended by John Dewey (1922) whose work and pedagogical insights inspired experience-based curricula and a shift of attention to 'how we think'.[46] Through discussion, exploration, encouraging students to think about the learning process, to reconsider their views, playfulness, the disruption of routine, Piaget's constructivism highlighted the merits of a process of learning as a path towards self-knowledge, personal growth and change.[47]

[43] Ernst von Glasersfeld noted that Jean Piaget is the great pioneer of the constructivist theory of knowing; see *Radical Constructivism: A Way of Knowing and Learning* (London: Falmer, 1995).

[44] Von Foerster, 'On Constructing Reality', pp. 41–61.

[45] Ibid., p. 60.

[46] John Dewey, *How We Think* (Boston, MA: Heath, 1933 [1910]).

[47] Nancie Arwell, 'Writing and Reading from the Inside Out' in J. Hansen, R. Newkirk and D. Graves (eds.), *Breaking Ground: Teachers Relate Reading and Writing in the Elementary School* (Portsmouth, NH: Heinemann, 1985); Catherine Twomey Fosnot, *Enquiring Teachers, Enquiring Learners: A Constructivist Approach for Teaching* (New York: Teacher College Press, 1989); Jean Piaget, *Psychology and Epistemology: Towards a Theory of Knowledge* (Harmondsworth, England: Penguin, 1972. For a good discussion of Piaget's thinking, see Howard Gardner, *Developmental Psychology*, 2nd edn (Boston, MA: Little, Brown, 1982) and *The Quest for Mind: Piaget, Levi-Strauss, and the Structuralist Movement* (Chicago, IL and London: University of Chicago Press, 1981).

Learning thus becomes a constructive activity; the classroom is transformed into a site of interaction which encourages students to reflect on ideas, reformulate them, draw connections and to develop their own unique insights. Accordingly, conversations replace instruction and active and collaborative learning replaces passive listening and the uncritical absorption of information. All this changes how teachers and learners are viewed. Learners are no longer passive listeners who need motivation and encouragement in order to acquire competencies. Teachers, on the other hand, become the orchestrators of dialogue and enquiry by using the curriculum as a platform for fostering deep understanding. Teaching is not conceived of as the end of the educational process; it is, instead, enacted and re-enacted in the classroom. The 'soul of enactment is the dialogue in which teachers and children inform, err, question, correct, self-correct, think aloud, repeat, make sense – in other words, develop together'.[48] In this respect, 'what empowers – what ought to empower – is the recognition that there is no "reality" that is unquestionably given, the same for everyone ... we can help students realise that reality must be understood as interpreted experience, that there can be multiple perspectives and multiple interpretations ... a reciprocity of perspectives'.[49]

The constructivist approach to education thus is premised on the existence of an intimate connection between supportive learning and the attainment of personal growth.[50] Both contribute to the free development of individuality and to the creation of critical citizens and moral selves.[51] The interactions of teachers and students qua individuals and as a group lead all of them to confront, and to re-examine, their own convictions and beliefs and to act as agents of change. Piaget was adamant that seeing learning as a one-way and top-down affair and encouraging obedience-based class environments would simply cultivate and perpetuate submissive behaviours and mindless conformity to regulations by others in adulthood. Accordingly, a morality of obedience could never develop into

[48] Celia Genishi, A. McCarrier and N. R. Nussbaum, 'Research Currents: Dialogue as a Context for Teaching and Learning', 65 *Language Arts* (1988), pp. 182–90, at p. 190.

[49] M. Greene, 'Landscapes and Meanings', 63(8) *Language Arts* (1986), pp. 776–84, at p. 782.

[50] Chomsky pays little attention to the formative role of the environment and has been criticised for not explaining adequately how individuals' capacities develop within environments saturated with meaning and symbols; Howard Gardner, *Frames of Mind: The Theory of Multiple Intelligences* (London: Fontana Press, 1984), p. 325. See Noam Chomsky, *Reflections on Language* (New York: Pantheon, 1975). Compare also Jerry A. Fodor, *The Modularity of Mind* (Cambridge, MA: MIT Press, 1983).

[51] John Dewey, *Moral Principles in Education* (Boston, MA: Houghton Mifflin, 1909).

a morality of reflection, including of self-reflection, which is the basis of moral judgments and of respectful engagement with others.[52]

One observes here that cognitive objectives are closely aligned to behavioural and moral dispositions. This makes the constructivist alternative to authoritarian- and discipline-based learning quite attractive in so far as the classroom becomes the seedbed for critical citizenship. The educational experience is thus part of a wider socio-moral experience of promoting free inquiry, experimentation with ideas, motivation to reason, interest in the implications of one's behaviour and empathetic interactions.[53] The same ethic of doubt, critical enquiry and openness to social change characterises Kincheloe's critical pedagogy. In his books (2001, 2005, 2008), he articulates a variant of constructivism which highlights the role of power in the construction of knowledge and emphasises the responsibility of 'educated' persons to effect social change. To this end, the struggles of the oppressed are unique repositories of knowledge and insights which could be utilised in the pursuit of social justice. Re-attachment to the plight of the weak and the oppressed, and not detachment from society and contemplation of the principles of justice in a state of reflective equilibrium, as Rawls envisaged, should thus guide social action.[54]

Within the discipline of psychology, on the other hand, Robert Rocco Cottone has articulated an ontology of relational realism which leads to the intertwining of reality and the observer. And although it is true that it is through experiential exchanges and social interaction that 'things' obtain meaning, Cottone slips into relativism in so far he believes that there exist only partial, consensual truths which are valid within specific interpretive communities or communities of understanding. An understanding of experience is socially constructed, but there exist different 'constructions' or interpretations of the same experience. Truth is also socially generated since it emerges within social interaction and not from the extra mundane world. As the settings of social interaction vary, it follows that

[52] Jean Piaget, *The Moral Judgement of the Child* (London: Free Press, 1965 [1932]); Rheta De Vries and Betty Zan, 'A Constructivist Perspective on the Role of the Sociomoral Atmosphere in Promoting Children's Development', in Fosnot (ed.), *Constructivism*, pp. 103–19.

[53] Robert L. Selman, *The Growth of Interpersonal Understanding* (New York: Academic Press, 1980); John Dewey, *Interest and Effort in Education* (Edwardsville, IL: Southern Illinois Press, 1975 [1913]).

[54] Joe L. Kincheloe, *Getting beyond the Facts: Teaching Social Studies/Social Science in the Twenty-First Century* (New York: Peter Lang; 1989); *Critical Constructivism Primer* (New York: Peter Lang, 2008); *Knowledge and Critical Pedagogy* (Dordrecht, The Netherlands: Springer, 2008).

truths are variable as well. Various standpoints give rise to many truths which are, then, pursued by various communities of understanding. There exists no perfect congruence between the individual and a community, since individuals have overlapping memberships in several communities. As this increases the possibility of collisions among various truth perspectives, individuals have no other option than to negotiate and to renegotiate understanding in their unique life processes.[55] Evidently, Cottone's position is close to Ernst von Glasersfeld's radical constructivism. Individuals take part in 'circularly conjoined' modes of understanding and acting; their own interpretation of experiences and ideas enables them to build knowledge bases and to obtain understanding. What actually occurs, or things 'as they really are', do not automatically lead to action.[56]

In sociological research, constructivist approaches follow divergent paths. Berger and Luckmann's agent-oriented constructivism, for example, differs from Bourdieu's more structuralist constructivism, Luhmann's epistemological constructivism and Beck's work on risk. Beck unravelled the 'construction' of risk; various actors perceive risk(s) differently and construct issues and problems as risks-ridden. Furthermore, one observes its spill-over effects from science-technology to society: 'science, having lost reality, faces the threat that others will dictate to it what truth is supposed to be'.[57] Accordingly, social knowledge cannot be objective; it is coloured by these constructions and the scientific agents' agendas.[58] In contrast, Luhmann leaves very little room for agency within his systems theory.[59] Influenced by cybernetics and Von Foerster's work on organisations

[55] Robert Rocco Cottone, *Toward a Positive Psychology of Religion: Belief Science in the Postmodern Era* (Winchester, IL: John Hunt Publishing, 2011). Compare E. Gillett, 'Relativism and the Social-Constructivist Paradigm', 5(1) *Philosophy, Psychiatry, & Psychology* (1998), pp. 37–48.

[56] Ernst von Glasersfeld, *The Construction of Knowledge: Contributions to Conceptual Semantics* (Seaside, CA: Intersystems Publications, 1987).

[57] Ulrich Beck, *The Risk Society: Towards a New Modernity* (Cambridge: Polity Press, 1992); *World at Risk* (Cambridge: Polity Press, 2007), p. 167.

[58] See also Edmond Wright, *Narrative, Perception, Language, and Faith* (Basingstoke: Palgrave Macmillan, 2005). It is noteworthy that Beck's approach to risk differs from the cultural theory of Mary Douglas. Her definition of risk takes into account the common norms and values of certain interpretative communities; it is the product of group specific ways of seeing. See Mary Douglas, *Risk and Blame, Essays in Cultural Theory* (Abingdon: Routledge, 1992); Mary Douglas and Aaron Wildavsky, *Risk and Culture: An Essay on the Selection of Technological and Environmental Dangers* (Berkeley, CA: University of California Press, 1983).

[59] Niklas Luhmann, *Social Systems* (Stanford, CA: Stanford University Press, 1995); *Die Wissenschaft der Gessellschaft* (Frankfurt: Suhrkamp, 1990).

as autopoetic systems, Luhmann paints a picture of the world as consisting of self-reproducing and quasi-independent subsystems characterised by their own rationality or internally constructed world views. The systems are guided by their own concerns for self-reproduction and display self-referentiality. Scientific knowledge is such a system, self-generating or autopoetic. It evolves in response to events, processes and systems. One cannot help but notice here that systems theory has more affinities with Talcott's structural functionalism than with the tradition of constructivism as discussed earlier. In this respect, it would not be incorrect to describe it as constructionist social systems theory.[60]

Constructivism captured the imagination of political scientists and international relations theorists in the 1990s. International relations has always been very rich in theoretical debates, but in the 1990s Emanuel Adler,[61] Freidrich Kratochwil,[62] Nicholas Greenwood Onuf[63] and Alex Wendt[64] sought to demonstrate in a dynamic way the fruitfulness of constructivism in explaining policy choices and the working of international institutions.[65] Among them, the European Union seemed to provide a confirmation of constructivist insights since it is the product of an institutional design premised on a transformational political vision.

The development of novel institutional arrangements in the European Union following the adoption of the Treaty on European Union (the so-called Maastricht Treaty) in 1992 (brought into force on 1 November 1993) inspired work on constructive citizenship in the EU in the mid and late 1990s.[66] Drawing on poststructuralism, social theory and normative

[60] See his *Erkenntnis als Konstruktion* (Bern: Benteli, 1988) and the last chapter in *Social Systems*.

[61] Emanuel Adler, 'Seizing the Middle Ground', 3(3) *European Journal of International Relations* (1997), pp. 319–63.

[62] Freidrich Kratochwil, *Rules, Norms and Decisions on the Conditions of Practical and Legal Reasoning in International Relations* (Cambridge: Cambridge University Press, 1989).

[63] Nicholas Greenwood Onuf, *World of Our Making: Rules and Rule in Social Theory and International Relations* (Columbia: University of South Carolina Press, 1989).

[64] Alex Wendt, *Social Theory of International Politics* (Cambridge: Cambridge University Press, 1999).

[65] For an excellent discussion of the similarities and differences, see Maja Zehfuss, 'Constructivism in International Relations: Wendt, Onuf and Kratochwil', in Karin M. Fierke and Knud Erik Jorgensen (eds.), *Constructing International Relations: The Next Generation* (New York: M. E. Sharpe, 2001) pp. 54–75.

[66] Dora Kostakopoulou, 'Towards a Theory of Constructive Citizenship in Europe', 4 *Journal of Political Philosophy* (1996), pp. 337–58; 'European Citizenship and Immigration after Amsterdam: Openings, Silences, Paradoxes', 24 *Journal of Ethnic and Migration Studies* (1998), pp. 639–56; 'Nested "Old" and "New" Citizenships in the EU: Bringing Forth the Complexity', 5 *Columbia Journal of European Law* (1999), pp. 389–413.

political theory, I blended theoretical work with applied research on citizenship, identity, sovereignty and democracy in the process of European integration. I then proceeded to apply the same constructivist approach to the intergovernmental cooperation in the context of the Union in Justice and Home Affairs.[67] I saw a constructive political potential in the new post-Maastricht institutional configuration which highlighted the need for a new thinking about the organising principles of political life in the late 1990s and the new millennium. Contrary to the existence of settled notions of community within national statist settings, the European Community cum European Union has not been a homogenous and unified body governed by a set of closed, coherent and fully theorised rules. Although Jean Monnet, the first president of the High Authority, was correct to note that the union of Europe cannot be based on goodwill alone and that nothing lasts without institutional rules, it is noteworthy that the latter are never completely settled and immune from debate and renegotiation. The master ideals of the European Community formed a legally distinct but at the same time flexible presuppositional framework within which national executives and supranational institutions alike declared their willingness to engage in a process of devising the rules and terms of their interaction without taking for granted commonalities, the existence and maintenance of common interests, shared beliefs about the 'common good' and shared dispositions. In this respect, the process of European integration with all its incrementalism, sudden turns, stagnation, upward trajectories, differentiated integration arrangements and so on is more akin to a generalised and bold conversation about institutional design. This conversation continually evolves as the parties, that is, supranational and national actors, engage in a collective quest for better solutions to common problems and for 'better' arrangements. And although the conversation does not mean the same things for all parties, since domestic constraints inform state preferences and shape the various interpretations of the European outputs, it is, nevertheless, shared within European Union institutional fora. But such a conversation can only be conducted within the auspices of an open and heterogeneous community that is not averse to disagreements, to critique, to new ideas and to collisions. It is true that strong disagreements and dissent often put pressure on the delicate institutional balances of the EU and disagreements about the scope of EU laws

[67] Dora Kostakopoulou, 'The 'Protective Union'; Change and Continuity in Migration Law and Policy in Post-Amsterdam Europe', 38(3) *Journal of Common Market Studies* (2000), pp. 497–518.

and policies take the form of disagreements about the EU itself in national arenas. In addition, the economic crisis has fuelled pressures for differentiated and asymmetrical arrangements. But at the same time, it has made clear that the EU can only exist if it is premised on a genuine commitment to continued partnership and to the ongoing creation, and modification, of common, albeit contested institutional realities.

Accordingly, a prominent feature of the political culture of the EU is the embracing of a politics of becoming. 'Becoming' means acceptance of equally legitimate perspectives, interests and opinions in a community of multifarious minorities – and not of majority government. The process of collective collaboration of diverse political communities cannot but induce fundamental changes in their workings and a generalised awareness of the contestability of their own positions and assumptions. This explains why European Union institutions are characterised by conditionality and reflexivity; they recognise their cognitive and coercive limits, seek to accommodate multiple and often contending visions even within a single provision or a legislative instrument and, more importantly, their outputs are open to review and revision. Profound disagreements co-exist with a deep commitment to shared ideas and common objectives.[68] Contestation is thus as much as a discursive process as an institutional fact. Disagreements and conflicts do not have a fleeting quality; they do not evaporate when Treaty amendments are agreed or when secondary legislation is published in the Official Journal. Rather, they continue as much after the deliberation as during and before it. European Union law becomes a surface for the inscription of disagreement and strife as well as a medium for the (co-ordinated) management and maintenance of dissent and antinomy. But this does not make the European Union a disorderly community. It merely affirms what it is, namely, a site for reflexive governance.

Thomas Christiansen, Knud Erik Jorgensen and Antje Weiner highlighted the significance of the building of such a polity beyond the nation-state. They articulated a number of very fruitful insights in 1998 by editing a special issue of the *Journal of European Public Policy* on the social construction of Europe.[69] Their approach was a social constructivist

[68] David Cameron's attempts to renegotiate the terms of the UK's EU membership attest this.

[69] Special Issue of the *Journal of European Public Policy*, 6(4), 01/1999, pp. 528–44. See also Markus Jachtenfuchs, Thomas Diez and Sabine Jung, 'Which Europe? Conflicting Models of a Legitimate European Political Order', 4(4) *European Journal of International Relations* (1998), pp. 409–45.

one; they emphasised the emergence and evolution of norms and processes through which norms become internalised by political actors and then sedimented. They noted the mechanisms for systemic transformation emerging from social learning, persuasion and normative dialogue. European integration has had a distinctive transformative impact on the European state system and on the identities of its constituent units. That was clear in the Europeanisation of domestic arenas and the development of European identities. Their conception of agency was distinctively Giddensian; actors reproduce structures in every day interactions and their interests and identities are endogenous to such interactions and thus socially constructed. Rules, norms, intersubjective meanings, institutions, routinized practices, unintended consequences of action, discourse; in brief, all the terms deployed by critical social theory and discourse ethics, became the crucial building blocks of changing social realities in Europe and beyond.

At that time, constructivism was seen to be a very promising approach to the study of international institutions and international relations in general.[70] It combined the material and ideational elements of the international reality and called for more attention to the discursive, institutional and normative realities of international governance.[71] Formal and informal rules and procedures had to be explored from the standpoint of a perspective that was sociologically sensitive and thus capable of explicating how institutions and role expectations could change actors' perceptions, interests and preferences in unanticipated ways.[72] The assumed centrality of given interests espoused by actors locked in processes of strategic bargaining became replaced by a scholarly interest in preference formation, the

[70] The term constructivism was first applied in IR by Nicholas Onuf in 1989; See his *World of Our Making*. See also Jeffrey T. Checkel, 'The Constructivist Turn in International Relations Theory', 50 *World Politics* (1998), pp. 324–48, and Stefano Guzzini 'A Reconstruction of Constructivism in International Relations', 6(2) *European Journal of International Relations* (2000), pp. 147–82.

[71] For a good discussion of the criteria of theory choice and for the application of different theoretical perspectives in IR, see Fred Chernoff, *Theory and Metatheory in International Relations: Concepts and Contending Accounts* (New York: Palgrave Macmillan, 2007); Compare also Charles Taylor, 'Interpretation and the Science of Man', 25(3) *Review of Metaphysics* (1971), p. 164.

[72] On the latter, see Robert Goodin (ed.), *The Theory of Institutional Design* (Cambridge: Cambridge University Press, 1996) and Paul Pierson, 'The Limits of Design: Explaining Institutional Origins and Change', 13(3) *Governance* (2000), pp. 475–99, at p. 483 et seq.

socialising effect of norms[73] and in identity construction.[74] Structures and procedures thus became more flexible, more plastic and thus processual. This led to a different treatment of supranational institutions; they could not be viewed as a 'passive transaction-cost reducing set of rules'.[75]

Wildavsky had already paved the way for the latter by suggesting that actors' preferences derive from their (political) cultural location and that cultural theory might have a lot to contribute to the constitution of political selves.[76] Legro utilised an organisational culture approach in order to study 'which norms matter' in World War II politics.[77] Similarly, a growing literature on international norms broadened the scope of research to include an analysis of ineffective norms, beliefs and patterns in international politics as well as norms' propensity towards institutionalisation.[78]

[73] Peter Hall, 'Policy Paradigms, Social Learning, and the State: The Case of Economic Policy-Making in Britain', 25(3) *Comparative Politics* (April 1993), pp. 275–96. Both lawyers and political scientists paid attention to the pluralisation of normative opportunities and the growth of international legal norms without adopting an explicit constructivist approach; see, for example, Charles Epp, *The Rights Revolution: Lawyers, Activists, and Supreme Courts in Comparative Perspective* (Chicago, IL: University of Chicago Press, 1998); Heinz Klug, *Constituting Democracy: Law, Globalism and South Africa's Political Reconstruction* (Cambridge: Cambridge University Press, 2000), Upendra Baxi, 'Taking Human Suffering Seriously: Social Action Litigation before the Supreme Court of India', in Neelan Tiruchelvan and Radhika Coomaraswamy (eds.), *The Role of the Judiciary in Plural Societies* (New York: St Martin's Press, 1987); Boaventura de Sousa Santos, *Toward a New Legal Common Sense* (London: Butterworths, 2002); Thomas Risse, Stepehn Ropp and Kathryn Sikkink (eds.), *The Power of Human Rights: International Norms and Domestic Change* (Cambridge: Cambridge University Press, 1999) and Anna-Marrie Slaughter, 'Judicial Globalisation', 40 *Virginia Journal of International Law* (2000), p. 1103; Ruti G. Heitel, *Humanity's Law* (Oxford: Oxford University Press, 2013).

[74] Jeffrey T. Checkel and Peter J. Katzenstein (eds.), *European Identity* (New York: Cambridge University Press, 2009).

[75] Andrew Moravcisk, 'Preferences and Power in the European Community: A Liberal-Intergovernmentalist Approach', 31(4) *Journal of Common Market Studies* (1993), pp. 473–524, at p. 508. One cannot but observe that this theorising is based on Oliver Williamson's (1975) pioneering work on transaction costs; *Markets and Hierarchies: Analysis and Antitrust Implications* (Chicago, IL: Free Press, 1975). Williamson argued organisations' development is driven by the efforts of rational actors to reduce transaction costs.

[76] Aaron Wildavsky, 'Choosing Preferences by Constructing Institutions: a Cultural Theory of Preference Formation', 81(1) *American Political Science Review* (1987), pp. 3–23.

[77] Jeffrey W. Legro, 'Which Norms Matter? Revisiting the "failure" of Internationalism', 51(1) *International Organisation* (Winter 1997), pp. 31–60.

[78] Robert O. Keohane, 'Neoliberal Institutionalism: A Perspective on World Politics', in R. O. Keohane (ed.), *International Institutions and State Power: Essays in International Relations* (Boulder, CO: Westview, 1989); Friedrich Kratochwil, 'Constructivism: What It Is (Not) and How It Matters', in Donattela Della Porta and Michael Keating (eds.), *Approaches and Methodologies in the Social Sciences: A Pluralist Perspective* (Cambridge: Cambridge University Press, 2008), pp. 80–98; E. Mariyani-Squire, 'Social Constructivism:

In 2002, Peter Haas and Ernst Haas put forward a pragmatic constructivist approach to international institutions.[79] Although they are viewed at times as rational actors, as realists and rational choice institutionalists would argue, Haas and Haas also considered them to be the locus for reflexive new practices and policies. In the place of a correspondence theory of truth, they envisaged a consensus-creating process mediated through and driven by institutions. A consensus theory of truth was premised on the distinction among three domains of knowledge, consisting of brute facts, social facts and hybrid facts. Transformative directions were thus closely aligned with the study of the existing structures of international governance.

The fruitful dialogue between constructivism, institutionalism and its variants and post-structuralism resulted in a typology of IR-based constructivism.[80] Wendt's sociological institutionalism alongside Checkel's[81] and Katzenstein's[82] identity-based constructivism became middle-ground constructivisms. These were, then, differentiated from rational choice constructivism, on the one hand, and what Smith called 'reflectivism' which was essentially radical postmodernism or discourse analysis, one the other.[83] Smith argued that despite the portrayal of social constructivism as

---

A Flawed Debate over Conceptual Foundations', 10(4) *Capitalism, Nature, Socialism* (1999), pp. 97–125; Michael N. Barnett and Martha Finnemore, 'The Politics, Power and Pathologies of International Organisations', 53(4) *International Organisation* (1999), pp. 699–733; Robert Jackson and George Sorensen, *Introduction to International Relations: Theories and Approaches* (Oxford: Oxford University Press, 1999). The pluralisation of the normative space and the interaction among various normative orders had captured the imagination of scholars in the 1980s as well. See inter alia Sally Engle Merry, 'Legal Pluralism', 22(5) *Law and Society Review* (1988), pp. 869–96; Peter Fitzpatrick, 'Law and Societies', 22 *Osgoode Hall Law Journal* (1984), p. 115; Boaventura de Sousa Santos, 'Law: A Map of Misreading; Toward a Postmodern Conception of Law', 14 *Journal of Law and Society* (1987), p. 274.

79 Peter M. Haas and Ernst B. Haas. 'Pragmatic Constructivism and the Study of International Institutions', 31(3) *Millennium* (2002), pp. 573–602.

80 For an explication of the dialogue between IR theorists and international law scholars, see Jutta Brunnee and Stephen J. Toope, 'Constructivist Approaches to International Law', in Jeffrey L. Dunoff and Mark Pollack (eds.), *Interdisciplinary Perspectives on International Law and International Relations: The State of the Art* (Cambridge: Cambridge University Press, 2012).

81 Jeffery T. Checkel, 'Tracing Causal Mechanisms', 8 *International Studies Review* (2006), pp. 62–70.

82 Peter J. Katzenstein, 'Introduction: Alternative Perspectives on National Security' in P. Katzenstein (ed.), *The Culture of National Security* (New York: Columbia University Press, 1996).

83 Steve Smith, 'The Discipline of International Relations: Still an American Social Science?', 2(3) *British Journal of Politics and International Relations* (October 2000), pp. 374–402.

distinct from both rationalism and reflectivism it shares methodological and epistemological assumptions with rationalism. He then observed that the term 'reflectivism' is often used to encompass both social constructivism and more radical accounts, such as critical theory, postmodernism and feminist theory.[84]

In the late 1990s, critical security studies provide a good example of the input of the constructivist school in international relations. Capitalising on a broadened and non-state centric agenda of security that emerged in the 1980s,[85] Ole Weaver, Barry Busan and Jaap de Wilde focused on processes of securitisation whereby ordinary issues become not only security concerns but existential threats to the survival of a community. In their book entitled *Security: A New Framework of Analysis*, which was published in 1998, they argued that securitisation is the product of speech acts enunciated by security actors seeking to convince their audiences that something is existentially threatened, thereby triggering exceptional measures of security management.[86] Their constructivist perspective triggered a healthy interest in processes of securitisation internally – i.e., in national arenas, in the EU and across the globe. It also sparked a fascinating debate with more Foucauldian perspectives characterising the so-called Paris School on security, centred on the work of Didier Bigo and Jeff Huysmans.[87] Despite their differences, both the Copenhagen and the Paris Schools saw desecuritisation, which is to say the disruption of the logics of survival of what is deemed to be under threat, and of exceptionality as the desirable alternative to securitisation strategies pursued by state officials and policy practitioners.

Compare also Robert O. Keohane, 'International Institutions: Two Approaches', 32(4) *International Studies Quarterly*, pp. 379–96; John G. Ruggie, 'What Makes the World Hang Together? Neo-utilitarianism and the Social Constructivist Challenge', 52(4) *International Organisation* (1998), pp. 855–85.

[84] Steve Smith, 'Social Constructivisms and European Studies: A Reflectivist Critique', 6(4) *Journal of European Public Policy* (1999), pp. 682–91.

[85] See North–South: The Report of the International Commission on International Development Issues (1980) which observed that a new, more comprehensive understanding of 'security' which would be less restricted to military aspects is needed; p. 124 et seq.

[86] Boulder, CO: Lynne Rienner, 1998.

[87] Didier Bigo, 'Security and Immigration: Toward a Critique of the Governmentality of Unease', 27 *Alternatives* (2002), pp. 63–92; Didier Bigo, 'Pierre Bourdieu and International Relations: Power of Practices, Practices of Power', 5(3) *International Political Sociology*, pp. 225–58; Jef Huysmans, *The Politics of Insecurity. Fear, Migration and Asylum in the European Union* (London: Routledge, 2006). But compare, William Walters, 'The Power of Inscription: Beyond Social Construction and Deconstruction in European Integration Studies', 31(1) *Millennium: Journal of International Studies* (2002), pp. 83–108.

2.4 Institutional Constructivism: The Contribution of the *Connexio Rerum* Model

Having mapped out the rich tradition of constructivism in art and social scientific disciplines, we can now proceed to examine in more detail the *connexio rerum* model suggested in the previous chapter. The suggested multivariable model, which has also underpinned my earlier writings,[88] includes agency, institutions, discourse, space-time and GIT. Readers might recall from the discussion in the previous chapter that GIT is Godel's incompleteness theorem,[89] and it is a constant. In brief, GIT is a reminder of the complexity of the inanimate and animate worlds. The natural world is much more complex than our interpretations of it. The social world, too, is quite ambiguous and messy. Human souls, minds and actions are in the main simultaneously understandable and inconclusive. If we add to all this the existence of fallibility in the reasoning and conduct of human beings and their ability to conceal their motives,[90] then Godel was absolutely correct to argue that logical analyses and carefully constructed exegeses also have parentheses or shadowy sides which might be neutral or not, visible or invisible at first sight. For the purposes of my discussion, Godel's incompleteness theorem thus reflects researchers' awareness that 'there is more than this' as well as their suspicion that 'we should be seeing more'.

All the other variables are internally connected; they are not externally related. They are important parts of an explanatory circuit, and treating agency, institutions, discourse and space-time in this way gives the model

[88] Dora Kostakopoulou, 'Ideas, Norms and European Citizenship: Explaining Institutional Change', 68(2) *The Modern Law Review* (2005), pp. 23–67; *Citizenship, Identity and Immigration in the European Union: Between Past and Future* (Manchester: Manchester University Press, 2001).

[89] Feferman et al. (eds.), *Kurt Godel*.

[90] As March has noted,

> 'Modern students of human choice frequently assume, at least implicitly, that actual human choice behaviour in some way or other is likely to make sense. It can be understood as being the behaviour of an intelligent bing or a group of intelligent beings. Much theoretical work searches for the intelligence in apparently anomalous human bahaviour. This process of discovering sense in human behaviour is conservative with respect to the concept of rational man and to bahavioural change. It preserves the axiom of rationality; and it preserves the idea that human bahaviour is intelligent, even when it is not obviously so'.

James G. March, 'Bounded Rationality, Ambiguity, and the Engineering of Choice', 9(2) *The Bell Journal of Economics* (1978), pp. 587–608, at p. 589. See also Herbert A. Simon, *Models of Man* (New York: Wiley, 1957) and A. Tversky and D. Kahneman, 'Judgment under Uncertainty: Heuristics and Biases', 185 *Science* (1974), pp. 1124–31.

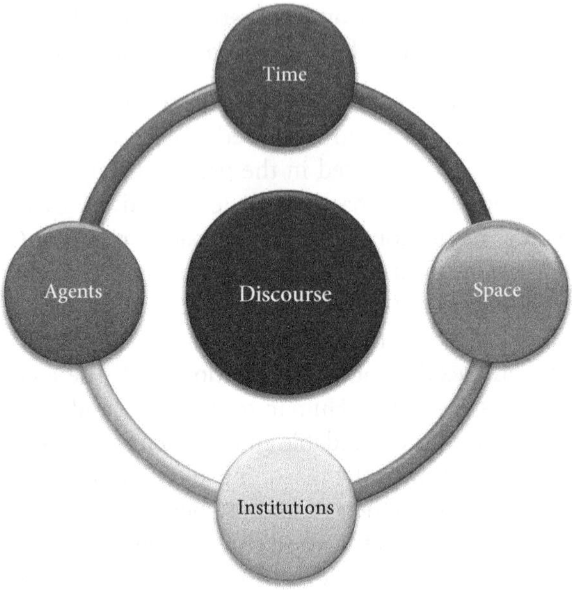

Figure 2.1 Variable connectivism

of institutional constructivism that I am proposing has the propensity to connect, illuminate and explain, and to yield fruitful insights. The anatomical nature of the model is thus one of connection and co-implication, be this direct or indirect. To put it differently, reflections on the nature of the variables need to take into account their relational and interactional dimensions. And this relation to one another is neither a linear nor a hierarchical one, it is not an 'order' established by the pre-eminence of one variable over the others, as is the case, for example, with structures in Marxism or agency in existentialist philosophy. Twining used Italo Calvino's Invisible Cities[91] as a tableau on which to map legal orders since Calvino's narrative evoked the complex, the multi-layered, the entangled and the muddled.[92] Both Calvino's complex topography and Twining's imaginative application of this to law are apposite to capturing the multivariable circuit I am proposing here. If I were invited to sketch this on a blackboard in an attempt to make it visible, I would have to draw it as follows (Figure 2.1).

In the drawing above, one does not have to start from the inner circle. For there exist, or can exist, several starting points. Like Calvino's cities, the outer and inner layers of the cities can converge. In this sense, the

[91] Italo Calvino, *Invisible Cities* (London: Vintage Books, 1997).

[92] William Twining, *Globalisation and Legal Theory* (London: Butterworths, 2000), p. 168 et seq.

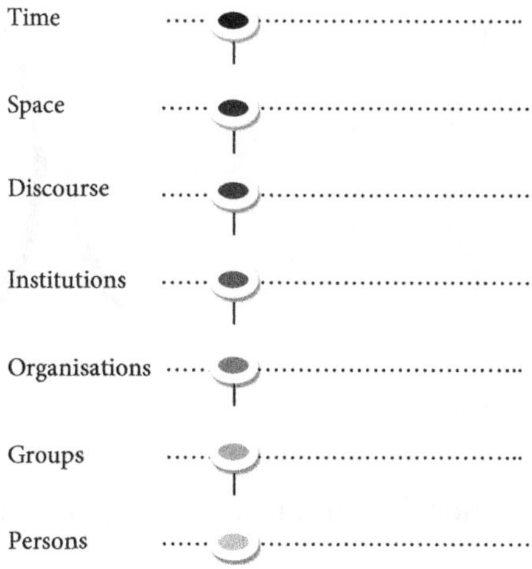

Figure 2.2 Entanglements

model is incorporative. In addition, because it is a multivariable model, it discourages easy voyages of discovery and premature solutions by definition. Reflections and thinking have to travel back and forth among the variables before one decides to zoom more in on one of them.[93] The same can be said about its levels of analysis, which are entangled, as depicted above (Figure 2.2).

Looking at the cochlea in more detail, we observe that there are no longer binary relations. Instead, there exist entanglements among several variables. The linkages among them never collapse, for, as I have already argued, each of the variables enfolds the others even when the enfoldment is not visible to the observer. This also means that the linkages do not switch off before or after the occurrence of an action; they exist throughout processes and impact on each other. The impact could be differential – thereby giving the impression that one of the variables is primarily responsible for the explanandum – but it is, nonetheless, real. So instead of focusing on institutions shaping individuals' choices and actions or on agents shaping institutional logics, one has to examine the impact of norms, conceptions, logics and ways of seeing things upon individuals

[93] It is also noteworthy that 'I', does not annul the fact that the individual is a social being. Similarly, 'I', for institutions, presupposes inter-institutional interactions and dialogue. Space (S) also presupposes interspatial and cross-spatial comparisons and time (T) includes intertemporal comparisons.

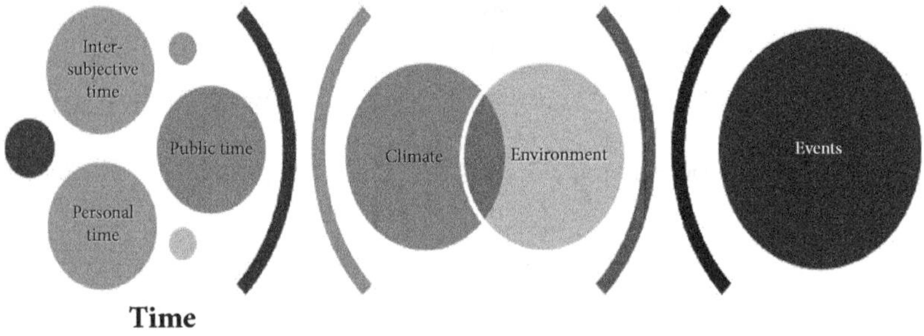

Figure 2.3 The time variable

acting within institutional environments and upon institutions within a given space-time.

The presence of time and space is essential. Space and time have been relatively neglected variables in social sciences and, in the main, tend to be viewed as either contextual presuppositions for actions and events or as irrelevancies. Very rarely have they been brought to the fore of social analyses.[94] And finally, the model shows that we do not have to focus on institutional disequilibria, crises or ruptures in order to understand change or the evolution of ideas, for the latter happen all the time. Individuals are simultaneously bearers, compliers, shapers and imaginers of institutional logics. In other words, agents are not just observers or spectators; they are actors, creators and problem-solvers, too.[95] The ensemble nature of the variables of time (Figure 2.3) and agency (Figure 2.4) could be sketched as follows.

Discourse cuts across the circular layers as it is defined in a broad way, incorporating ideas – mental images, conceptions, beliefs, assumptions, syllogisms, postulates, ideological templates and non-institutionalised norms, i.e., statements of 'ought'. Statement of ought are conceptions which encapsulate the desirable, the worthy and the obligatory, and thus influence an agent's action. The 'oughtness' they prescribe is derived from their importance in the process of coordinating human activity, the accomplishment of the purposes of socio-political life and the advancement of individual flourishing. They are part of the 'sovereignty of the good',[96] both

[94] See the Report of the Gulbenkian Commission, Introduction, above, pp. 26 and 76.

[95] Compare, here, James S. Coleman, 'Social Theory, Social Research and a Theory of Action', 91 *American Journal of Sociology* (1986), pp. 1309–35.

[96] The term is borrowed by Iris Murdoch, *The Sovereignty of the Good* (London: Routledge and Kegan Paul, 1970).

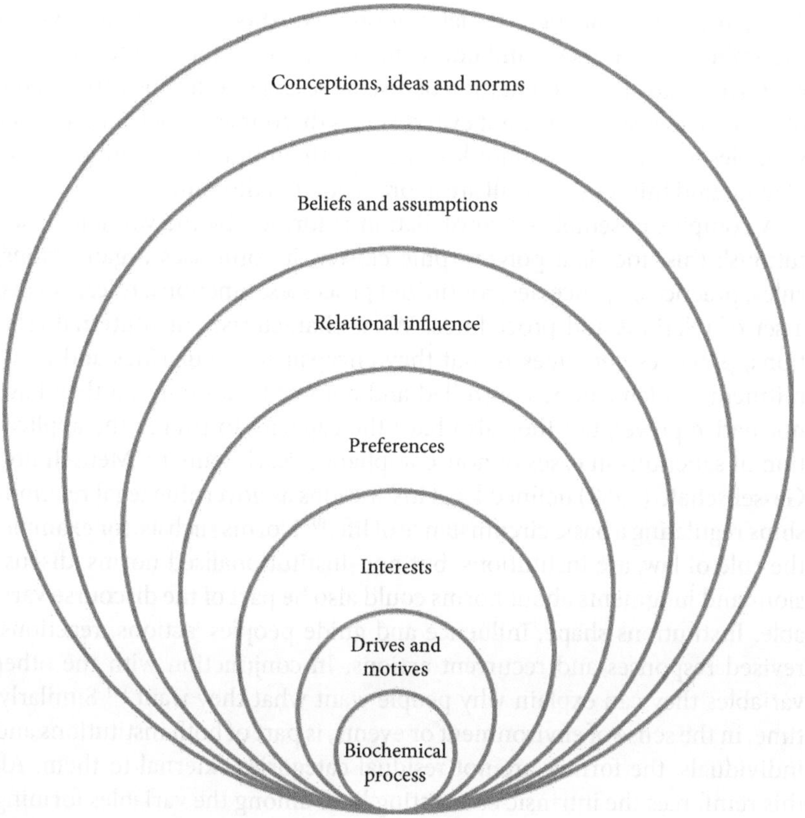

Figure 2.4 The agent variable

of the social good and the personal good, and are subject to evolution and redefinition.[97] And notwithstanding their abstract character and their grand positioning, it is also important to recognise that individuals make, and unmake, norms with their conduct and their chosen course of action. Similarly, standards of all sorts (good governance, social responsibility, democracy and so on) are part of the discursive ensemble to the extent that they have not been institutionalised thereby forming soft law directives or hard law commands. For example, the 'responsibility to protect' in international law was an emerging norm in the later 1990s and early

[97] Compare, Prosper Weil, 'Towards Relative Normativity in International Law', 77 *AJIL* (1983), pp. 413–42.

2000s and still awaits precise elaboration.[98] For this reason, it falls within the ambit of 'discourse' – and not within the ambit of the 'institution' variable. The pictorial representation of discourse as a line cutting through the other variables shows that not everything is discourse; in fact, all the other variables are not – we cannot lose sight of them in our account of them. Having said this, however, all are apprehended in discourse.

A complex ensemble or constellation is formed by the variable 'institutions'; this, too, is a polymorphic cluster. It comprises organisations, rules, practices,[99] processes, routinized processes, functions, roles, norms, a set of relations and procedures. What characterises institutional relations, practices and rules is that they encapsulate regularities and commitments which can be controlled and enforced. Not only do they have normative power, but they also have the capacity to trigger the application of sanctions in cases of non-compliance. Karl Renner's 'Mensch und Gessellschaft' (1952) defined legal institutions as governing legal relationships regulating a basic circumstance of life.[100] Norms such as, for example, the rule of law, are institutions, but non-institutionalised norms, discussions and judgments about norms could also be part of the discourse variable. Institutions shape, influence and guide peoples' actions, reactions, revised responses and recurrent actions. In conjunction with the other variables they can explain why people want what they want.[101] Similarly, time, in the sense of environment or events, is part of both institutions and individuals; the former are not residual categories external to them. All this reinforces the intrinsic connecting lines among the variables forming a reflexive circuit.

In the subsequent chapters, I discuss further the main premises of the institutional constructivist model by applying it to EU citizenship and integration. Before proceeding with its application, however, I should

[98] For a discussion of this principle as an emerging global constitutional norm, see the chapter written by Anne Peters on Membership in the Global Constitutional Community in Jan Klabbers, Anne Peters and Geir Ulfstein, *The Constitutionalisation of International Law* (Oxford: Oxford University Press, 2009), pp. 154–262, at p. 188 et seq.

[99] An emphasis on practices seems to characterise recent work which resonates with some constructivist assumptions; see, for example, Adler and Pouliot (eds.), *International Practices*; Rebecca Adler-Nissen, 'Towards a Practice Turn in EU Studies: The Everyday of European Integration', 54(1) *Journal of Common Market Studies* (2016), pp. 87–103.

[100] Verlag der Wiener Volksbuchhandlung (January 1, 1952).

[101] See Wildavsky, 'Choosing Preferences by Constructing Institutions', pp. 3–21. Wildavsky argued for the importance of cultural theory in explaining people's preferences, desires, values and ideals, but exaggerated the role of (political) culture by arguing that culture constitutes our political selves.

mention that the constructivist epistemological journey does not rule out normative analyses and moral philosophical reflection. 'Getting to see and to know' things, persons, places and the cosmos and responding to them are often punctuated by 'might have beens' and 'musts'. Understanding and imagining, delving into realities and constructing new ones are convergent activities. Indeed, the main argument of the first section of this chapter was that constructivism is a theory of cognition, action and imagination.

2.5 Conclusion

The discussion in this chapter travelled many roads. It unearthed the constructivist 'world view' in the early part of the twentieth century and examined constructivist perspectives in several social scientific disciplines. Notwithstanding their considerable divergence, these nevertheless converge on the reality of human ingenuity, the belief in human malleability and perfectibility, and on a critical approach to the social world. That there is no separation between the knower and the known and that human beings have the capability to reflect, construct images and new representations of things and to imagine new arrangements are also accepted by all. As constructivisms were mapped out in special fields of learning, the discussion proceeded to show that the blending of institutionalism with constructivism and the interconnection of five variables are promising roads towards an enhanced methodological approach in social sciences.

Critics might be quick to observe here that my suggested model is simply a more complex constructivist approach and that what appears to differentiate the *connexio rerum* model from other epistemological perspectives in social sciences is the inclusion of the dimensions of space, time and discourse. Others might suggest that it is just another partial epistemological point of view. I would disagree with these observations. *Connexio rerum* is as an alternative to both monism and dualism; it is based on multiplicity and complexity. In addition, it does not rely on the combination or juxtaposition of previously explicated variables – it does not draw sharp lines among them. Instead, it is premised on the transcendence of any separation and absolute distinction among them. We cannot conceive of one variable without the play, and impact, of the others. It would also be incorrect to argue that numerical additions, that is, the presence of more variables, make all the difference. This is because the additional dimensions are the by-product of a different way of conceiving agents, their place in the world, and their role in world-making. So what is really at stake is something bigger: *connexio rerum* is premised on a different relation between being, reflecting, knowing and acting in an open, futureful and interdependent world. As the five variables of time, space, discourse, institutions and agency interact, unfold and enfold, the distinction between internality and externality[102] collapses. All reveal themselves to be intrinsic parts of a model of cognition for social sciences.

But by making apparent their interrelationships into an integrated model, one cannot sidestep the possibility of 'incompleteness', that is, the importance of Godel's theorem (GIT). When we seek to account for things *a posteriori* and for things far way and long ago, humility needs to guide the search for new knowledge. We can make connections, understand actions, explain outcomes and *see new* processes, but there always exists something more in all of them which we might not be able to fathom. Irrespective of what one might call this,[103] Godel's shadow is always present to remind us of the incompleteness of the conceptual framework we develop or the analysis we articulate. This does not give cause for pessimism. It does not make our inquiries pointless or inadequate. GIT merely points to the necessity of leaving room for 'something more' in what took place and thus for 'something more' to pursue or to be pursued at a future point.

Knowledge proceeds in increments and meaning is a woven and incomplete tapestry.[104] A similar realisation takes place every time we recall, relive or revive the past. Irrespective of our painstaking attempts to capture every single detail of a past experience, there always has been something more in what we did or felt or saw which escapes us. Sometimes, we refer to it as 'the magic of the moment' since a memory of it is always a re-enactment, a re-presentation and interpretation – and not the actual experience – of being, feeling, seeing, touching, doing and so on. In such cases, we look at the past from the outside; we do not live in it.

The discussion in this chapter has been suggestive. I hope that readers will be encouraged to experiment with the model of institutional constructivism by applying it to their own research areas. Experimentation and more probing thought underpin the subsequent chapters as well. In what follows, I address the issue of institutional change before applying the model to European Union citizenship and integration. Having said this, it also possible that certain readers might wish to use the model as a mere point of reference in the pursuit of their favoured methodology, or might

[102] Compare Winch, *The Idea of a Social Science and Its Relation to Philosophy*, p. 10 et seq.

[103] We might wish to term it 'the excess' or 'the incomplete' or 'the contingent' or 'the element of doubt' or Heidegger's 'uncanny'.

[104] Compare here Hans Georg Gadamer's 'fusion of horizons'; *Truth and Method* (New York: Continuum, 2002 [1979]).

indeed find that they implicitly assume what I have made explicit here. Such a varied reception would not be regrettable. On the contrary, the very idea of a conceptual scheme presupposes a variable use and multifarious adaptations.[105] I would be very pleased if my efforts led to an appreciation of even the reference potential of institutional constructivism as a way of seeing and knowing.

[105] The notion of a conceptual scheme is borrowed from Donald Davidson, 'On the Very Idea of a Conceptual Scheme', *Proceedings and Addresses of the American Philosophical Association* (1973–4), pp. 5–20. Compare also Philip Kitcher, 'Theories, Theorists and Theoretical Change', 87(4) *The Philosophical Review* (October 1978), pp. 519–47.

3

Theorising Institutional Change: A Dynamic Theory of Process

3.1 Introduction

Although we are embedded within institutions of all sorts[1] and it is impossible to lead our lives outside their control or regulation or, at least, their shadow, we tend to view them as monolithic and soulless entities. In our ordinary conversations, we may praise or moan about them but, essentially, we tend to depict them as part of the world as we found it, as Wittgenstein would argue.[2] We have grown accustomed to the idea that institutions represent a 'world without time'. And 'a world without time' is, inevitably, a 'world without actors'. Institutions are thus part of this world, but they are not part of our world. Otherwise put, they have objective facticity, but do not have subjective relationality.

I have often wondered why we tend to adhere to timeless (one might also wish to use, here, terms such as ahistorical or structuralist) depictions of reality, for if we pause to think more deeply about them we quickly realise the flaws in our conceptions. Irrespective of whether we wish to concede it or not, we are part of institutions. 'Their world' is 'our world'. In addition to this limitation, by being attracted to a rather soulless and static view of institutions, we tend to suffocate both 'the actual' and 'the potential' in them. By 'the actual', I mean the subtle layers that by piling on each other constitute an institutional reality and its gradual evolution (Chapters 1 and 2).

[1] I adhere to a broad definition of institutions encompassing formal as well as informal practices, rules, norms, procedures and organizations facilitating human cooperation and coordinated action. For such a definition, see Norgaard, 'Rediscovering Reasonable Rationality in Institutional Analysis', pp. 31, 29; Armstrong and Bulmer, *The Governance of the Single Market*, p. 56. But compare John Searle's preference for 'institutional facts' instead of addressing the question 'what is an institution?'. As he put it, 'an institution is any collectively accepted system of rules (procedures, practices) that enable us to create institutional facts'; 'What is an Institution?', 1(1) *Journal of Institutional Economics* (2005), pp. 1–22, at p. 2 et seq. and p. 21.

[2] Ludwig Wittgenstein, *Tractatus Logico-Philosophicus*, trans. D. F. Pears and B. F. McGuinness (London: Routledge, 1961 [1921]).

Institutions are multilayered constructions that are subject to ongoing change in space-time, as will be shown in the subsequent discussion. Change happens all the time irrespective of whether we are inclined to observe it. From moment to moment, from past to present to future, various institutional dimensions, be they essential or non-essential, mutate, expand or just become replaced by others.

When we discuss the institution of citizenship, for instance, we tend to refer to the abstract, formal rights we have and more often than not we tend to ignore the everyday realities of citizenship practice and citizenship making. But, as the subsequent chapters show, formal citizenship rights cannot be thought of without formal and informal citizenship making practices, that is the processes of citizenisation, which we could accentuate, accelerate, change or contain. In other words, we imagine, and describe, institutions as being outside ourselves; we do not see ourselves alive inside them. In reality, however, neither the 'thereness' nor the 'timelessness' of institutions is justified. As the foregoing discussion on constructivism has shown, all institutions[3] are co-created. And the co-creation or co-construction of reality involves both the activist – in the sense of participatory – and the activity-based, practice-oriented construction of all institutional realities.

Yet, discussions on institutional change tend to display a structuralist bias. Even the various forms of institutionalism tend to favour stability and system maintenance over fluidity and change.[4] This might be partly due to the fact that much of our thinking, and writing, is necessarily time bound. And time boundedness by its nature does not allow us to see institutional change as part of a wider process of socio-political change. In the West, the dominance of capitalism and the political relations underpinning it have amplified the 'change question'. The lively debate concerning revolutionary change versus systemic reform that characterised social and political life in the latter part of the nineteenth century and most of the twentieth century seem to be part of our historical repertoires, and not of contemporary political life.

[3] I do not distinguish, here, between institutions and organisations; I use the terms interchangeably. I have provided definitions of institutions in the preceding discussion. It may be worth noting, here, that Elinor Ostrom defined organisations as 'composites of participants following rules governing activities and transactions to realise particular outputs'; *Strategies of Political Inquiry* (London: Sage, 1982), p. 193.

[4] In the subsequent discussion, I argue that neither structural determinism, nor assumptions about the 'overdetermination' of structure, nor the notion of an unencumbered or 'acontextual' agency can lead to a nuanced understanding of why and how societal, political or institutional change takes place.

Viewing institutional change as a subset of socio-political change, however, would enable us to study social life as a whole and to see institutions and their workings as generated by, and connected to, the dynamics of this whole. In other words, such an approach would require a zooming in on, and out of, institutional change, or a back and forth movement between the general and the particular, in an attempt to grasp the general modalities of socio-political change and the more specific characteristics of institutional change. At the same time, because institutional change in institutions-as-organisations might unfold in a different way from institutional change in institutions-as-systems or established policies or routinised procedures and practices, one would need to draw a typology of the pathways of change.

The discussion in this chapter entails both endeavours; namely, I zoom out to examine how institutional change relates to wider processes of social change, and then I zoom in on institutional change in order to theorise its activating factors and modalities as well as implications. I will thereby address the latter from various standpoints; that is, the standpoint of organisations, the standpoint of norms or sedimented policies and so on. It seems to me that it is important to separate these standpoints initially and to try to unify them afterwards. In seeking to accomplish my two aims, I will intentionally integrate sociological, political, philosophical and legal perspectives. The advantage of integrating a multidisciplinary literature is that it may allow for the development of a more systematic perspective on – and an alternative way of thinking about – institutional change.

3.2 Sociological and Philosophical Guideposts

Chapter 2 unravelled the basic premises of constructivism. Among them is the assertion that the way we think about various phenomena and people (including ourselves) shapes our perception of them (and ourselves). The subsequent chapters on European Union citizenship and judicial decision-making will confirm this assertion. In the same vein, the way we think about socio-political change shapes our perception of it. Because not much attention has been given to how we think about change, I would like to look more closely at various perspectives on socio-political change, commencing with the pragmatist one.

Following the publication of *Social Organisation* in 1909,[5] Charles Horton Cooley devoted his next book to the study of the 'social process'.

[5] Charles Horton Cooley, *Social Organisation*.

In *Social Process*, Cooley explored in depth the issue of social change by linking it to larger processes of physico-organic change in both humans and nonhumans.[6] He believed that change has direction and that this is, more often than not, an upward one. After all, the movement of life is onward.[7] He wrote:

> the whole thing appears to be a kind of growth, and we might add that it is adaptive growth, meaning by this that the forms of life we see – men, associations of men, traditions, institutions, conventions, theories, ideals – are not separate or independent, but that the growth of each takes place in contact and interaction with that of others. Thus any one phase of the movement may be regarded as a series of adaptations to other phases.[8]

Having said this, it is also true that he also considered 'negative' or 'non-beneficial' changes. These can cause degeneration, dislocations and erosion. Influenced by Aristotle and the ancient Greek belief that kinesis, or motion, is inherent in all things and beings, but also by Darwin's evolutionary theory, Cooley made 'growth', in its many forms, the paradigmatic modality of change. He discussed in detail the 'sympodial' model of growth which characterises the grapevine. Like grapevines, which can only grow if there is support for the shoots, human beings can best flourish in supportive environments. 'A shoot which thus gets a hold grows rapidly and sends out more tendrils; if it fails to get a hold it by and by sags down and ceases to grow'.[9] Some of their activities will find congenial conditions and will grow while others will be stifled and repressed. Cooley saw the grapevine as the perfect analogy for the equilibrium he believed had to exist between *structures* and *social action* or between conditions and activities and decisions. A habitat conducive to innovation, experimentalism, and the democratic method can encourage change, while a habitat characterised by conventionalism and fixity cannot. Both the habitat and social action, however, were linked in 'an endless system of reciprocal growth'.[10]

This 'botanical model' led Cooley to make adaptive growth, or what we call today incremental change, as the main mode of change. Unlike the revolutionary fervour that characterised other parts of the world at that time, American sociologists were concerned with changes in the institutions that were congruent with the limiting conditions of

[6] Charles Horton Cooley, *Social Process* (Carbondale and Edwardsville: Southern Illinois University Press, 1966[1918]).

[7] Ibid., p. 3.

[8] Ibid., p. 3.

[9] Ibid., p. 9.

[10] Ibid.

the environment. Change had to be adaptive; that is, it had to be slow, gradual and contained. It could not be radical, since that would require substantial change in the surrounding environment and this might have catastrophic results. Radical change was seen to be unnatural. After all, as Hinkle remarked in the introduction to the *Social Process*, Cooley and other sociologists at that time, such as Ward, Sumner, Keller and Small, believed in the dictum 'natura non facit saltum' which is translated as 'nature does not jump or leap'.[11]

Humankind develops, progresses, evolves and improves. Social change, social process, social evolution and social development were terms that were used interchangeably. We all change and can change for the better. And by changing ourselves we are changing our environment that conditions us. In other words we instigate double change; we construct better selves in a reformed environment that allows these selves to actualise themselves. According to Cooley, the individual could not be separated from the society; both constitute one 'living' whole and every self is by definition a social self. As Hinkle observed,

> the outcome of daily interaction can be viewed as a gradual growth, or as a trial and error in adjusting to the situation through the heritage of the past, or as an experiment to adjust the past to the present. Even in ordinary circumstances, each person does things a little differently from everyone else, is more or less novel or innovating, and unconsciously modifies everything that he transmits. Yet, he is no more aware of what is going on than he is of the selective action of his digestive organs. Members do not recognise change or the innovating consequences of their own individualities in applying, combining, and recombining ideas in relation to their situations. Conformity seems to prevail. Deviation is not perceived. Yet, these imperceptible variations tend to accumulate over time and become what Alvin Gouldner has termed 'creeping transformations'.[12]

Change can have different phases, such as inception, incorporation and dissemination. It is also characterised by rate, magnitude or size, amplitude or range and direction. Variability in the above-mentioned characteristics is triggered by the surrounding structure or system; 'the variations which can be incorporated as modifications are restricted by the continuity of the system with its antecedent or prior historical experiences'.[13] For Cooley structures both enable and delimit change,[14] but, under the

[11] Ibid., Introduction written by Hinkle, p. xvii.
[12] Ibid., p. xxxvi.
[13] Ibid., p. xxviii.
[14] Compare Giddens's notion of the 'duality of structure'.

influence of the Darwinian bio-organicist evolution, he also believed that structures survive, decay or degenerate.

While Cooley's theory of change is based on botanical analogies and the notion of an organism's fitness within the surrounding environment, Karl Marx's theory of change focuses on progressive evolution. History progressively unfolds in stages and each stage is nothing other than a 'progressive epoch' in the 'economic formation of society'.[15] The key for unlocking this progressive evolution is class conflict. Although the very idea of class conflict places human activity at the centre of attention, Marx's evolutionary logic often imports assumptions related to mechanism. In mechanism, there always exists an underlying, unfolding logic destined to lead to the envisaged outcome irrespective of conditions, altered environments and the decisions made by agents. It is endogenous and automatic – entailed by the system itself. Otherwise put, it is immanent change.[16] For Marx, the implosion of the deeply contradictory capitalist mode of production was destined to lead to the dictatorship of the proletariat and, then, to socialism and communism. Change was thus perceived to be endogenous. The inherent structured contradictions between productive forces and relations of production would be progressively overcome through class struggle.

Commenting on immanent change, David Lockwood has noted that dialectical materialism is a variant of functionalism.[17] Notably, functional theory[18] is also underpinned by a mechanistic view of change – change is seen to be a slow, evolving process of compensating for the differentiated interaction among elements while maintaining the unity of the system.[19] Talcott Parsons highlighted the functional imperatives

[15] See Karl Marx, 'Preface to A Contribution to the Critique of Political Economy' in *Marx and Engels: Selected Works in One Volume* (London: Lawrence and Wishart, 1968), p. 183.

[16] Robert M. MacIver, *Social Causation* (Boston, MA: Ginn, 1942).

[17] David Lockwood, 'Some Remarks on "The Social System"', 7 *British Journal of Sociology* (1956), pp. 134–46.

[18] Functional theory first emerged within the domain of anthropology and is linked to attempts to understand societies, their membership and their 'survival'. Malinowski and Radcliffe-Brown (1935) have been important protagonists; the former put emphasis on individuals and their needs while the latter emphasised the survival of the group. See Bronislaw Malinowski, *Magic, Science and Religion and Other Essays* (Glencoe, IL: The Free Press, 1954 [1925]) and Alfred R. Radcliffe-Brown, 'On the Concept of Function in Social Science', 37 *American Anthropologist* (1935) New Series, p. 396. Durkheim and Parsons developed structural functionalism.

[19] See John C. Harsanyi, 'Explanation and Comparative Dynamics in Social Sciences', 5 *Behavioural Science* (1960), pp. 136–45.

of social systems[20] and his theory is premised on conceptually closed systems of variables which are associated in specific ways so as to serve the ends of the system.[21] In contrast to organicism, which examines the results of change in light of its impact on the environment, mechanistic accounts of change place emphasis on stable equilibria and systems in balance. Hence the existence of a sense of inevitability; the certainty that change will come and will take root irrespective of the soil on which it will fall.[22]

Dialectical materialism differs somewhat from the above-mentioned strand of the functional account of change as social homeostasis or a moving equilibrium in so far as it focuses on systemic contradictions. Lockwood has used the term 'system malintegration' in order to highlight the incompatibility between the dominant institutional order and its material base.[23] The disfunctionality of the system is thus instrumental in leading to systemic change.

In Marxism, if systemic strains and contradictions are not capitalised upon by the proletariat in order to bring about change, then it is assumed that agents have become interpellated by the system.[24] This means that they fail to recognise their real interests and misrecognise their actual interests for their real interests. In both Marxist canonical accounts and certain post-Marxist perspectives, it is thus assumed that human beings are either structural or cultural automata due to the hegemony of the dominant ruling class ideology. It might be objected, here, that Marx's thought was more complex and nuanced, and I am pleased to concede this. In his writings, automatism was combined with social action of a radical kind. In fact, since revolutionary action was seen to be the engine of history, one might argue that Marx embraced a combinatory theory of change.

[20] Talcott Parsons, *Structure and Process in Modern Societies* (Glencoe, IL: The Free Press, 1960). Compare also Marlon J. Levy, Jr, *The Structure of Society* (Princeton, NJ: Princeton University Press, 1952) and David Arbele et al., 'The Functional Prerequisites of a Society', 60 *Ethics* (1950), pp. 100–11.

[21] Functionalism has been criticised for being static; see *inter alia* Ralf Dahrendorf, 'Out of Utopia', 64 *American Journal of Sociology* (1958), pp. 115–27; Lockwood, 'Some Remarks on "The Social System"'. But compare, Francesca Cancian, 'Functional Analysis of Change', 25(6) *American Sociological Review* (1960), pp. 818–27.

[22] Darhendorf, 'Out of Utopia'; Lockwood, 'Some Remarks on "The Social System"'.

[23] David Lockwood, 'Social Integration and System Integration', in George K. Zollschan and Walter Hirsch (eds.), *Explorations in Social Change* (London: Routledge and Kegan Paul, 1964), pp. 244–57.

[24] Louis Althusser, 'Ideology and Ideological State Apparatuses', in *Lenin and Philosophy and other Essays*(), trans. Ben Brewster (New York and London: Monthly Review Press, 1971), pp. 121–76.

A given generation inherits changeable forces of production, capital and conditions. Human beings are thrown into realities, but also possess the power to alter them and construct new ones. As Marx noted in *The German Ideology*, conditions create human beings in the same way that human beings create conditions.[25] As C. Wright Mills has observed, 'Marx, using historical materials with superb mastery, takes as his unit of study entire epochs. The values of social scientists generally lead them to accept their society pretty much as it is; the values of Marx led him to condemn his society – root, stock and branch.'[26] Accordingly, capitalism suffers from internal contradictions and is prone to crises that then become opportunities for the proletariat to change the prevailing relations of production and to emancipate human beings. As Marx noted, what is needed is the toppling of all circumstances under which man is a demeaned and abandoned being[27] and 'to create conditions which make man truly human.'[28]

In both orthodox and revisionism Marxism, the past carries within it a critique and the present gives rise to the responsibility to overcome the past. Indeed, in *Passato e Presente*[29] (1951), Garmsci argued that what makes Marx's focus on socio-political change laudable is that he did not confine his analysis to the modification of political and economic institutions and the relations of productions underpinning them, but he embarked upon the redesign and the building of a whole new political order which, in line with all messianic narratives, promised a happy ending for human beings. Gramsci had set a more modest ambition for himself. He discussed the 'double relation' of the present and the past which is manifested in taking up a critical stance towards the past and transcending its limitations while

[25] Ibid.

[26] Charles Wright Mills, *The Marxists* (New York: Dell Publishing Co., 1962), pp. 10–11. It is noteworthy that Mills criticised biological explanations of human behaviour and the notion of change as adaptation to an environment on the ground that it displays insensitivity to the structural origins of interests and class disparities. Focusing on Dewey's notion of adaptation, Mills wrote that 'the biological model is associated with 'a politics of reform of the situation'; *Sociology and Pragmatism* (New York: Oxford University Press, 1964), p. 382. The latter was his PhD dissertation which was originally entitled 'A Sociological Account of Pragmatism'. For a critical assessment see J. L. Simich and Rick Tilman, 'Radicalism vs. Liberalism: C. Wright Mills' Critique of John Dewey's Ideas', 37(4) *American Journal of Economics and Sociology* (1978), pp. 413–30.

[27] Introduction to the Critique of Hegel's Philosophy of Law, in Karl Marx, *Early Writings*, trans. T. B. Bottomore (New York: McGraw-Hill, 1964), p. 52.

[28] The Holy Family, in Marx, *Early Writings*, p. 176. Marx made this clear in 'The Holy Family' that through his/her intervention in the world and by changing it, the human being changes simultaneously his/her nature.

[29] Antonio Gramsci, *The Present and the Past*, Greek Translation (Athens: Stochastis, 1974).

at the same time acknowledging its presence or its traces in the present. Changing existing realities is thus a constant theme permeating his *Prison Notebooks*, and *Passato e Presente* concludes with a short essay on 'motion and intention' in which he notes that the intervention of human beings is a decisive factor in historical evolution.[30] Notably, Marx and Engels had made the same observation: 'History is nothing but the activity of men in pursuit of their ends'.[31]

Cooley's model of change was characterised by incrementalism and adaptation while Marx's dialectical materialism combined evolution with revolution, quiet and latent change with sharp, deep and radical change. In the place of piecemeal reconstruction, it sketched the possibility of a novel socio-economic order. True, this variation should not lead us to believe that such perspectives on socio-political changes have to be necessarily dichotomous. For some sense of continuity could co-exist with rupture and qualitatively different reforms. True, the former works in tandem with the conditions (material causes) while the latter stands against the prevailing conditions. Equally true, the former connects the past and present and makes everything a transition while the latter emphasises ruptures, break and radical overhauls. The former embeds the new within existing relations, whereas the latter changes and reconstructs those relations. Irrespective of their explicit and subtle differences, however, it seems to me that any convincing paradigm of change would have to accommodate both gradual change and unanticipated radical transformations. It would have to leave room for both spectacular revolutionary moments and unspectacular everyday changes, for continuous and discontinuous change and for transitions and ruptures. All the above are manifestations of change in socio-political organisations.[32]

In his pioneering book, entitled '*Institutions, Institutional Change and Economic Performance*', Douglass North (1990) sought to incorporate

[30] Ibid.

[31] Karl Marx and Frederick Engels, *The Holy Family* (Moscow: Progress Publishers, 1956), p. 125. Wright Mills also made a similar observation: 'Publics live in milieux but they can transcend them – individually by intellectual effort; socially by public action. By reflection and debate and by organised action, a community of publics comes to feel itself and comes in fact to be active at points of structural relevance'; *The Power Elite* (New York: Oxford University Press, 1956), p. 321.

[32] Giddens referred to 'time-space edges' in relation to discontinuous change. The former 'refer to forms of contact or encounter between types of society organised according to variant structural principles. They are the edges of potential or actual social transformation, the intersections between different planes and societal organisations'; see *A Contemporary Critique of Historical Materialism*.

institutional analysis and economic history into neoclassical economic theory.[33] He attempted to grapple with change over time and to capture the dynamics of both gradual and discontinuous institutional change. Gradual change, which, in his opinion, is 'the dominant way by which societies and economies have evolved', is the result of two main mechanisms; namely, change in relative prices and changes in actors' preferences. The subjectivity implied by the latter is thus coupled with objectivity associated with the former. And both may have exogenous as well as endogenous parameters. As he put it, 'the agent of change is the individual entrepreneur responding to the incentives embodied in the institutional framework. The sources of change are changing relative prices or preferences. The process of change is overwhelmingly an incremental one'.[34] Within a generally stable institutional system, adjustments take place constantly. A change in relative prices will lead to an altered agreement or contract which in turn cannot take place without a restructuring of a higher set of rules which in turn will lead to a change in tastes and the erosion of a norm and its replacement by another norm. Change from the micro to the macro is quite slow but certainly directional; as North put it, 'change is overwhelmingly incremental'.[35] Because radical change is associated with high costs it is relegated to the realm of the exception.

It may be observed, here, that the system North has in mind is predisposed to stability. Its participants are endowed with 'the comfortable feeling of knowing what we are doing and where we are going' and therefore can bring about adjustments. In this incremental process of institutional change, the fittest – in the sense of the most efficient – institutions will survive: efficient institutions adapt to changing environments.[36] Adaptation is thus the key to achieving successful economic change and path dependence is correlative to understanding institutional change. Paths do not alter frequently and the pattern of change is 'system maintaining'; 'change takes the form of marginal adjustments or adaptation in the margin'.[37] But in addition to 'ordinary' institutional change, one may also come across discontinuous institutional change. This is the product of wars, revolutions,

[33] New York: Cambridge University Press, 1990.

[34] Ibid., p. 83. See also Kathleen Thelen and Frank Longstreth (eds.), *Structuring Politics: Historical Institutionalism in Comparative Analysis* (Cambridge: Cambridge University Press, 1992). But compare, Pierson, 'The Limits of Design', pp. 474–99.

[35] North, *Institutions, Institutional Change and Economic Performance*, p. 89.

[36] Douglass North, 'Economic Performance through Time', 84(3) *American Economic Review* (1994), pp. 359–64, at p. 367. Compare also *Understanding the Process of Economic Change* (Princeton, NJ: Princeton University Press, 2005).

[37] North, *Institutions, Institutional Change and Economic Performance*, p. 101.

conquests and natural disasters[38] – in other words, of exceptional and spectacular instances. Such events are 'system disrupting' rather than simply 'path altering'.[39]

While North's account of institutional change succeeds in blending institutional analysis with 'static' neoclassical economic theory, and his notion of path dependence, which is the product of 'the increasing returns mechanisms that reinforce the direction once on a given path'[40] has been influential in both economics and political science,[41] one discerns the influence of Darwinian notions of organic evolution in his schema. As a consequence, his theory leaves little room for shocks and systemic turbulence. In other words, it is difficult to account for change that departs from the ordinary[42] and for the re-visitation of the drawing board in terms of institutional and constitutional design.

In political science, too, institutions more often than not are associated with stable ensembles that posit constraints on actors' behaviour or correct asymmetries in the information they possess. There is a close correlation between stability and constraints since constraints on human conduct ensure the stability of expectations, predictable outcomes and the maintenance of the overall institutional framework. In fact, it is this overall stability of the system that guarantees stable patterns of social interaction, rule governed ways of doing things and the increasing utility of social cooperation in all its settings. This does not rule out change in all the above. Rules change, organisations evolve despite the incessant mobility of their members and systems have to adapt to pressures from both within and outside. There exist endogenous pressures for adjustment, better rules and regulation, growth and more efficient structures. But change takes place within a clear geometry, within the pre-given boundaries of conditions. This has been highlighted by the important work produced by Powel and DiMaggio (1991), Hall and Taylor (1966), Thelen (1999) and others.[43] But

38 Ibid., p. 89.

39 Ibid.

40 Ibid., p. 112.

41 North notes that alterations in the path come from unanticipated consequences of choices, external effects, and sometimes forces exogenous to the analytical framework. A reversal of paths (from stagnation to growth or vice versa) may come from the above-described sources of path alteration.

42 Compare here the essays in Wolfgang Streek and Kathleen Thelen (eds.), *Institutional Change in Advanced Political Economies* (New York: Oxford University Press, 2005).

43 Walter W. Powell and Paul DiMaggio (eds.), *The New Institutionalism in Organisational Analysis* (Chicago, IL: Chicago University Press, 1991); Peter A. Hall and Rosemary C. R. Taylor, 'Political Science and the Three New Institutionalisms', 44(5) *Political Studies*

in the same way that American sociologists in early twentieth century anchored change on notions, such as equilibrium, consensus and social control, thereby placing it within an ordered universe of incremental steps and slow adaptations, American political scientists at the end of the twentieth century theorised change as developments within a relatively stable system. They focused on change within, and not of, the system. Path dependence is prevalent in historical institutionalism.[44] There exists an implicit or explicit preference for stasis and an ensuing emphasis on the constraining, rather than the enabling, dimensions of (resilient) structures of all sorts.

The same pattern can be found in law. The need for predictability, settled meanings, correct imagined outcomes and, generally speaking, the fixity associated with the settled nature of legal norms does not appear to be hospitable to contingency and processes. After all, legal meaning thrives in objectification and the authoritative pronouncement of the 'right' answer. Legal regulations need to be controlled, secured and clearly set out in advance of the malfunctioning of legal relations. Legal norms and regulations are part of the legal system which must be in equilibrium and capable of neutralising both disruptions and threats to its stability.

Yet the matrix of fixed and predefined meanings cannot contain the multiplicity of meanings that human creativity and social action generate. Nor can it foil legal permutations. For law is not confined to authoritative commands, specific institutions and carefully designed procedures. It incorporates all the above, but also exceeds them; it becomes part of the conscious project of deliberating, testing, inquiring and approaching many questions of juridico-political life from a practical starting point. Otherwise put, law is lived,[45] that is, cannot be thought of separately from the agents, both laypersons and officials, actualising it in everyday life. This performative dimension inherent in law transforms agents into central actors since the institutional reality surrounding them becomes inseparable from their realities and the whole system maintains its equilibrium by internal, agency-related motion. It is in this process of 'living

(1966), pp. 936–57; Kathleen Thelen, 'Historical Institutionalism and Comparative Politics', 2 *Annual Review of Political Science* (1999), pp. 369–404.

[44] Pierson, 'The Limits of Design'; Arthur, L. Stinchcombe, 'On the Virtues of the Old Institutionalism', 23 *Annual Review of Sociology* (1977), pp. 1–18.

[45] By writing this I do not wish to invoke Robert Cover's exaltation of the rich world of culturally informed communal meanings beyond the nomos; 'The Supreme Court, 1982 Term – Foreword: Nomos and Narrative', (1983), Faculty Scholarship Series. Paper 2705, http://digitalcommons.law.yale.edu/fss_papers/2705

law'[46] that limitations and gaps are revealed and demands for improvement or institutional change arise. The parameters of what is possible, and what is normatively desirable, become broadened owing to agents' actions and claims-making. One often appreciates this better, if she or he steps out of the present and takes on a diachronic view of legal realities; this can be done, for example, by paying attention to the history of legal provisions as well as the politics associated settled legal norms and forms (see Chapter 4). By timing law, that is, by situating law in time, one attains a clear view of its processual nature and its historically unfolding evolution.

Contingency, on the other hand, does not merely signal the presence of events, unruly behaviour or unpredictable emergences which unsettle the unification of legal meaning. It also captures the various complex, and often not easily accounted for, processes of meaning making and meaning attributing which can threaten existing regulations and state sanctioned settlements. And because the state and its law have monopolised the political and academic worlds, the location of both state and its law within both broader and subaltern contexts has not received the attention it deserves.[47]

In reality, however, state law is always nested and floating. It is part of a bigger normative universe built on complex relations and intellectual horizons.[48] It is also constantly undergoing change, both volitional and by chance, due to the simultaneous interaction, and sometimes collision, of various spheres; for example, in my past work the spheres that have been relevant have been the European Union, national-statist orders, exogenous developments of a more global nature, and actors' normative expectations, complaints and claims. The system comprising of these four spheres is thus neither closed nor open; rather, it is in constant flux. All of them are changing, and thereby triggering changes and mutations to one another. Rules are located within the context which, in turn, is nested

[46] Eugen Ehrlich, *Fundamental Principles of Sociology of Law*, vol. 19, trans. by Walter L. Moll (New Jersey: Transaction Publishers, 2001 [1936]).

[47] Neil Walker, *Global Law* (Cambridge: Cambridge University Press, 2014); Wibren van der Burg, *The Dynamics of Law and Morality* (Farnham: Ashgate, 2014); Neil MacCormick, 'Law as Institutional Fact', 90 *The Law Quarterly Review* (1970), pp. 102–29. But compare Herbert L. A. Hart, *The Concept of Law* (Oxford: Clarendon, 1961); Joseph Raz, *The Concept of a Legal System: An Introduction to the Theory of Legal System* (Oxford: Clarendon, 1970); Hans Kelsen, *General Theory of Law and the State* (Cambridge: Harvard University Press, 1945).

[48] Rafael Domingo, *The New Global Law* (Cambridge: Cambridge University Press, 2010); William Twining, *General Jurisprudence: Understanding Law from a Global Perspective* (Cambridge: Cambridge University Press, 2009); *Globalisation and Legal Scholarship* (Nijmegen: Wolf Legal Publishers, 2011).

within a larger context and this, in turn, is nested within a larger environment. All of them are interlinked and are capable of triggering ripples of change. In this sense, context does not merely point to entailment, detail and causation.

In the light of the above discussion, it may be concluded that change is not something that happens to law. Instead, it is part of law's existence. This is because law is always at crossways, institutionally set, as well as lived and unfolding in time. Being at crossways implies relationality, that is, connectedness with other things and interactional dimensions upwards, downwards and sideways. Connectedness brings forth possibilities. Quite often, possibilities are hardly known and appreciated until after all the interactions have occurred – until they become actualities. And games of chance may become necessities or the by-products of a rational fulfilment ex post facto. Law's correlativity also means that legal change cannot be contained; not only can it easily leak outside a specific domain but it also has a ripple effect. This makes law what it is, namely – just like art – a *poesis*, that is, an act of creation. If I am correct on this, then the question that arises is why legal studies do not pay sufficient attention to correlational change and to time, or – to be more specific – to correlational change in time. It is this question that I will now examine.

3.3 How We Think about Change: The Conversion Fallacy and How To Overcome It

Although politics is essentially the means of regulating processes and outcomes of collective action,[49] governmental instrumentalities, including law, are considered to be institutional facts.[50] As institutional facts, they tend to be endowed with fixity and stability. This is important because, as noted in the previous section, social agents experiencing, and taking into account, such institutional facts need to have stable expectations. They need to know what to get, where and when and to entertain the antecedent belief that their prospective course of action will be followed by certain reciprocal actions or reactions by other agents. In addition, they need to know that officials are likely to take the appropriate remedial action to

[49] A rather more reductive definition of politics may be associated with Ashby's dictum that 'governing is reducing variety in behaviour' cited in G. R. Boynton, 'On Getting from Here to There', in Elinor Ostrom (ed.), *Strategies of Political Inquiry* (London: Sage, 1982).

[50] Neil MacCormick, *Institutions of Law: An Essay in Legal Theory* (Oxford: Oxford University Press, 2007); Vincent Ostrom, *The Political Theory of the Compound Republic* (Lincoln: University of Nebraska Press, 1971).

enforce their rightful claims if they are wronged. In other words, they rely on hypothetical, yet real, sequences of events and on the predictability entailed by the contemplation of such sequences of events.

This is understandable. Imagine, for example, the countervailing scenario. Although agents may have a correct appreciation, and sound knowledge, of institutional facts, they also believe that there may be breaks in the envisaged sequence of events. By the latter I mean that their actions might not be followed by the anticipated reactions and thus may never have, or never be allowed to have, the envisaged outcomes. Moreover, the consequences of those outcomes escape their control since contingency can be neither anticipated nor controlled. Their powers are simply exhausted in the performance of a certain action. In such a hypothetical situation, individuals would feel insecure and quite disoriented. And contingency, ambiguity and uncertainty would be unbearable.

Although in much of our real world we find the presence of both stable courses of action and expectation, on the one hand, as well as of contingency, on the other, we nevertheless find it difficult to recognise and come to terms with the latter. Our lives must go on as if most institutional forms and social selves were fathomable and thus rather stable and predictable.[51] Our minds tend to transform the moving, changing, multiple, incomplete, foggy and uncertain world around us into an unchanging, fixed, predictable, unified and complete reality. We thus tend to convert change into unchange and motion into stasis. A fluid world becomes a static world.[52] Similarly, when we examine ourselves, we tend to bracket the unfolding and projective nature of our selves in the world. We hold on to the fiction of a given, complete and unified self. This makes us feel more assured since any changes appear to be both controlled and manageable.

Yet, if we pause to reflect on all this, we realise that everything is continuously changing and a great deal surrounding these changes is beyond our control. As we struggle to come to terms with this, we are confronted with two options. We either need to seek stability and order by constructing cocoons, be they in our private world or in small collective groups, or we must embrace the fiction of a changeless or slowly changing world in

[51] On the philosophy of 'as if' see Hans Vaihinger's 'Die Philosophie des Als Ob'; for a good summary of his philosophy, see Havelock Ellis, *The Dance of Life* (New York, NY: Modern Library, 1929).

[52] In the illusionary static world, developing processes can only take place as a result of exceptional interventions; namely, catastrophes, ruptures and breakdowns. When the latter happen, there is a shift from one paradigm or period or historical epoch to another. If one adopts a diachronic view of history, one thinks of successive periods as a series of separate compartments, and not as phases that slide into one another or as a continuous flowing movement.

a conscious way. So we pretend that the moving world is changeless. In such circumstances, fiction becomes real because it is functional, that is, either convenient or necessary or therapeutic since it makes our lives less stressful.

This is simply a conversion fallacy: the moving, changing, developing reality is transformed into an unmoving, unchanging and essential reality. Heisenberg pinpointed this fallacy at the turn of the twentieth century by postulating his uncertainty or indeterminacy principle and thus repeating the Heraclitean flux of happening.[53] And following Heisenberg, Dewey commented: 'The need for security compels men to fasten upon the regular in order to minimise and to control the precarious and fluctuating. In actual experience this is a practical enterprise, made possible by knowledge of the recurrent and stable, of facts and laws'.[54] Andy Gasset added:

> And that complex of certainties which, in thinking about the environment, we build for ourselves – like a raft in the tempestuous and enigmatic sea of our surroundings – this complex is the world, the vital horizon. Whence it happens that in order to live man needs, whether he likes it or not, to think, to form convictions for himself – or, what is the same thing, to live is to react against the basic insecurity of life by constructing the security of a world, by believing that the world is like this or like that so that we may direct our lives with due regard for it, so that in view of it we may live.[55]

A related fallacy is the perception of change as a loss: an element or a dimension is lost and our sight is stubbornly concentrated on this. The fact that what is lost is replaced by something new is sidestepped. Change is primarily seen as an abstraction or reduction – and not as an addition and, possibly, as an enrichment. In this respect, change and continuity are considered to be antithetical stages; very rarely, they are seen as dimensions of

[53] Werner Karl Heisenberg (1901–76) was a distinguished physicist.

[54] John Dewey, *Experience and Nature* (New York: W. W. Norton and Company, 1929), p. xi. Compare, also, Jose Ortega y Gasset, *Man and Crisis* (Ruskin House: George Allen and Unwin Ltd, 1958), pp. 34–5.

[55] Ibid., p. 34. Compare also John Dewey, *Reconstruction in Philosophy* (Mineola, NY: Dover edition, 2004, unabridged republication of the edition published by The Beach Press, Boston, 1948), pp. 54–5:

> The world in which philosophers once put their trust was a closed world, a world consisting internally of a limited number of fixed forms, and having definite boundaries externally. The world of modern science is an open world a world varying indefinitely without the possibility of assignable limit in its internal make up, a world stretching beyond any assignable bounds externally.

See also his *The Quest for Certainty: A study of the Relation of Knowledge and Action*, the Gifford Lectures 1929, [1929] (New York: Capricon Books, 1960); and 'What I believe', in Gail Kennedy (ed.), *Pragmatism and American Culture* (Boston, MA: D.C. Heath and Company, 1950), pp. 26–7.

the same thing. In reality, however, we find that both the old (o) and the new (n) can co-exist. And they can co-exist not only in combination (i.e., o+n) or in their difference from one another, but as a unit or a system (on). Furthermore, this state of 'on' often is a transition and a metamorphosis.

Our quest for certainty and for reciprocal actions and smooth complementary expectations[56] in turn relies on: (a) a belief in some form of strong or weak determinism, (b) a tendency to simplify reality and thus to embrace monistic explanations (see Chapter 1) and (c) the abrogation of our (either strong or weak) responsibility to act and to react since it is more convenient to conserve our energies. These tendencies are intimately related; the former is likely to be accompanied by the presence of the latter two. In fact, determinism in its various forms more often than not rules out both the occurrence of chance and of conscious human intervention. Nothing is ambiguous because everything can be explained and predicted; causation creates realities (see the discussion in Chapter 1). Fixity generates principles and formulae; and the latter point towards predictability. As Dewey put it, 'Whenever the thought of fixity rules, that of all-inclusive unity rules also'.[57] Accordingly, we tend to give prevalence to facts and adhere to all-embracing meanings. We do not note possibilities and 'might have beens', things which could have been different, serious errors in judgement and statements of regret or failed interventions.

Constraints and opportunities thus become attributes of structures which appear as solid blocks. As such, they are presumed to be objective and knowable – they assume an existence before agents experience them. They seem to posit an obstacle and thus an impediment to further progress (a constraint) or to lay a smooth path towards a goal (an opportunity). Accordingly, constraints and opportunities oblige and disoblige, block or allow even before a course of action is taken. In reality, however, something reveals itself as either a constraint or an opportunity in the process of performing the relevant act. Assumptions about the existence of constraints and opportunities before a relevant act takes place are merely assumptions and speculations. Embarking upon a course of action is therefore a process filled with potentiality and possibility and thus a certain degree of indeterminism.

Let us assume, for example, that I am competent to do *x*, decide that is worth striving to attain *x* and, subsequently, I attain *x*. In this case I possess

[56] The term 'complementary expectations' was used by Talcott Parsons and Edward Shils, *Toward a General Theory of Action* (Cambridge: Harvard University Press, 1951), p. 64.

[57] Dewey, 'What I believe', at p. 26.

facultas. But it may also be the case that I am competent to do *x*, but *x* is never attained either because I cannot attain it or the circumstances do not allow me to do so. In the latter case I possess an aptitude. There is no linear progression from competence to attain *x* to the attainment of *x*. In addition, in both cases, I might modify *x*, decide to do *x* as well as *y*, choose other means of doing *x*, cease to desire *x* or to redeploy the same means to do *y*. One hardly knows, and thus cannot anticipate, the numerous possibilities that a single act may entail and the extent to which possibilities may be stretched unless one engages in flowing action. The latter is surrounded by ambiguity, indeterminism, wishful thinking, error, unexpected occurrences and unforeseen consequences. This is not regrettable; a determinist world would be a world without potentiality and without possibility.

John Dewey and the other pragmatists at the turn of the twentieth century criticised determinism quite strongly.[58] In their view, even when we are focusing on simple human conduct it is hardly possible to talk about fixed and equivocal ends and settled means. Both ends and means may be imbued with different meanings, can be revised and rethought, selected and deselected. Individuals can only devise *ends in view* which are revisable and attainable by various means. As they contemplate their achievement, infer possible consequences and embark upon action, they may form other ends in view, consider new information and revise things accordingly, realise the fallacy of their preconceptions and, finally, change their course of action. Motion and change are inherent in this process. This implies neither a Parmenidean undifferentiated motion nor an Aristotelian motion (kinesis) toward a fixed end (entelechy) as 'substance' metaphysics have postulated. It is akin to a Heraclitean notion of flux, a process of becoming by doing (and by failing). Dewey captured this point nicely: there is always 'a false, unnatural separation between process and product, between activity and its achieved outcome'.[59] And further,

> when an individual is engaged in doing or making something (the activity not being of such a mechanical and habitual character that its outcome is assured) there is an analogous situation. Something is going to come of what is present to the sense, but just what is doubtful. The plot is unfolding towards success or failure, but just when or how is uncertain.[60]

[58] See, *inter alia*, 'Time and Individuality' in Douglas Browning (ed.), *Philosophers of Process* (New York: Random House, 1965), pp. 208–24.

[59] John Dewey, *The Way We Think* (Lexington, MA: D.C. Heath, 1910) p. 164; *How we Think* (Memphis: Central Books, 2012), p. 59.

[60] Dewey, *The Way We Think*, p. 194.

If change is present at a micro level, that is, in our personal conduct, the same holds for the meso and macro levels of a pluralistic and restless universe. Certainty, a belief in clearly visualised and predictable outcomes is contestable. Settings, conditions, states of affairs, the significations and meanings we create about all the above, ends in view, and actors all are subject to change. And change means surpassing what exists. Change is also correlational because nothing happens disconnectedly in the same way that nothing is intelligible by itself alone (*connexio rerum*, Chapters 1 and 2). There exist intrinsic relations between the world and the self because the self is in the world, interacts with it and changes it through his or her actions. In addition, by so doing, one changes oneself. The self is always projective and one has to navigate seas of change without the luxury of fixed anchorages.

For this reason, the conversion fallacy needs to be resisted, notwithstanding the discomfort and restlessness that such resistance will create. We are left with the realisation that the frames and categories we use in order to think are not flexible enough to capture the complexity and fluidity of the world. Openness in our mind sets, a willingness to embark upon reflective and experimental thinking, to accept the existence of alternative ways of doing things and to change course are all essential in social actions mobilised towards solving problems in processes of social cooperation. This, as William James noted, 'leaves the creative mind subject to the law of time'.[61]

The two dimensions discussed above, namely, (a) the presence of dynamic and restless change on multiple levels and the dynamics of changeable realities and (b) the involvement of a *social self in action*,

[61] William James, 'The Dilemma of Determinism', in Browning (ed.), *Philosophers of Process*, pp. 112–38, at p. 136. Creation, which has its etymological root in the Latin verb *creare*, is an act of bringing forth something new, of producing, bringing about the emergence of something and therefore of ultimately having faith in the openness of the future. As James noted,

> indeterminism, on the contrary, says that the parts have a certain amount of loose play on one another, so that the laying down of one of them does not necessarily determine what the others shall be. It admits that possibilities may be in excess of actualities, and that things not yet revealed to our knowledge may really in themselves be ambiguous. Of two alternative futures which we conceive, both may now be really possible; and the one becomes impossible only at the very moment when the other excludes it by becoming real itself. Indeterminism thus denies the world to be one unbending unit of fact. It says that there is a certain ultimate pluralism in it; and, so saying, it corroborates our ordinary unsophisticated view of things. To that view, actualities seem to float in a wider sea of possibilities from out of which they are chosen; and, somewhere – indeterminism says – such possibilities exist, and form a part of truth.

The Will to Believe and Other Essays in Popular Philosophy (London: Longmans, Green and Co., 1910), p. 151.

accurately reflect Dewey's understanding of society and agents as forming a restless and fully integrated system. Indeed, according to Dewey, we are parts of a moving, dynamic, interactive system: 'We, who are also parts of the moving present, create ourselves as we create an unknown future'.[62] An individual's action in a given context thus 'serves both to create who I become and to a degree what the context becomes'.[63] This conception of the world leaves ample room for creative endeavours, transformative social change and responsibility placed on the lap of individuals; 'for now there is responsibility to choose not only for one's self but for the environment defining and creating that self'.[64]

3.4 Structuration, Structuation and Co-creation

In contrast to Dewey's conception of 'the social self in action', structural theories of social action depict agency and structure as separate entities. In addition, there appears to be a hierarchical relation among them; structures dominate. They have the capacity to determine the scope, direction, effectiveness and magnitude of social action. One can hardly talk about the existence of a dialectical relation or a relation of co-determination between them. There appears to be no mutual implication; one-dimensional causality and necessity prevail. In Althusserian Marxism we discern the 'overdetermination' of structure and in orthodox Marxism the 'base/superstructure' schema. Mechanistic perspectives also highlight automatic developments procuring change, while for determinists fixed laws govern the emergence of the new. All these approaches leave little room for creative, unexpected and de novo possibilities or for revisable purposes and goals. Since systems and structures of domination envelop our lives, patience is required until either mechanistic or evolutionary or determinist change eventually brings about societal betterment and the emancipation of human beings from the evils and the unfreedom of this world.

In these accounts, structures and agents are seen as already formed, fixed and unified. Structures are perceived to be rigid and objective, as

[62] John Dewey, *Individualism Old and New* (Amherst, New York: Prometheus Books, 1999), p. 83.

[63] David Hildebrand, *Dewey* (Oxford: ONEWORD publications, 2008), p. 112.

[64] Ibid., p. 112. In continental philosophy, too, one can find a similar conception in Gilles Deleuze's thinking. Compare his belief that differentiation is never a negation, but a creation and that difference is never negative but essentially positive and creative; *Bergonism*, trans. Hugh Tomlinson and Barbara Habberjam (New York: Zone, 1988), p. 101.

opposed to constructions that can be remade and reconfigured. They are emptied of their fluid qualities and of the relations that constitute and ultimately dovetail them. Yet, in reality, structures are crystallised 'action patterns into which individual actions congeal'.[65] As such, they cannot exist without people. They can also change if people decide to act in different ways. Because structures are often seen in monolithic terms, any change is seen to unsettle, disrupt and to threaten what exists. Accordingly, collisions and conflicts between agency (what I may wish to do) and structure (what the 'system' permits me to do) are treated as occurrences that separate agency and structure – not as manifestations of their mutual interaction and co-implication.

Although we tend to perceive structures as blocks, if we pause to reflect on their origins and evolution, that is, if we situate them within their spatio-temporal context, we realise that they reflect sedimented or crystallised processes, practices[66] and events. Giddens's emphasis on the time-space constitution of social systems has exemplified this; 'social systems are hence constituted of situated practices'.[67] And processes and practices, including the differing logics on which they may be premised, cannot take place without the involvement of human beings. Even events, which are happenings outside human beings' control, depend on agents' conception of, and reaction to, them. In other words, human beings in the process of social cooperation and strife make and unmake structures which, in turn, house, direct and shape their ongoing actions. Interestingly, in 1950 John R. Commons defined an institution 'as collective action in control, liberation, and expansion of individual action'.[68] Similarly, Giddens has defined institutions 'as practices which stretch over long time-space distances in the reproduction of social systems'.[69] So subsequent acts sustain the continuity of processes which, in turn, sustains the continuity of structures.

[65] Emile Durkheim had noted this too in *The Rules of Sociological Method*; cited in Stark, *The Fundamental Forms of Social Thought*, pp. 248–9. Stark warned against treating 'social action and social institutions as separate phenomena since they are a continuum'. Compare also Lon Fuller's interactional account of the law, 'Human Interaction and the Law', 14 *American Journal of Jurisprudence* (1969), pp. 1–36.

[66] For recent scholarship on this, see Adler and Pouliot (eds.), *International Practices* (Cambridge: Cambridge University Press, 2011); Adler-Nissen, 'Towards a Practice Turn in EU Studies', pp. 87–103.

[67] Giddens, *A Contemporary Critique of Historical Materialism*, p. 26.

[68] Commons, *The Economics of Collective Action*. See also his book entitled *Legal Foundations of Capitalism* (Madison: University of Wisconsin Press, 1959).

[69] Giddens, *A Contemporary Critique of Historical Materialism*, p. 28.

If my understanding of structures is correct, then it can be further argued that the difference between the maintenance of a structure and change is inexact. The reason being that change is inherent in the ways of doing things and thus it is only the intensity and magnitude of it that will make us perceive a multitude of changes as 'change'. At a certain point, agency would have to intervene decisively to increase the intensity of changes, to reorganise practices and eventually to restructure systems. Influenced by the Chicago School of Sociology in the early twentieth century, Buckley pinpointed that systems are inherently 'structure-elaborating and changing': 'the "structure" is an abstract construct, not something distinct from the ongoing interactive process but rather a temporary, accommodative representation of it at any one time. These considerations lead to the fundamental insight that socio-cultural systems are inherently structure-elaborating and changing; for some, the terms "process" and "change" were synonymous'.[70] Bohm also noted that the Latin root of the word 'structure' denotes something that grows and evolves and that the Latin suffix *ura* 'originally meant the action of doing something'.[71] This etymological observation led Bohm to introduce the verb 'to structuate'. To structuate means 'to create and dissolve' structures.

As David Bohm noted in another context, 'each relatively autonomous and stable structure is to be understood not as something independently and permanently existent but rather as a product that has been formed in the whole flowing movement and what will ultimately dissolve back into this movement. How it forms and maintains itself, then, depends on its place function within the whole'.[72] To put it differently, structures contain the deposits of past actions and, in turn, are containers of present actions as well as springboards for new imagined actions and thus new (or reconstructed) structures. They can obstruct, restrict and limit but can also prepare, facilitate and condition. They are, and can be, made to measure since, ultimately, agency brings structures into being and phases them out of being. But, if we lift structures out of their historical dynamics, thereby bracketing time and the processes that gave rise to them and that sustain them, then we are inevitably led to structuralist or functionalist or structural functionalist explanations. And the latter tend to have a system

[70] Walter Buckley, *Sociology and Modern Systems Theory* (Englewood Cliffs, NJ: Prentice-Hall, 1967), p. 18.

[71] David Bohm, *Wholeness and the Implicate Order* (London: Routledge, 1980), pp. 151–2.

[72] Ibid., p. 14.

maintaining or conserving orientation, since change is seen to be risk- or threat-ridden.

The processual dimension entailed by structures identified in the foregoing discussion can also be applied to human agency. For the agents involved in processes of structuration, to borrow Anthony Giddens' notion, are never complete, fully formed beings.[73] Their selves are always in formation, changing, adapting and fusing new and old dimensions in often contradictory, but also more enriched, configurations. Although their existence is biologically and socially shaped, it is also in motion and formation until death. Their past, present and future all become one since their environing conditions both affect and shape them, but neither determine nor cage them. As noted throughout the discussion in Chapters 1 and 2, there exists a projective, prospective self that emerges out of the dialectical play of agency and structure. Selves and structures are constantly in the making and in interaction. The relation among them is one of co-evolution and co-implication. This means that human rationality[74] is both bounded and, thus, incomplete as well as unbelievably creative.[75]

[73] This is not to underestimate the existence of what may be called 'a double parallel subjectivity'; the subjectivity instigating action in the world and the subjectivity of the observer of that action. As Riker has observed in another context, 'all observation contains a subjective element – namely the demarcation undertaken for the purpose of uttering particular sentences. This is why it is erroneous to attribute the slow development of social science to the subjectivity of social observation. Where subjectivity a barrier to knowledge, we would have no science at all'; in Alt and Shepsle (eds.), *Perspectives on Positive Political Economy*, at p. 169. Similarly there exists a double parallel objectivity; namely the objectivity of a changing reality which will continue to unfold outside, and without the gaze of the observer, and the objectivity that our gaze attributes to it in the sense of constructing the world which is then the object of our perception. My argument here differs from Margaret Archer's mutually constitutive agents, structures and institutions over time since in her schema agents transform or reproduce social structures rather than create them; Margaret Archer, *Realist Social Theory: The Morphogenetic Approach* (New York: Cambridge University Press, 1995), p. 197.

[74] By this I refer to the ability to examine circumstances, set goals, contemplate alternative courses of action and weigh up their consequences, desired outcomes and biased preferences, mobilise one's resources to achieve one's ends and so on.

[75] Taking actors seriously means that we recognise that they can make rational choices as well as irrational ones. They also make mistaken choices and often act on impulse or as if they had no choice (that is without a prior consideration of possible alternatives and the formation of a preference for a course of action as opposed to b course of action). There exists no single human quality that can explain or capture the totality of human activity and existence. And if one such quality is singled out, be this rationality or emotion, then this is bound to conceal the multidimensional character of the self. Sociality, morality, reflexivity and intense feeling all are bound up with rationality and individuality and in

More importantly, rationality unfolds within a temporal continuum and a socio-spatial context. In this continuum the various instances (i.e., next second, next minute, next hour, next day, next week, next month, next season, next year and so on) can only be artificially separated. This is because every instance, within which an agent's action unfolds, flows from what has preceded it, feeds back into the preferences and interests formed in the previous one, occasions a rethinking and often a reconstruction of the previous one, prepares the ground for the next one and feeds forward into future action and projection. Rationality thus must be related to the totality of a given situation. For in the process sketched above not only is the present lived and re-imagined, but also the past that lies behind is continuously reconstructed in order to give velocity to the present and to firmly install it within the future. As Mead has noted in another context, 'as the condition of the present, the past then will vary as the present varies' and new paths will 'arise behind us' in the course of evolution as each present 'marks out and in a sense selects what has made its own peculiarity possible'.[76] In this respect, change is not only prospective; it is also retrospective. And irrespective of the arrow of its direction, it is endemic in agents and their surrounding environment. If we are thus to develop a sound theory of institutional change, we need to connect everything together (*connexio rerum*). Agents cannot be placed outside structures and the world, nor can they be considered to be overdetermined or actionless, passive recipients of the world's stimuli. Being-in-change is being-in-action and being-in-action is, in turn, being-in-formation. Active and activist human agency is our living reality. Indeed, as Homans has argued in another context, 'the world and its meaning are always negotiating with one another, with experience as the go-between'.[77] Perhaps, herein lie the building blocks for a theory of institutional change.

fact converge to making the person. Instants cannot capture flow, reason cannot capture processes of knowing, judging, acting, and parts do not reflect the sum. Nor do they reflect the complex process involved in deliberating and acting and redeliberating and reacting or adjusting continuously to new and unforeseen conditions. See Robert C. Lieberman, 'Ideas, Institutions and Political Order: Explaining Institutional Change', 96 *American Political Science Review* (2002), pp. 697–712; Jens Beckert, 'Agency, Entrepreneurs, and Institutional Change: The Role of Strategic Choice and Institutionalised Practices in Organisation', 20 *Organisation Studies* (1999), pp. 777–99.

[76] George Herbert Mead, *The Philosophy of the Present* (London: The Open Court Company, 1932), p. 23.

[77] George C. Homans, *The Human Group* (London: Routledge and Kegan Paul, London, 1968 [1951]), p. 13.

3.5 But Change of What? The Significance of the Particular

Having made explicit the implicit assumptions underpinning our bias towards stability, fixity and order, and thus the ensuing underestimation of processes and change, it is, nevertheless, important to distinguish among the units of analysis undergoing change. For although there exist general modalities and characteristics of change, there also exist distinctive features and peculiarities among the entities-in-change or the various processes-in-change. It would thus be wise to differentiate *inter alia* policy change from organisational change or a change in norms. By focusing on the particular-in-change, we would thus be in a position to develop distinctive conceptual tools for a more accurate understanding of processes of change.

The table below seeks to map the distinctive patterns of change that may accompany distinctive units of analysis; namely, organisations, systems, policies, beliefs, norms, rules, practices, procedures, cultures, societies and modes of governing. As shown below, change in organisations will exhibit different dynamics from wider processes of cultural change. And the process of change in substantive policy areas is unlikely to display the same pattern one may find in societal or political transitions; such as, for example, the one generated by the fall of communism. This serves to illustrate that patterns of change found in the study of one unit of analysis may not be perfectly migratory (Figures 3.1 and 3.2).

Adaptive emulation is a result of diffusion processes which lead to the dissemination of a practice or a policy and its adoption in different contexts. A number of factors will influence the diffusion of a policy, including spatial ones, such as geographical proximity[78] of the settings or contexts, the impact of interrelations among the actors and contexts and the existence of networking activities, and the presence of an overarching political setting which facilitates and encourages diffusion and policy learning. In other words, both spatial and communicational contiguity will play an important role in determining the pace and the extent of the diffusion process.[79] In the same vein, factors which will impede diffusion are the

[78] For an overview of the diffusion literature, see David Strang and John W. Meyer, 'Institutional Conditions for Diffusion', 22 *Theory and Society* (1993), pp. 487–512; David Strang and Sarah A. Soule, 'Diffusion in Organisations and Social Movements: From Hybrid Corn to Poison Pills', 24 *Annual Review of Sociology* (1998), pp. 265–90.

[79] Both Hall and Jenkins-Smith and Sabatier differentiate among 'different layers' of policy change. For Hall, the latter could include the instruments used, the setting and the overall goals of a policy; Hall, 'Policy Paradigms, Social Learning, and the State', pp. 275–96. H. Jenkins-Smith and P. Sabatier, on the other hand, examine whether the normative core of a policy has been altered or the policy core, that is, policy choices for achieving the deep

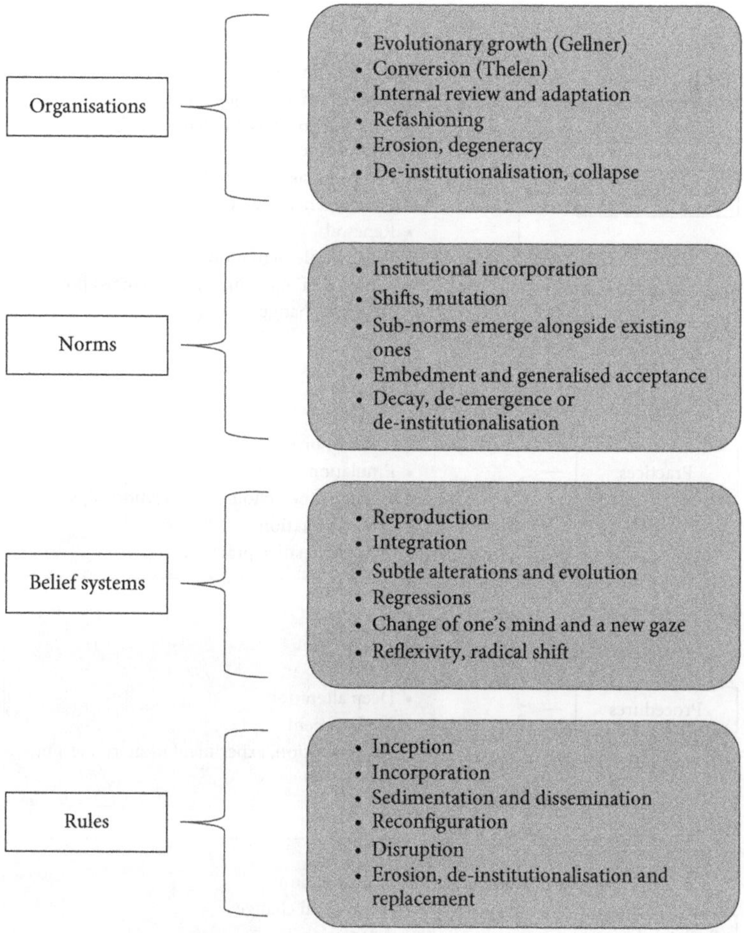

Figure 3.1 Patterns of change 1

presence of costs, strong domestic interests, institutional opposition or organisational rivalry, cultural scripts and practices that show resilience and opposition to the new policy or practices, the degree of openness or closure of an organisation or system and the rule of elites with different ideological beliefs and scepticism towards reform.

normative core, or just secondary aspects designed to implement the policy core; *Policy Change and Learning: An Advocacy Coalition Approach* (Boulder, CO: Westview Press, 1993). Both templates relate to the depth of policy change; for an excellent discussion of all this, see Florian Trauner and Ariadna Ripoll Servent (eds.), *Policy Change in the Area of Freedom, Security and Justice* (Abingdon: Routledge, 2014), pp. 11–31.

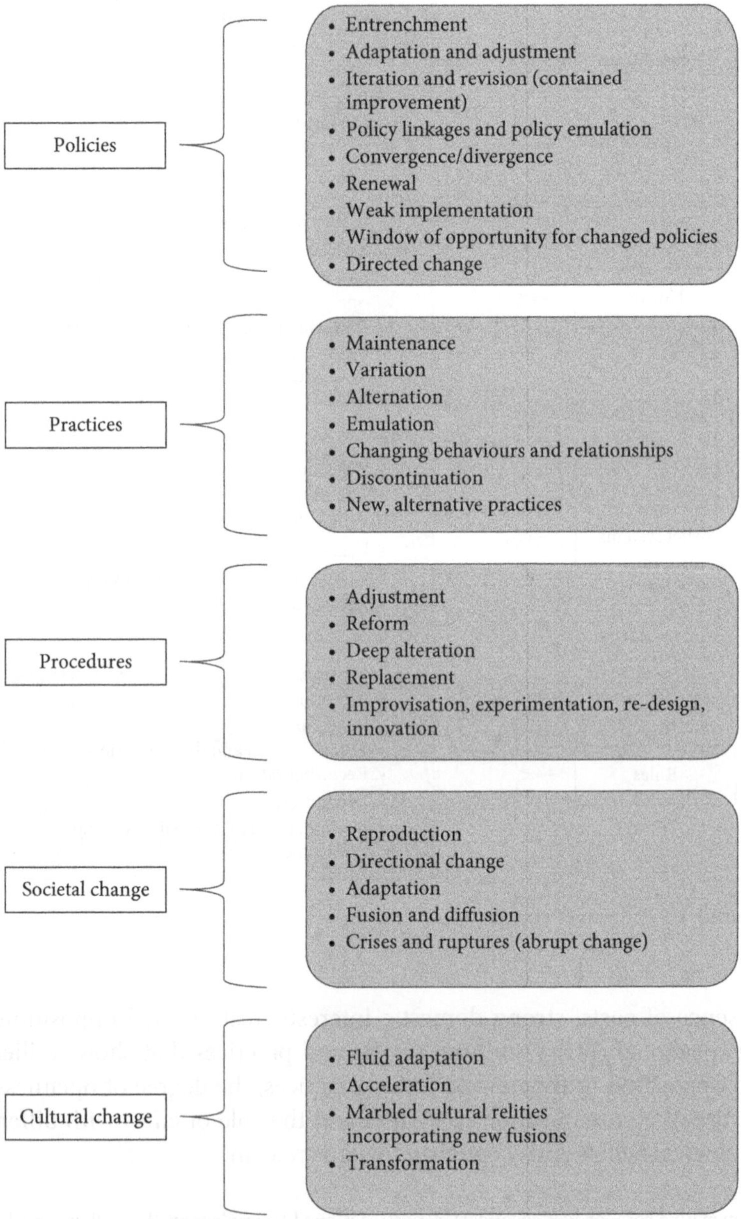

Figure 3.2 Patterns of change 2

3.6 General Modalities of Change

Having highlighted the importance of distinguishing the various units of analysis and discussing the mechanisms of change, in this section I zoom out in order to focus on general modalities of change. By this I mean characteristics of change which are general enough and thus applicable to autonomous, yet interdependent, fields. If one examines institutional change in general, one will discern that it is characterised by a number of characteristics: namely, (i) form or quality, (ii) rate, including urgency and duration, (iii) magnitude or depth, (iv) amplitude or range and (v) direction. 'Form' refers to step change, radical breaks, ruptures as well as incremental and adaptive changes. Direction, on the other hand, reflects understandings of change as either linear (Comte, Marx, Darwin) or cyclical or spiral, that is, as having upward and backward dimensions or back and forth oscillations. The former 'upward' dimension captures change as growth or development while the latter 'backward' dimension refers to change as regression (epistrophe or backsliding), change as decline or decay (fthora) or de-emergence (metaptosis) or de-institutionalisation. Sorokin made a distinctive contribution in this area by identifying three principal 'patterns of direction' of change, namely, linear – subdivided as unilinear, oscillating, spiral and branching; cyclical; and variably or creatively recurrent direction, which may be approximately paraphrased as 'cycles with trend'.[80]

It is true that more often than not most of the above-mentioned characteristics will be clearly visible following the culmination of processes of change. The unpredictability of socio-political life and human limitations make it difficult to obtain a full understanding of the depth, range and direction of change while it is occurring. It is as if the depth, range and direction of change are covered by a fog; a clear view of 'the road behind and in front' emerges when processes of change settle. In addition, it is often the case that while change unfolds, agents continue to prioritise and value the 'stable' over the 'precarious' and thus tend to resist or underplay change. Dewey perceptively remarked that, if we think more deeply about things, we will realise that, despite the appearance of fixity, they always evolve. With respect to structures, he noted that 'the fact is that all structure is structure of something; anything defined as structure is a

[80] Cited in Wilbert E. More, 'A Reconsideration of Theories of Social Change', 25(6) *American Sociological Review* (1960), pp. 810–18, at p. 816.

character of events, not something intrinsic per se'.[81] But fixity exists 'for the time being'; beneath the layer of stasis or solidity, micro- and macro-changes always take place. One does not have to adhere to an organic view of social structures or to a functionalist institutional perspective in order to appreciate the processual nature of things. In fact, as I argued in the previous sections, since structures are formalised and solidified arrangements of processes, practices and events, it would be misguided to believe that structure and process stand apart or that processes unfold outside of structures.

The interactionist and interconnected view of structures and processes prompt a shift of attention away from a functional assessment of change[82] which centres on questions, such as what is change for?, why do we need it?, which forces does it serve? It is to an appreciation of the rhythms of change. And rhythms include both microtones – something that has just started but which is not fully shaped, and overtones – the loud or 'noisy' elements that capture attention. It may also lead to an understanding that change more often than not is not singular. Instead, it is plural and variable. In other words, one may be able to trace parallel processes of change within change per se which might well be asynchronic. Some may start while other processes unfold or approach cessation. This is the case of the non-simultaneity of simultaneous sub-processes of change.

The above observation opens up an opportunity for me to explain why the above-mentioned list of the modalities of change does not include a reference to the 'reception' or the 'acceptance' of change. In drawing the list, I decided to exclude this variable because it essentially relates to the external effects of change rather than to its 'internal' unfolding. However, irrespective of whether one focuses on the (internal) characteristics of change or on its implications, one would have to acknowledge that processes of change depend on congenial environing conditions (this will become very clear in Chapter 6 with respect to Brexit). Without the latter, change itself cannot unfold. Nor can it take root. It could easily evaporate if the setting within which it unfolds is not elastic enough to adjust profitably to it. In brief, both its range and depth would be limited. Rigid systems are more likely to resist change, co-opt new processes, but also, because of their rigidity, to experience change as a crisis or a rupture. This is for two

[81] Ibid., p. 247.

[82] As noted above, the term function and its dissemination in social sciences are associated with the works of the anthropologists A. R. Radcliffe-Brown and B. Malinowski.

main reasons. First, rigidly ordered systems do not have the inbuilt adjustment capability to accommodate change easily. Second, because they tend to rely on a predetermined set of relations among units/entities, they do not encourage the spontaneous growth of relations which can absorb change. If systems are hierarchically structured and command-based, suggestions for internal review and change will be perceived as threatening the authority of central agents who direct the activities. Conversely, in 'plastic' systems, that is, systems where centralised commands and superior inferior relations are replaced by polycentric nodes of coordination and decision-making, change is less likely to be seen as a threat thereby triggering defence mechanisms.

Writing about a wholly different context, Polanyi juxtaposed pyramids of authority or 'corporate orders' to 'spontaneous orders'.[83] This juxtaposition enabled him to highlight the creative possibilities inherent in spontaneous orders, such as a highly adaptable coordination of participants' activities, easy adjustments and an ability to cope better with complex tasks. Polanyi used the distribution of passengers over the compartments of a train in which the seats are not reserved[84] as an example of a spontaneous order and observed that the main attraction of the spontaneous order is that it can multiply the connections and relations among the participants, thereby promoting self-adjustments. Conversely, in a pyramid or a hierarchical system the relations are mostly confined to given sets; the superior issues authoritative orders to those they control who then re-command these to their subordinates. People are placed into specifically prescribed positions instead of taking part in mutual self-adjustments. Of course, Polanyi was preoccupied with the limits of Soviet central planning and economic development. But his distinction between self-adjusting systems or polycentric orders,[85] on the one hand, and 'dominocracies', on the other, is, nevertheless, insightful for the purposes of the discussion here. In spontaneously ordered systems change finds a fertile ground.

In fact, one could argue that spontaneous orders and their inbuilt adjustments resemble kaleidoscopes. A simple shake of the kaleidoscope changes the components or the relations among the components thereby producing a different image. A new image and thus a new structure – when

[83] Michael Polanyi, *The Logic of Liberty: Reflections and Rejoinders* (London: Routledge and Kegan Paul, 1951).

[84] Ibid., p. 115.

[85] Ibid., p. 170 et seq.

the image is frozen – are formed as a result of the re-arrangements of the previous forms or part-images. The relationships among the parts are thus always conditional and can be re-arranged by a simple act of motion. Spontaneously ordered systems allow for kaleidoscopic change and can easily develop strategies for procuring, accepting and accommodating new relations and processes and for managing the ensuing tensions. Such strategies may include: a regular reflection on the purposes, objectives and expectations of the systems; building capacities for strategic thinking and the evaluation of alternatives; a 360 degree gathering of information; encouraging experimentation and rewarding it; improvisation; the diffusion of conflicts; emulation and policy-learning; and the incorporation of new agents, new goals and new capacities of action.[86] They are thus more creative. By doing 'original work' they help to determine what the future shall become.[87]

3.7 Conclusion

Although the foregoing discussion on the 'generative' templates of institutional change may give rise to further questions about their efficacy[88] in diverse disciplinary domains, its essential premise has been that processualism and a holistic approach yield a better understanding of our institutional and social worlds. Processualism captures the long-duree of things[89] which is, in the main, beyond the ambit of harmonising certitude. Holism, on the other hand, refers to institutional change's spatial and ideational contexts. True, space and time cannot be separated neatly from a perceptual point of view. This is not only because it is impossible to perceive time a-spatially, that is, without being situated somewhere, but also because change, be it institutional, socio-legal or political, cannot be studied in an isolated way.

Bringing time back into our thinking, in line with the *connexio rerum* model, necessarily involves three inter-related processes: (i) the need to pay attention to the evolving dynamics of institutions due to changing

[86] As Alvin Boskoff noted: we could approach change 'as the product of the variable capacity of social systems for generating and channelling innovative processes'; 'Functional Analysis as a Source of a Theoretical Repertory and Research Tasks in the Study of Social Change' in Zollschan and Hirsch (eds.), *Explorations in Social Change*, pp. 213–43, at p. 239.

[87] I borrow, here, from pragmatist perspectives and, in particular, from William James.

[88] The term is borrowed from Bourdieu, *Outline of a Theory of Practice*, p. 97.

[89] The term is borrowed from Henri Bergson; See his 'The Idea of Duration' in Douglas Browning (ed.), *Philosophers of Process*, pp. 6–43.

relations, practices and unforeseen developments; (ii) the intertwining of micro and macro levels, that is, the interlacing of agency, actions and relations, processes, practices and structure and (iii) an examination of the continuously changing environment that surrounds an evolving institution. In this respect, even if the main unit of analysis is a particular institution or one phase in its development, one needs to resist: (a) static and unrefined depictions of it (see also Chapters 1 and 2), (b) the erasure of agency in processes of change (Chapters 2 and 4) and (c) assumptions about relatively stable and changeless surrounding environments (Chapters 5 and 6). Institutions, and their contexts, are subject to perpetual motion and studying this requires an attention to the past, that is, to the effects of past time, and to the future, that is, to how they will be affected by future time. Otherwise put, there exists no spaceless time and no timeless space. Our analyses must be nuanced enough to capture this.

For this reason it is advisable to examine the context of change as well as the context generated by change, or in other words, change's relational and constitutive effects in the fields in question. The context of change is important because the surrounding environment often affects the effect, rate and direction of change itself; the environing conditions are likely to make change felt, important and effective. Effectiveness essentially means the perception of change as something more than a happening in time *t*, a mere occurrence. Change(s) will thus produce ripples of change in the adjacent environment. For this reason, it is not wise to lift it out of its connections with other fields and to study it in isolation. All changes, transitions, reforms and radical breaks are always part of a greater whole. Systems are not isolated; they are coupled and they co-evolve. Coupling implies connectedness as well as frictions and irritations. To ignore this and to study change as a system evolution or growth leads to a partial understanding of the reality around us. No space is closed off, and attempts to introduce some empirical or cognitive closure are bound to fail. In fact, without this broader point of view we might fail to appreciate the mingling of the stable and the new, the discrete and the novel and thus to assess change adequately, be it a clearly visible derogation from the past (rupture) or an enhancement of it (adaptation and acceleration) or an epistrophe to it (regression).

The foregoing chapters demonstrated the reality of 'nested' changes and changes 'in', 'of' and 'to' something. By so doing, they showed the merits of the adoption of a processual and holistic perspective on institutional change. Although this focus opens up very interesting windows in social science research, it is beyond the scope of my discussion to elaborate on evaluative assessments of change. I hope readers will pardon me for this. As I mentioned in the introduction, that question is the subject matter of a rather different discussion, and of a separate volume devoted to the 'change for' question.

The reader may recall that an advantage of the constructivist approach, as I argued in Chapter 2, is that it aligns perception, action and imagination in order to bring about positive change in the social world and to facilitate human flourishing. Attention to the temporal spread quite often tends to confirm the rationale for an institution's existence and continuation. Institutions exist and continue to evolve because they have specific purposes and these purposes cannot be judged in isolation from the human activities or the needs or the interests they serve. Indeed, questions such as what an institution does or whether it evolves in the right direction would always have to be addressed on the basis of its potency to meet human needs well enough. Admittedly, the latter judgement brings us beyond the domain of social scientific research; it brings us to the real, everyday world that is populated by ordinary things and people – in other words, by everything that really matters. And such a yardstick is normative in nature and remains relatively unaffected by time and space relativity.[90] I use the term relatively, because I believe that anything that reduces human life or constricts it or limits its potential is unlikely to last for an extended period of time.

Institutions are neither self-serving nor self-maintaining. In fact, if one takes human beings 'out of them', that is, either as input or output or purpose, they are nothing else than empty shells or empty frames. And if they themselves 'turn away from human beings' in a quest for abstract goals and in pursuit of imposed ideal rationales, they become 'unreal' and useless. They cannot operate functionally, evolve, re-map, re-organise, re-structure, re-frame and so on. In other words, they will not be able to create congenial conditions which will lead to better operations, better practices, and to new developments. When the latter are impeded or restricted and

[90] Interestingly, Frei has noted: 'The purpose of government is to fulfil the needs of the citizens and of the population at large as best as possible'; Bruno Frei and Reiner Eichenberger, *The New Democratic Federalism in Europe: Functional, Overlapping and Competing Jurisdictions* (Northampton: Edward Elgar, 1999), p. ix. Compare, Aristotle's belief that 'The city comes into existence in order that men may live; it persists that they may live well'; *Politics*, I, 1, 1252b12.

the evolution of an institution is brought to a halt, then its very existence will be at stake. Self-deception, coercive power and ideology can only conceal disfunction for a certain period of time.[91] Turning away from human beings, having no interest in the ordinary details of human existence or even pursuing institutional change for change's sake all undermine the capacity of institutions to serve human beings and society.

[91] Sadly enough, this observation more often than not flows from 'distance' judgments and following periods of reflection, and not from 'contact assessments' which often have a rather demoralising effect.

Part II

Applied Aspects of Institutional Constructivism

4

Ideas, Norms and European Citizenship

4.1 Introduction*

In the previous chapters I discussed the shortcomings of monistic and dualistic paradigms in social science research. In Chapter 1, I laid the foundations for a multivariable model, the *connexio rerum* model, which *inter alia* attributes importance to human beings as institutional designers and agents of socio-political change. The discussion in Chapter 2 developed the model, situated it within the tradition of constructivism and highlighted the advantages of maintaining the interdependence of agency, institutions, discourse and space-time in studying social problems and political phenomena. In what follows, I wish to illustrate the fruitfulness of institutional constructivism in explaining the institutional dynamics of European Union citizenship and the black box of judicial decision-making. This discussion, in turn, will prepare the ground for a more sustained attention to institutional change in EU citizenship and the contestation of supranationalism in Chapters 5 and 6.

The introduction of Union Citizenship by the Treaty on European Union (1 November 1993) shattered prevailing economic approaches to European integration[1] and generated debates concerning issues of polity formation, such as European democracy and legitimacy, European constitutionalism, the formation of a European demos and the design of a

*This chapter is a revised version of an article which appeared in the *Modern Law Review* (2005), Vol. 68(2), pp. 233–67. It was written with the support of the British Academy, the Thank-Offering to Britain Fund and the AHRB and it was my first exploration of institutional constructivism.

[1] For early accounts, see Andrew Durand, 'European Citizenship', 4 *European Law Review* (1979), pp. 3–14; Andrew Evans, 'European Citizenship: A Novel Concept in EEC Law', 32(4) *American Journal of Comparative Law* (1984), pp. 674–715.

European public sphere.[2] As such, it featured centrally in what has been termed 'the normative turn' in European studies.[3] Certain scholars saw European citizenship as an important – albeit skeletal – institutional structure on which more flesh had to be grafted. The mere fact that citizenship had 'burst' its statist and national bounds[4] sparked intriguing questions, such as what citizenship might mean in a supranational context, how it may affect the development of a non-statal form of governance and how citizenship per se might be transfigured in analytical and institutional terms.[5] Constructivist approaches addressed these questions and sought to capture the transformative potential of European citizenship.[6]

[2] See Joseph Weiler, 'Does Europe Need a Constitution? Reflections on Demos, Telos and the German Maastricht Decision', 1(3) *European Law Journal* (1995), pp. 219–58; 'To Be a European Citizen – Eros and Civilization', 4(4) *Journal of European Public Policy* (1997), pp. 495–519; Grainne de Burca, 'The Quest for Legitimacy in the European Union', 59(3) *Modern Law Review* (1996), pp. 349–79; Deirdre Curtin, *Postnational Democracy: The European Union in Search of a Political Philosophy* (The Hague: Kluwer, 1997); Carlos Closa, 'The Concept of Citizenship in the Treaty of European Union', 29 *Common Market Law Review* (1992), p. 1137; 'Supranational Citizenship and Democracy: Normative and Empirical Dimensions', in M. La Torre (ed.), *European Citizenship: An Institutionalist Challenge* (The Hague: Kluwer, 1998); Elizabeth Meehan, *European Citizenship* (London: Sage, 1993); Kostakopoulou, 'Towards a Theory of Constructive Citizenship in Europe', pp. 337–58; 'European Citizenship and Immigration after Amsterdam', pp. 639–656; Ulrich Preuss, 'Two Challenges to European Citizenship', XLIV *Political Studies* (1996), pp. 534–52; Josephine Shaw, 'The Many Pasts and Futures of Citizenship in the EU', 22 *European Law Review* (1997), pp. 554–72; Antje Wiener, 'Assessing the Constructive Potential of Union-Citizenship – A Socio-Historical Perspective', 1(17) *European Integration On-line Papers* (1997) (http://eiop.or.at/eiop/); Antje Wiener and Vincent Della Sala, 'Constitution-Making and Citizenship Practice – Bridging the Democracy Gap in the EU?', 35(4) *Journal of Common Market Studies* (1997), pp. 595–614; Richard Bellamy and Dario Castiglione, 'The Communitarian Ghost in the Cosmopolitan Machine: Constitutionalism, Democracy and the Reconfiguration of Politics in the New Europe', in Bellamy and Castiglione (eds.), *Constitutionalism, Democracy and Sovereignty: American and European Perspectives* (Aldershot: Avebury, 1996); Ian Ward, 'In Search of a European Identity', 57(2) *Modern Law Review* (1994), pp. 315–29.

[3] Weiler, 'To Be a European Citizen'.

[4] I borrow this metaphor from Derek Heater, *What is Citizenship?* (Oxford: Polity Press, 1999).

[5] See Meehan, *European Citizenship*; Elizabeth Meehan, 'Political Pluralism and European Citizenship', in P. Lehning and A. Weale (eds.), *Citizenship, Democracy and Justice in the New Europe* (London: Routledge, 1997); Gerard Delanty, 'Models of Citizenship: Defining European Identity and Citizenship', 1(3) *Citizenship Studies* (1997), pp. 285–303; Siofra O'Leary, *European Union Citizenship: The Options for Reform* (London: IPPR, 1996).

[6] Theodora Kostakopoulou, 'Nested "Old" and "New" Citizenships in the European Union: Bringing Forth the Complexity', 5(3) *Columbia Journal of European Law* (2000), pp. 389–413; *Citizenship, Identity and Immigration in the European Union*; Antje Wiener, *Building Institutions: The Developing Practice of European Citizenship* (Oxford: Westview, 1998); Josephine Shaw, 'The Interpretation of European Union Citizenship', 61(3) *Modern Law*

This had much to do with the fact that citizenship was no longer a single status; instead, it was multiple. As Meehan remarked, 'the identities, rights and obligations associated ... with citizenship are expressed through an increasingly complex configuration of common Community institutions, states, national and transnational voluntary associations, regions, alliances of regions'.[7] This unprecedented complexity and, generally speaking, the interaction of nested and interlocking 'old' (i.e., national) and 'new' (i.e., supranational) citizenships held out the promise of transforming the scope and nature of 'old' and 'new' citizenships over an extended period of time.[8]

However, this perspective was not embraced by everyone. Certain scholars saw European citizenship as a purely decorative and symbolic institution, and a mirror image of pre-Maastricht 'market citizenship'.[9] For instance, it was observed that Union citizenship had added little substantially new to existing Community law, with the exception of electoral rights at European Parliament and local elections and the right to diplomatic and consular protection. Others argued that since European citizenship was essentially a mercantile form of citizenship designed to facilitate economic integration, it would only be relevant to 'favoured EC nationals', that is, to a minority of European citizens who possess the necessary resources required for intra-EU mobility.[10] Reflecting the subtle influence of the intergovernmentalist repertoire, certain authors have proceeded to dismiss Union citizenship as empty rhetoric or a lofty proposal designed to enhance either the Union's social legitimacy or the Commission's promotional agenda. Notwithstanding their differences, all these perspectives

---

Review (1998), pp. 293–317; Ursula Vogel, 'Emancipatory Politics between Universalism and Difference: Gender Perspectives on European Citizenship', in Lehning and Weale (eds.), *Citizenship, Democracy and Justice in the New Europe*, pp. 142–60.

7 Meehan, *European Citizenship*, p. 1.

8 Andrew Evans, 'Nationality Law and European Integration', 16(3) *European Law Review* (1991), pp. 190–215; Kostakopoulou, *Citizenship, Identity and Immigration in the European Union*.

9 Michelle Everson, 'The Legacy of the Market Citizen', in J. Shaw and G. More (eds.), *New Legal Dynamics of European Union* (Oxford: Clarendon Press, 1995); J. d'Oliveira, 'Union Citizenship: Pie in the Sky?', in A. Rosas and E. Antola (eds.), *A Citizens' Europe: In search of a New Order* (London: Sage, 1995); Percy Lehning, 'European Citizenship: A Mirage?', in Lehning and Weale (eds.), *Citizenship, Democracy and Justice in the New Europe*, pp. 175–99; Tony Downes, 'Market Citizenship: Functionalism and Fig-Leaves' in R. Bellamy and A. Warleigh (eds.), *Citizenship and Governance in the European Union* (London: Continuum, 2001), pp. 93–106.

10 See the three separate categories of residence rights established by Directive 2004/38 OJ 2004 L 158/77 (30 April 2004).

entail a minimalist conception of European citizenship. Generally speaking, minimalism focuses on a few selective characteristics of the whole, thereby bracketing the context out of which European citizenship emerged and the context that its institutional development may help create. On the basis of the above assessments, minimalist European citizenship was not enough to induce real institutional change. Despite such assessments, however, institutional change has occurred.

The discussion here charts, analyses and explains the process of the institutional development of Union citizenship. In what follows, I argue that, following the establishment of Union citizenship, the Court of Justice of the European Union made tactical interventions, which procured incremental, transformative institutional change. By adopting a phased approach, the Court has strengthened the constitutional importance and substance of European citizenship in-between Treaty revisions. The judicial institutionalisation of Union citizenship[11] does not only show that much of the 1990s' literature on European citizenship incorrectly underestimated its conceptual resources and wide-ranging transformative potential, but it also highlights and refines the role of institutions in the process of the construction of reality (Chapter 2). Ideas, concepts, precepts, norms and strategies are nested in, shaped and altered by institutions and the institutional power to shape, mould and extend the above via discursive practices and strategies that create new intersubjectively shared meanings is a powerful tool (Chapters 1 and 2). On this particular point, Haas and Haas observed that 'the constructivist ontology invests institutions with a political potential that is mainly overlooked by scholars from other approaches'.[12] Institutions are thus catalysts for change and agents of change, rather than unitary entities with fixed preferences that are difficult to change.

Although at first sight institutional constructivism could be seen as blending social constructivism with the sociological institutionalist

[11] Institutionalisation may be defined as the incremental and long-term process by which an institution acquires meaning, specificity and value. The term 'specificity' refers to the clear differentiation of an institution from others, while the term 'value' captures the centrality that an institution acquires. Polsby had added 'internal complexity' as a characteristic of the institutionalisation of organisations; N. W. Polsby, 'The Institutionalisation of the US House of Representatives', *American Political Science Review* (1968), p. 145. See L. D. Longley, 'Parliaments as Changing Institutions and as Agents of Regime Change: Evolving Perspectives and a New Research Framework', 2(2) *Journal of Legislative Studies* (1996), p. 24 and Jepperson's essay in Powell and DiMaggio (eds.), *The New Institutionalism in Organisational Analysis*.

[12] Haas and Haas, 'Pragmatic Constructivism and the Study of International Institutions', pp. 573–602, 576.

approach of treating institutions as independent variables including ideas, norms and value that constitute identities and preferences, this view overlooks the subtle, but important, differences among these perspectives. For instance, institutional constructivism attributes greater salience to the institutional creation of reality and is much clearer about the role of institutions in the construction of ideas, norms, cognitive templates, identities and accounts than social constructivism.[13] At the same time, by emphasising actors' creative capacities to produce, construct, change and transform discursive landscapes, which inform and shape, but do not determine their identities, it helps overcome the structuralist bias inherent in the institutionalist literature, as attested by its emphasis on stable, reproductive processes and patterns of behaviour,[14] institutional 'stickiness'[15] and the privileging of structure over agency.[16] This approach thus opens up space for an actor-based theory of non-linear, incremental and transformative institutional change (Chapter 3). Agents have the capacity to capitalise on the normative surplus of meaning and the progressive possibilities already present in accepted logics and existing conceptual resources nested within institutions in order to develop new conceptions, to construct, communicate and extend norms and to act in complex environments. On this basis, institutional change is not iterative, that is, reproducing the same ideas, norms, patterns and practices. It is, instead, more fluid, contingent, unpredictable and, more importantly, transformative.[17]

[13] My account is different from Checkel's 'middle ground' constructivism; 'The Constructivist Turn in International Relations Theory', p. 324.

[14] See Huntington's chapter in Goodin (ed.), *The Theory of Institutional Design*.

[15] Pierson, 'The Limits of Design', pp. 474–99; North, *Institutions, Institutional Change and Economic Performance*. But compare Simon Bulmer and Martin Burch, 'The "Europeanisation" of Central Government: The UK and Germany in Historical Institutionalist Perspective', in G. Schneider and M. Aspinwall (eds.), *The Rules of Integration* (Manchester: Manchester University Press, 2001). Bulmer and Burch depart from deterministic accounts of historical institutionalism by arguing that Europeanisation has transformed the character of government in Bonn/Berlin and Whitehall.

[16] Notwithstanding the existence of variations, it is generally acknowledged that sociological institutionalism privileges structure over agency, whereas historical and rational choice institutionalisms exhibit a stronger structural determinism. On the three institutionalisms, see Hall and Taylor, 'Political Science and the Three New Institutionalisms', pp. 936–57.

[17] Following Hall and Taylor's distinction, although sociological institutionalism explains both institutional design and compliance, it has difficulties in explaining how and why norms change thereby effecting institutional change. Historical institutionalists argue that significant change is associated with critical junctures. It is worth noting here that Bulmer and Burch have suggested the concept of 'critical moments' that give rise to opportunities for significant change. 'Such opportunities may not be realised or exploited, but if they are, the outcome is a critical juncture at which there is a clear departure from previously

The discussion in this chapter is structured as follows. In the first section I uncover existing templates for conceptualising European Union Citizenship, while in Section 4.2 I analyse its judicial institutionalisation by distinguishing three phases; namely, judicial minimalism (1993–7), signalling intentions (1998–2000) and engineering institutional change (2001–9). In searching for conceptual tools that capture the key factors that influence European judges' decisions not only to effect qualitative institutional change, but also to bring about 'a change' in such a way that extension of the change is possible in the future, I put forward a model that reflects the weight of various variables on judicial decision-making. The model together with the dynamics of institutional change and the implications of the study are discussed in the final section.

4.2 Models of European Citizenship: Uncovering Templates

The scope and dynamics of institutional change depend on quasi-objectified ways of seeing European citizenship and its role in the evolving Community legal order. These normative and interpretive frames are important because they shape perceptions, priorities, and understandings of the meaning of citizenship and its implications. Five conceptualisations of European citizenship may be noted, as follows:

Market Citizenship. Drawing on the individualistic variant of liberalism, this mode depicts European citizenship as comprising a core of entitlements designed to facilitate market integration.[18] This owes much to the generalised belief that 'the Union is still predominantly a market and most of its freedoms to move are of interest only to property and commodity owners'.[19] Such an approach draws on the liberal conception of citizenship as a status bestowed on morally autonomous individuals

---

established patterns ... In theory, at each critical moment the opportunities for institutional innovation are at their widest'; Schneider and Aspinwall (eds.), *The Rules of Integration*. Rational-choice institutionalism sees institutional change as the result of changes in the actors or the bargaining power of actors or in the distributional implications of existing institutional arrangements. See also Lieberman, 'Ideas, Institutions and Political Order', pp. 697–712. Besides institutionalism, functionalist and neo-functionalist perspectives account for incremental change within an overall stable environment. Change is mostly exogenously induced and threatens to render existing institutions dysfunctional.

[18] Everson, 'The Legacy of the Market Citizen'.

[19] See Klaus Von Beyme, 'Citizenship and the European Union', in K. Eder and B. Giesen (eds.), *European Citizenship, National Legacies and Transnational Projects* (Oxford: Oxford University Press, 2001), pp. 61–85, 80.

who pursue their chosen forms of life.[20] This conception, however, overlooks that economic transactions do not take place in a vacuum. Instead, they are embedded within a social and political context. The latter does not only regulate them but, rather crucially, shapes the frames though which economic transactions are understood. Rights related to economic transactions thus have implications for a broader spectrum of socio-political relations. This has been made clear by the European Court of Justice, which has pronounced the right to free movement as an intrinsic part of affirming workers' human dignity and a means for the improvement 'of their living and working conditions and promoting their social advancement'.[21] Arguably, if European citizenship is conceived of as a 'market citizenship',[22] then it does not, presumably, require the full range of 'constitutional essentials'.[23] Adding new rights to European citizenship might lead to 'rights saturation',[24] and attribute 'a fake legitimacy on the essentially autocratic mode of governance of the Union'.[25] However, such arguments sidestep the fact that European citizenship is not a free-standing institution that is emptied of political content. In fact, a cursory glance at the ECJ's jurisprudence suggests that free movement rights have turned 'aliens' into associates, opened up possibilities for the Community nationals' active involvement and participation in the socio-political life in the Member State of residence, and have activated redistributive policies designed to enhance their effective exercise.[26]

Civic Republican European citizenship. A civic republican model of European citizenship would champion an expressly political, dynamic and participatory conception of citizenship.[27] This model draws on the civic

[20] On the liberal conception of citizenship, see I. Berlin, *Four Essays on Liberty* (Oxford: Oxford University Press, 1969); Reinhard Bendix, *Nation-Building and Citizenship* (New York: Wiley, 1964); John Rawls, *A Theory of Justice* (Cambridge, MA: Harvard University Press, 1971).

[21] See Advocate General Trabucchi's Opinion in Case C 7/75 *F V Belgian State* [1975] ECR 679, and Advocate General Jacobs' Opinion in Case C-168/91 *Konstantinidis* [1993] ECR I-1191.

[22] Everson, 'The Legacy of the Market Citizen'.

[23] d'Oliveira, 'Union Citizenship: Pie in the Sky?'.

[24] Weiler, 'To Be a European Citizen', p. 501.

[25] Rainer Baubock, 'Citizenship and National Identities in the European Union' (1997) *Harvard Jean Monnet Working Paper* 4/97.

[26] This coheres with the Marshallian sociological paradigm of citizenship which views citizenship as an institution that contains capitalist inequalities and social rights as a precondition for full membership in a community.

[27] Richard Bellamy and Dario Castiglione, 'The Normative Challenge of a European Polity: Cosmopolitan and Communitarian Models Compared, Criticised and Combined' in

republican conception of citizenship as practice; that is, as active engagement and participation in common affairs.[28] Such a conception would necessitate the strengthening and expansion of both formal and informal participatory mechanisms in the EU coupled with reforms to remove constraints on access to citizenship, and initiatives to increase transparency and accountability in decision-making.[29] A civic republican approach to European citizenship could take either the form of liberal communitarianism, thereby praising belonging, solidarity and fairness in a political community, or of a thicker notion of citizenship – one that embodies a common identity, common political values and shared final ends. Whereas the latter form raises the spectre of Euro-nationalism[30] with all its undesirable repercussions for ethnic migrants, refugees and their families, the former clearly recognises peoples' various subject positions and their engagement in various projects and associative relationships at the local, national or supranational levels.[31] Undoubtedly, both variants would be criticised by those who value the cultural particularity of national communities and believe that the territorial nation state is the natural locus of democracy and citizenship.

Deliberative European citizenship. This model is strongly associated with Habermas' emphasis on creating a supranationally shared political culture based on the rule of law, separation of powers, democracy, respect for human rights, and so on. Such a political culture would guarantee the flourishing of equally legitimate cultural forms of life.[32] The model is based on a strong notion of participatory democracy[33] and champions active

A. Follesdal and P. Koslowski (eds.), *Democracy and the European Union* (Berlin: Springer-Verlag, 1998); E. Tassin, 'Europe: A Political Community?' in C. Mouffe (ed.), *Dimensions of Radical Democracy: Pluralism, Citizenship, Community* (London: Verso, 1992).

[28] Adrian Oldfield, *Citizenship and Community: Civic Republicanism and the Modern World* (London: Routledge, 1990); Stephen Mulhall and Adam Swift, *Liberalism and Communitarianism* (Oxford: Blackwell, 1996).

[29] Compare Adrienne Heritier, 'Elements of Democratic Legitimation in Europe: an Alternative Perspective', *Journal of European Public Policy* (1999), pp. 269–282.

[30] By putting emphasis on a shared citizenship identity, common heritage and a shared way of life, this approach champions a particularistic identity which undercuts egalitarianism.

[31] Federico Mancini, 'Europe: The Case for Statehood', 4(1) *European Law Journal* (1998), pp. 29–42.

[32] Jurgen Habermas, 'Citizenship and National Identity: Some Reflections on the Future of Europe', 12 *Praxis International* (1992), pp. 1–19; *Between Facts and Norms: Contributions to a Discourse Theory of Law and Democracy* (Cambridge: Polity, 1996); 'Reply to Grimm' in P. Gowan and P. Anderson (eds.), *The Question of Europe* (London: Verso, 1997). See also Closa, 'The Concept of Citizenship in the Treaty of European Union'.

[33] Compare Agnes Heller and Ferenc Feher, 'Citizen Ethics and Civic Virtues' in Heller and Feher, *The Post-modern Political Condition* (Cambridge: Polity, 1988); Jean Cohen and Andrew Arato, *Civil Society and Political Theory* (Cambridge, MA: MIT Press, 1992).

dialogic participation and the flourishing of a European public sphere. In practical terms, this would seem to require, among other things, the development of European political parties and the adoption of a framework regulation on their legal status based on Articles 191 and 'the elastic clause' (formerly 235 EC), the recognition of the right of association within the context of the Union citizenship provisions and the disentanglement of demos from ethnos.[34]

Although these reforms are worthwhile, constitutional patriotism fails to convince scholars and observers for several reasons. It will suffice to mention only two here. First, constitutional principles are not ethically neutral; they have a particularistic anchoring in so far as they are rooted in interpretations derived from the perspective of the nation's historical experience and the majority culture. Although this does not preclude critique and the mutual adjustment of political culture, it does confine critical exchanges within the 'architectonics of the constitutional state'. Within such a context, migrants are expected to 'engage in the political culture of their new home',[35] as it has been defined by the dominant group. Migrants should not, publicly, call into question the culturally and historically specific understandings embodied by it.

Second, Habermas tends to assume that 'pre-constituted' individuals enter the public sphere in order to devise the rules that bind them, and that agreement on these rules is possible under conditions of undistorted communication. Since the worlds people inhabit are multiple, fragmentary and contradictory, and the prospects for unimpeded communication are rather slim in the real world – even more so in the EU where communication and deliberation is often seen by participants as an opportunity to hold on to their entrenched positions in order to meet domestic political expediencies and not to succumb to the force of the better argument, a deliberative model of citizenship would appear to have limited chances of success. Instead of conditioning the European polity on a supranational political culture, it might thus be preferable to start from the premise of heterogeneous, internally differentiated and contested communities taking part in an ongoing quest for procedures, principles and institutions, which accommodate their differences and meet their common needs and aspirations.

Corrective European Citizenship. If a deliberative European citizenship is incapable of eliciting subjective identification with the EU, the mixed

[34] Kostakopoulou, 'Nested "Old" and "New" Citizenships in the European Union'.

[35] Habermas, 'Citizenship and National Identity', p. 17.

approach adopted by Weiler and others may be a more attractive one.[36] This approach shares the normative premise of constitutional patriotism, but, at the same time, it appreciates the ethno-cultural traditions of Member States. As such, it reflects the fusion between liberal and communitarian approaches that characterised political theory in the 1990s and the development of communitarian liberalism.[37] National identities are valued as symbols for collective action, resources for identity building and markers of intergenerational projects promising collective immortality. According to Weiler, a European civic public can co-exist with national publics without threatening to displace them. Whereas national citizenship would be the realm of affinity and nationhood, European citizenship would be the realm of law and Enlightenment ideals.[38] Double membership of individuals in national organic and supranational, value-driven communities would tame nationalism, which is prone to expressions of intolerance and xenophobia.[39] On this reading, European citizenship 'serves as a civilising force which keeps the eros of nationalism at bay'.[40] True, Weiler makes concrete suggestions for empowering European citizens by enhancing their participation in the process of European governance, such as the European legislative ballot coinciding with elections to the European Parliament, Lexcalibur, the creation of a European Constitutional Council and so on.[41] However, the crux of the point is that the notion of corrective European citizenship as a rational overlay of deeply rooted national identities and a check on the dysfunctions of national political processes tends to overrate 'the embeddedness' of individuals within national cultures and, consequently, underrates the prospects of their transformation into European Union citizens.

Bellamy and Castiglione also share the idea of a corrective European citizenship. They argue that in the European 'mixed commonwealth' communitarian commitments and distinctive identities can coexist with a cosmopolitan regard for universal principles of rights and fairness (cosmopolitan communitarianism).[42] But this begs the question of whether the tension generated by these opposing elements can be so easily overcome.

[36] Weiler, 'To Be a European Citizen'.

[37] John Rawls, *Political Liberalism* (New York: Columbia University Press, 1993); Charles Taylor, *Liberalism and the Moral Life* (Cambridge, MA: Harvard University Press, 1989).

[38] Weiler, 'To Be a European Citizen'.

[39] Ibid., pp. 508–9; See also Joseph Weiler, 'European Citizenship – Identity and Differentity' in La Torre (ed.), *European Citizenship*, pp. 1–24.

[40] Weiler, 'To Be a European Citizen', p. 527.

[41] Ibid.; Weiler, 'European Citizenship', pp. 20–24.

[42] Bellamy and Castiglione (eds.), *Constitutionalism, Democracy and Sovereignty*, p. 267.

The subjugation of European citizenship by quasi-nationalist definitions of membership does not rule out the possibility that the Europeanisation of the nation-state may be accompanied by the 'nationalisation' of the European supranational community. The exclusion of third country nationals from Union citizenship and the Schengenising of migration law and policy are also good cases in point.

Constructive European Citizenship. This approach conceives of the EC/EU as the product of evolutionary and reflexive institutional design.[43] It draws on radical theories of citizenship, namely, on feminist, post-structuralist and post-colonial perspectives. Radical theories of citizenship diverge from both conventional liberal and communitarian approaches in so far as they regard citizenship not as an issue of either the Right (individual rights) or the Good (the community), but as a matter of calling into question the constructed senses of community and the self underlying such politics.[44] Accordingly, European citizenship is conceived of as both a process and a project to be realised as the 'grand conversation' about the political restructuring of Europe continues. This means that the meaning of European citizenship exceeds the rights enumerated in the Treaties. This owes much to the fact that European citizenship has called into question traditional ways of thinking about membership and community, and entails possibilities for new transformative politics beyond the nation-state.

Several reforms could actualise the potential of Union citizenship. For instance, the rules on residence could be updated.[45] Existing formal and informal mechanisms of participation[46] could be strengthened with a view to giving Union citizens full franchise in their State of residence. European citizenship could also be disentangled from state nationality, and be conditioned on domicile. This would lead to the inclusion of approximately 18 million long-term resident third country nationals (TCNs) within

[43] George Ross, *Jacques Delors and European Integration* (Cambridge: Polity Press, 1995), at p. 6; G. Marks et al., *Governance in the European Union* (London: Sage, 1996); James Caporaso, 'The European Union and Forms of State: Westphalian, Regulatory or Post-modern?', 43(1) *Journal of Common Market Studies* (1996), pp. 29–52.

[44] Iris Marion Young, *Justice and the Politics of Difference* (Princeton, NJ: Princeton University Press, 1990); Carol Pateman, *The Sexual Contract* (Oxford: Blackwell, 1988); Paul Gilroy, *There Ain't No Black in the Union Jack: The Cultural Politics of Race and the Nation* (London: Hutchinson, 1987).

[45] Jorg Monar, 'A Dual Citizenship in the Making: The Citizenship of the European Union and Its Reform', in La Torre (ed.), *European Citizenship*, pp. 167–83.

[46] Proposal for a Council Decision *establishing a Community action Programme to promote active European citizenship (civic participation)*, COM/2003/0276/ final.

its personal scope.[47] The inclusion of TCNs into Union citizenship has been defended on several grounds: the need to remedy the civic inclusiveness deficit of European political membership;[48] the creation of a European 'open republic';[49] concern about the social integration of TCNs and social harmony within the Union;[50] a commitment to a liberal democratic order which sets limits to the community's right of collective self-determination;[51] dual citizenship;[52] and the need to eliminate divergent conditions of access to European citizenship owing to different nationality laws.[53] Finally, given the dynamic and open-ended character of European citizenship, new provisions could be added within its ambit, such as the protection of social rights and the development of an anti-poverty strategy, the promotion of forms of substantive equality between the sexes, consumer rights, the protection of health and the environment, and the rights of association and assembly. Finally, European citizenship could be made meaningful to citizens who have never exercised their Community law rights of free movement, thereby wearing down the 'purely internal' rule.[54]

Inspiring as these reforms and challenges might be for some, it is true that national executives see them as a mission impossible. There is, on the whole, a generalised apprehension about decoupling European citizenship from nationality. But if the goal of European citizenship is to transform the residents of Europe whose lives have been monopolised by national collectivism into critical Union citizens, then the European political community

[47] National executives have succeeded in grafting their notions of who the Europeans are in the emerging European institutions. Although EC Treaty referred to workers of the Member states as recipients of the free movement rights, the Member States' interpretation of article 48 EC as referring to workers qua nationals became sedimented, thereby cancelling out of existence alternative juridical options (i.e., conditioning free movement on domicile). This made almost 'natural' the confinement of special rights and, subsequently, of Union citizenship to nationals of Member States.

[48] Kostakopoulou, 'Nested "Old" and "New" Citizenships in the European Union'; *Citizenship, Identity and Immigration in the European Union.*

[49] Rainer Hofmann, 'German Citizenship Law and European Citizenship: Towards a Special Kind of European Nationality?', in La Torre (ed.), *European Citizenship*, pp. 149–66.

[50] Alvaro Castro Oliveira, 'The Position of Resident Third Country Nationals: Is It Too Early to Grant Them Union Citizenship?', in La Torre (ed.), *European Citizenship*, p. 98.

[51] Rut Rubio Marin, 'Equal Citizenship and the Difference That Residence Makes', in La Torre (ed.), *European Citizenship*, p. 226.

[52] Monar, 'A Dual Citizenship in the Making'.

[53] Marie-Jose Garot, 'A New Basis for European Citizenship: Residence?', in La Torre (ed.), *European Citizenship*, pp. 232–3.

[54] Niamh Nic Shuibhne, 'Free Movement of Persons and the Wholly Internal Rule: Time to Move On?', 39 *Common Market Law Review* (2002), pp. 731–71.

should be disentangled from quasi-nationalist trappings. This would make both majority and minority communities rightful shapers and makers of the public culture and Europe's possible futures. In addition, there is a pressing need to ensure inclusiveness in the practice of European citizenship by decoupling enjoyment of the rights of movement and residence from socio-economic status, and by making European citizenship meaningful even to immobile European citizens by providing a set of rights that could make a difference to their lives.

4.3 The Indeterminate Trajectory of European Citizenship

4.3.1 Phase 1: 1993–1997; Judicial Minimalism[55]

National courts provided the initial fora in which the meaning and full implications of European citizenship were to be tested. In *R* v. *Secretary of State for the Home Department, ex parte Adams*,[56] *R* v. *Secretary for the Home Department, ex parte McQuillan*,[57] and in *R* v. *Secretary of State for the Home Department, ex parte Vitale*[58] the issue of the direct effect of Article 21 TFEU (formerly 18 TEC) was raised but, unfortunately, no definite answer was reached. In Adams, the reference was withdrawn when Mr Adams' exclusion order was lifted, and in Vitale no preliminary ruling reference was made to the European Court of Justice. It is true to say that the latter adopted a cautious approach in 1993–7. Undoubtedly, the Court was aware of the constitutional significance of Union citizenship. In its Report on *Citizenship of the Union*, the Commission had stated that European Citizenship had led to a conceptual metamorphosis of the Community rights of free movement and residence 'by enshrining them in the Treaties themselves'.[59]

Advocate General Leger, in his opinion in *Boukhalfa*, also pinpointed the 'promise' of Union citizenship inherent in the constructive model outlined in the previous section:

> Admittedly the concept embraces aspects which have already largely been established in the development of Community law and in this respect it represents a consolidation of existing Community law. However, it is for the Court to ensure that its full scope is attained. If all the conclusions

[55] I borrow the term from Cass Sunstein's, *One Case at a Time: Judicial Minimalism on the Supreme Court* (Cambridge MA: Harvard University Press, 1999).
[56] [1995] All ER (EC) 177.
[57] [1995] 4 All ER 400.
[58] [1996] All ER (EC) 461.
[59] COM(93) 702 final, 21/12/93.

> inherent in the concept are drawn, every citizen of the Union must, whatever his nationality, enjoy exactly the same rights and be subject to the same obligations. Taken to its ultimate conclusion, the concept should lead to Citizens of the Union being treated absolutely equally, irrespective of nationality. Such equal treatment should be manifested in the same way as among nationals of one and the same Member State.[60]

But the European Court of Justice opted for a 'consolidating', rather than 'constitutionalising' approach to Union citizenship, that is to say that European citizenship was used as supplementary basis in order to reaffirm existing Community law. Although European judges knew that Union citizenship was not a market citizenship, they nevertheless embarked upon a process of 'adaptive stabilisation' of its meaning. In *Uecker and Jacquet*, the Court ruled that Article 8 was not intended to alter the scope ratione materiae of the Treaty so as to cover internal situations.[61] In *Skanavi*, the question of whether holders of driving licences need to exchange their licences for licences in the host Member State within one year of taking up normal residence in order to remain entitled to drive a motor vehicle there was answered by recourse to Article 49 TFEU, and not Article 21 TFEU (formerly Art. 18 TEC).[62] Similarly, *in Stober and Pereira* the Court did not use Union citizenship in deciding that German legislation, which required the children of self-employed workers to reside in Germany in order to qualify for dependent children's allowance, was incompatible with the Treaty.[63] In *Kremzow*, European citizenship was invoked, but without success.[64] The Court confirmed its treatment of purely internal situations by ruling that the sentence of imprisonment imposed on *Kremzow* by an Austrian criminal court did not fall within the scope of the application of the Treaty.

How can one thus explain the judicial minimalism during the period 1993–7? It is true that European judges were well aware of national executives' apprehension about the possible implications of Union citizenship. Such fears found expression in the Danish opt out Declaration which stated 'nothing in the TEU implies or foresees an undertaking to create a citizenship of the Union in the sense of citizenship of the nation-state.

[60] Case C-1214/94 *Boukalfa* v. *Federal Republic of Germany* [1996] ECR I-2253.

[61] Cases C-64 and 65/96 *Kari Uecker* and *Vera Jacquet* v. *Land Nordrhein-Westfalen* [1997] 3 CMLR 963;[1997] ECR I-317.

[62] Case C-193/94 *Skanavi* and *Chryssanthakopoulos* [1996] 2 CMLR 372; [1996] ECR I-929.

[63] Joined Cases 4/95 and 5/95 *Stober and Pereira* v. *Bundesanstalt Fur Arbeit* [1997] 2 CMLR 213; [1997] ECR I-511.

[64] Case 299/95 *Friedrich Kremzow* v. *Austria* [1997] ECR I-2629.

The question of Denmark participating in such a development, therefore, does not arise.'[65] European judges also knew that the Member States would be wary of the movement of non-active economic actors without strong assurances that such persons would not become a burden on their social welfare services. Furthermore, various governmental proposals in circulation, which were designed to limit the authority and independence of the ECJ prior to the 1996 Intergovernmental Conference, had alerted the ECJ to national executives' dissatisfaction with its influential institutional operation. Evidently, European citizenship's time had not come. European judges saw radical change as difficult, premature and costly in view of post-Maastricht reactions and governmental opposition. As a consequence, the conceptual resources inherent in the institution of Union citizenship were not utilised.

Besides the fact the political climate did not favour change (the notion of Kairos mentioned in Chapter 2), it is true to say that the cases considered by the European Court of Justice during the first phase did not provide an opportunity for institutional change. The cases did not bring forth a real dissonance between European citizenship norms and concrete reality, and settled jurisprudence offered coherent and complete answers to the questions posed, thereby making reliance on Union citizenship provisions indirect and subsidiary. In sum, in the period 1993–7, there was neither an interest nor an opportunity for bringing about qualitative change in the meaning and implications of Union citizenship.

4.3.2 *Phase 2: 1998–2000; Signalling Intentions*

Although the Court did not derive new rights of residence directly from Article 21 TFEU in the second phase, it nevertheless highlighted the constitutional importance of European citizenship by bringing citizens within the scope of the protection afforded by the non-discrimination clause (Article 18 TFEU). The political climate was conducive to a constructive conception of Union citizenship and the extension of citizenship norms. In its second report on *Citizenship of the Union*, the Commission had stated that Union citizenship 'raised citizens' expectations as to the rights that they expect to see conferred and protected'.[66] The European Parliament's Resolution on the Commission's second report also noted that Union citizenship constitutes 'the guarantee of

[65] OJ C348/4, 31/12/94.
[66] COM/97/0230.

belonging to a political community under the rule of law'.[67] Finally, in its Communication to the European Parliament and the Council *on the follow-up to the recommendations of the High-Level Panel on the Free Movement of Persons*, the Commission had also stated that free movement rights 'are becoming an integral part of the legal heritage of every citizen of the European Union and should be formalised in a common corpus of legislation to harmonise the legal status of all Community citizens in the Member States, irrespective of whether they pursue a gainful activity or not'.[68] To this end, the Commission proposed a Council Regulation amending Council Regulation 1612/68 and a Council Directive amending Council Directive 68/360 on 12 November 1998.[69] Both proposals were designed to adapt the provisions of Council Reg. 1612/68 and Council Dir. 68/360 to the new socio-economic and political conditions of the Union, and provided a right of residence for third country national spouses of Union citizens who have resided in a Member State for three consecutive years on the event of the dissolution of marriage.[70]

This discursive interaction and the Commission's entrepreneurship provided impetus for judicial activism. In *Martinez Sala* the ECJ held that lawful residence of a Community national in another Member State is sufficient to bring her within the scope of ratione personae of the provisions of the Treaty on European citizenship. Sala, a Spanish national who was a lawful and long-term resident in Germany and received social assistance

[67] COM (97) 0230 C4-0291/97, OJ C 226, 20.7.1998, p. 61.

[68] COM/98/0403 final.

[69] Proposal for a European Parliament and Council Regulation Amending Regulation (EEC) No. 1612/68 of 15 October 1968 on freedom of movement for workers within the Community (COM(1998) 394 – COD 98/0229; OJ C 344, 12.11.1998, OJ C 344); Proposal for a European Parliament and Council Directive Amending Directive 68/360/ EEC on the abolition of restrictions on movement and residence within the Community for workers of Member States and their families (COM(1998) 394) – COD 98/0230, OJ C 344. Other legislative initiatives include: Proposal for a European Parliament and Council Decision establishing an Advisory Committee on freedom of movement and social security for Community workers and amending Council Regulations (EEC) No. 1612/68 EEC 1408/71 (COM/98/0394 OJ C344, 12/11/1998 final) and Commission Proposal for a Council Regulation amending Regulation 1408/71 as regards its extension to nationals of third countries (COM (1997) 561 final, submitted on 10 December 1997.) The ECJ has extended the personal scope of the Regulation to refugees and stateless persons resident in a Member State and to their non-EU relatives on the grounds that such an inclusion is ancillary to Article 48 TFEU objectives and the international obligations of the Member States; Cases C-95/99 to 98/99, *Khalil, Chaaban, Osseili and Nasser*, and C-180/99 *Addou*, Judgement of 11 October 2001.

[70] Articles 10(4) and 4a(1) respectively.

under Federal Social Welfare Law,[71] was refused a child raising allowance on the grounds that she did not possess a residence permit. The allowance was a non-contributory benefit granted to non-German nationals who had a dependent child, but did not have a full time job. If Sala were a worker or a self-employed person under Regulation 1408/71, her treatment would activate Articles 45 or 48 TFEU respectively. If the national court concluded that Sala did not fall in either of these categories, her status as a Union citizen, lawfully residing in another Member State, could bring her within the personal scope of the Treaty. By examining the material scope of the Treaty the Court also concluded that the allowance came within the scope of EC law, as either a social advantage under Council Regulation 1612/68 or a family benefit under Regulation 1408/71, thereby activating the non-discrimination clause (Article 18 TFEU).[72] Hence, the Court stated that, since Sala had been authorised to reside in Germany, the requirement of the 1985 Federal Law that a Community national had to produce a residence permit in order to receive a child-raising allowance, when that state's own nationals were not required to produce any document of that kind, amounted to unequal treatment prohibited by Article 18 TFEU. In other words, Sala was entitled to receive non-discriminatory treatment on the grounds of nationality as a European citizen lawfully residing in another Member State.

By putting 'flesh on the bones of European Union Citizenship', the Court displayed its capacity to attach a new constructive meaning to the status of citizenship of the Union, thereby overriding the interests of Member States.[73] More importantly, it did so by calling into question the link between the existence of citizen status and economic activity or self-sufficiency.[74] And although the Sala ruling raised expectations that benefits reserved for active economic actors (workers) under Council Regulation

[71] Sala was protected by the European Convention on Social and Medical Assistance; European Treaty Series 14; Case C-85/96 *Sala* v. *Freistaat Bayern* [1998] ECR I-2691.

[72] As J. Shaw and S. Fries have argued, if a provision is not covered by the rules of the free movement of workers, establishers and service providers, Article 18 provides an alternative route: 'Citizenship of the Union: First Steps in the Court of Justice', 4(4) *European Public Law* (1998), pp. 533–59. The Court's jurisprudence concerning article 12 EC includes: Case 185/87 *Cowan* [1989] ECR 195; Case C-43/95 *Data Delecta* [1996] ECR I-4661; C-323/95 *Hayes* [1997] ECR I-1711; Case C-122/96 *Saldanha* [1997] ECR I-5325); Case C-274/96 *Bickel and Franz* [1998] ECR I-7637; Case C-172/98 *Commission* v. *Belgium* [1999] ECR I-3999; and Case C-411/98 *Ferlini* [2000] ECR I-8081.

[73] Siofra O'Leary, 'Putting Flesh on the Bones of European Union Citizenship', 24 *European Law Review* (1999), pp. 68–79.

[74] As the Advocate General stated, 'the limitations in Article 8a (now 21 TFEU) itself concern the actual exercise but not the existence of the right'; Case C-85/96 at para. 18.

1612/68, such as social advantages, could be granted to job-seekers, in *Collins* the Advocate General foreclosed this possibility by suggesting that 'Community law as it now stands does not require that an income-based social security benefit, intended for jobseekers, be provided to a citizen of the Union who enters the territory of a Member State with the purpose of seeking employment while lacking any connection with the State or link with the domestic employment market'.[75]

In *Bickel and Franz* the Court held that the right to free movement in Article 18 EC would be enhanced if citizens of the Union were able to use a given language to communicate with the administrative and judicial authorities of a state on the same footing as its nationals.[76] As potential recipients of services and EU citizens exercising their right to free movement, Bickel and Frantz fell within the scope of the Treaty and could thus challenge their unequal treatment based on nationality. In this respect, the right to use their mother tongue in criminal proceedings in the Italian province of Bolzano, a right that was available to German speaking residents of Bolzano, was derived from Article 18 TFEU. As A. G. Jacobs stated in his opinion, Union citizenship implies a 'commonality of rights and obligations uniting Union citizens by a common bond transcending member state nationality'.[77]

Following *Sala* and *Bickel and Frantz*, the Court used its settled jurisprudence in order to resolve issues relating to Union citizenship. In *Donatella Calfa*, the Court did not use Union citizenship,[78] while in *Kaba* it interpreted Article 7(2) of Council Regulation 1612/68 narrowly. There, it stated that national legislation which imposes differential residency requirements for the spouses of Community nationals and the spouses of nationals who are 'present and settled' in the United Kingdom for the grant of indefinite leave to remain does not constitute discrimination on the grounds of nationality.[79] It relied on what the 'objective difference' between persons enjoying an unqualified right of residence and Community nationals whose right of residence is limited by the Treaty and secondary legislation.

[75] Case C-138/02 *Brian Francis Collins* v. *Secretary of State for Work and Pensions*, Opinion of Advocate General D. Ruiz-Jarabo Colomer on 10 July 2003. The ECJ confirmed that the right to equal treatment did not preclude legislation which made entitlement to a job-seeker's allowance conditional on a residence requirement, in so far as it could be justified on the basis of objective considerations that were independent of nationality and met the test of proportionality; Judgement of the Court of 23 March 2004.

[76] C-2774/96, 24 November 1998.

[77] Ibid. at paras. 23–24.

[78] Case C-348/96 *Danatella Calfa* [1999] ECR I-0011.

[79] Case C-365/98, Judgement of the Court of 11 April 2000, [2000] ECR I-2623.

And although it refrained from addressing directly the question whether 'indefinite leave to remain' constitutes a social advantage within the meaning of Article 7(2) of Regulation 1612/68, it stated that even if the former right constituted a social advantage, British legislation did not contravene Community law.[80] It is noteworthy here that the Court reiterated its decision in the second reference for a preliminary ruling made by the Immigration Adjudicator. It ruled that the qualified right of residence enjoyed by Community nationals cannot be compared to the unqualified right of residence enjoyed by persons who are 'present and settled' in the United Kingdom under UK immigration rules.[81]

In July 1998, the Court took issue with the political participatory aspects of Union citizenship. The Kingdom of Belgium had failed to comply with the Council Directive 94/80 EC laying down detailed arrangements for the exercise of the right to vote and to stand as a candidate in municipal elections by Union citizens in the Member State in which they reside and to transpose it into national law within the prescribed period. Although the Belgian Government submitted that the non-transposition was due to the need to revise Article 8 of the Belgian Constitution and that progress had been made in implementing the Directive, the ECJ dismissed the defence concerning difficulties in the internal legal system in accordance with its jurisprudence, and ruled that Belgium had failed to fulfil its obligations under the first paragraph of Article 14 of the Directive.[82]

Finally, in *Elsen* the Court highlighted the importance of Union citizenship.[83] Elsen, a German national who had transferred her residence form Germany to France and acquired the status of frontier worker employed in Germany, was refused validation of the periods spent rearing her son as periods of insurance for the purpose of an old age pension on the grounds that the child rearing had taken place in another Member State. The Court ruled that although the Member States retain the power to organise their social security schemes, they must, nonetheless, comply with Community law and in particular with the Treaty provisions on freedom of movement for workers or Union citizenship. The German provisions put Community nationals, who had exercised their Community law rights of free

[80] Ibid. For a critical view, see Steve Peers, 'Dazed and Confused: Family Members' Residence Rights and the Court of Justice', 26 *European Law Review* (2002), pp. 76–83.

[81] Case C-466/00 *Kaba* v. *Secretary of State for the Home Department*, Judgement of the Court of 6 March 2003.

[82] Case C-323/97 *Commission* v. *Kingdom of Belgium*, Judgment of the Court of 9 July 1998.

[83] Case C-135/99 *Ursula Elsen* v. *Bundesversicherungsanstalt fur Angestellte*, Judgment of the Court of 23 November 2000.

movement and resided in another Member State while continuing to work in Germany, at a disadvantage. The Court thus used Union citizenship in conjunction with the free movement provisions in order to highlight the constitutional importance of free movement.

The Court's rulings in this phase show that institutional change is not a linear, unidirectional process (see also Chapter 3). In *Sala* the Court seized the opportunity to give more substance to Union citizenship,[84] whereas in *Kaba* it acknowledged the Member States' competence in enlarging or narrowing the scope of the right of residence on the basis of nationality and migration law differentials. In *Sala*, nationality would not justify differential conditions in the enjoyment of an allowance, whereas in *Kaba* nationality was a relevant factor in determining migration statuses. Undoubtedly, there exists an important difference between the two cases. As *Sala* had been legally authorised to remain in Germany, the Court had to decide whether it would allow a European citizen resident to be treated differently than German nationals. In the absence of any justification, Sala's unequal treatment contravened Article 18 TFEU. *Kaba*, on the other hand, raised the spectre of judicial direct interference with states' competence in the field of migration control. Although European judges knew that the introduction of citizenship of the Union raised expectations that citizens of the Union will enjoy equality, at least before Community law, and in *Sala* they capitalised on the opportunity to transcend the language of the European citizenship provisions by advancing a new constructive interpretation, they were also aware of the strong criticism they would ultimately face if indefinite leave to remain were granted to the spouses of Community nationals resident in Britain. This leads me to argue that although the judges' interests did not coincide with the preferences of national executives, and Union citizenship exerted a normative pull,[85]

[84] Compare here Wincott's assessment of the quiet, routine and salient process of advancing integration in-between the grand bargains negotiated by national governments; D. Wincott, 'Institutional Interaction and European Integration: Towards an Everyday Critique of Liberal Intergovernmentalism', 33 *Journal of Common Market Studies* (1995), p. 4. Hence, Rasmussen's assessment that the Court shifted to a more 'self-restrained' course in post-Maastricht Europe does not apply to the field of Union citizenship; Hjalte Rasmussen, *European Court of Justice* (Copenhagen: Gadjura, 1998); Norbert Reich, 'The "November Revolution" of the European Court of Justice: Keck, Meng, and Audi Revisited', 34(3) *Common Market Law Review* (1994), pp. 459–92.

[85] Joseph Weiler, 'Community, Member States and European Integration: Is the Law Relevant?', 31 *Journal of Common Market Studies* (1992), pp. 39–56; Anne-Marie Burley-Slaughter and Walter Mattli, 'Europe before the Court: A Political Theory of Legal Integration', 47(1) *International Organisation* (1993), 41–76; Alec Stone Sweet and Thomas L. Brunell,

other variables, such as the anticipated costs of an integrationist ruling and the organisational climate, played a crucial role in the judicial decision-making process. As a result, institutional change in this second phase was not as robust as would have been anticipated. In *Sala* and *Bickel and Frantz*, the ECJ signalled its intention in a powerful way to advance the Union citizenship norm. It was not until a year later that the ECJ drew on the transformative potential of Union citizenship (Section 4.1) and moulded skeletal norms into concrete, binding rules which became locked in and difficult for governments to change. By so doing, the ECJ's expansive logic to the strengthening of Union citizens' rights would initiate a process of vertical normative socialisation through which national executives would have to embrace the constructive interpretation of Union citizenship and the new practices set in motion by it.

4.3.3 *Phase 3: Engineering Institutional Change*

In this phase European citizenship norms not only matter, but also European judges become more explicit as to the ways they matter in opposition to the preferences of Member States.[86] Acknowledgement of the fundamental status of Union citizenship is accompanied by new normative templates and a policy-oriented approach, despite the absence of societal mobilisation and sustained pressures for policy reform by organised interests.[87]

On 7 December 2000, the Charter of Fundamental Rights of the European Union was proclaimed at the European Council meeting in Nice.[88] Article 45 of the Charter entailed the possibility of extending Union citizenship to 'nationals of third countries legally resident in the territory of a Member State'. Article 45 thus signalled that the 'declaration' phase of Union citizenship had been superseded by a 'proposal' phase, that is, by a willingness on the part of Community institutions to suggest concrete measures for institutional reform. In May 2001, the Commission presented a proposal for a European Parliament and Council Directive on the right

'Constructing a Supranational Constitution: Dispute Resolution and Governance in the European Community', 92 *American Political Science Review* (1998), pp. 63–81.

[86] See Geoffrey Garrett, 'International Cooperation and Institutional Choice: The European Community's Internal Market', 46 *International Organisation* (1992), pp. 533–60; Geoffrey Garrett, Daniel Kelemen, and Heiner Schulz, 'The European Court of Justice, National Governments, and Legal Integration in the European Union', 52 *International Organisation* (1998), pp. 149–76.

[87] Compare, Lisa Conant, *Justice Contained* (Ithaca, NY: Cornell University Press, 2002).

[88] [2000] OJ C364.

of citizens and their family members to move and to reside freely within the territory of the Member States.[89] The Commission's proposal sought to prepare the ground for a comprehensive and coherent set of rules on the free movement of all Union citizens and their families, irrespective of economic motives. The draft directive, which explicitly referred to the 'new legal and political environment established by citizenship of the Union',[90] suggested a 'phased' approach to the disentanglement of residence from economic activity, whereby non-active economic actors would have to satisfy the self-sufficiency and possession of sickness insurance conditions in the first four years of residence in the host state. Thereafter, non-active economic actors would enjoy a permanent and unqualified right of residence and 'virtually complete equality of treatment'.[91] According to the Commission's proposal, the right of permanent residence would entail security of residence by providing immunity from expulsion and access to social welfare in the host Member State.[92]

Although these initiatives were not associated with the existence of a 'critical juncture', that is, of a critical moment of crisis which could be resolved by shaking off the institutional past,[93] they nevertheless provided impetus for constructive interpretations of Union citizenship and the extension of citizenship norms by the Court. It thus comes as no surprise that in *Grzelczyk* Advocate General Alber stated that:

> Citizenship of the Union took on greater significance, in contrast to the perception of individuals as purely economic actors which had underlain the EC Treaty. The conditions on which freedom of movement may depend are now no longer economic in nature, as they still were in the 1990 directives. The only 'limitations and conditions' attached to freedom of movement now are imposed on grounds of public policy, public security and public health.[94]

[89] COM (2001)257 final; Brussels 23.5.2001.

[90] COM (2001) 257 final, para. 1.3 of the explanatory memorandum.

[91] Ibid., Article 14.

[92] Ibid., Articles 26 and 21(1).

[93] Critical junctures play an important role in historical institutionalist analysis, as mentioned above.

[94] Case C-184/99 [2001] ECR I-6913 at para. 52. Compare A. G. Geelhoed's statement that in special cases in which a right to move and reside does not exist under other provisions of EC law, it can be derived directly from Article 18(1) EC; Case C-413/99 *Baumbast and R* v. *Secretary of State for the Home Department*, Opinion delivered on 5 July 2001. In *Commission* v. *Italy* (Case C-424/98 [2000] ECR I-4001), the Court ruled that the condition of economic self-sufficiency entailed by the three Residence Directives (i.e., 93/96, 90/365, 90/364) has the meaning of resources that are higher than those below which the host state grants social assistance to individuals. If the state does not grant social assistance then the

Let me now chart the process of transformative institutional change in more detail.

In *Kaur*, the Court reaffirmed the Michelletti ruling.[95] It upheld the validity of the 1972 and 1982 declarations on the definition of the term UK national for Community law purposes made by the UK Government[96] and stated that 'it is for each Member State, having due regard to Community law, to lay down the conditions for the acquisition and loss of nationality'.[97] As Kaur, a British overseas citizen under the 1981 British Nationality Act, did not have the right of abode in the United Kingdom, she was excluded from the personal scope of the EC Treaty.

In *Grzelczyk*, the Court clearly demonstrated why and how the institution of European citizenship matters. Grzelczyk, a French national studying physical education in Belgium, who during his first three years of his study had supported himself through various jobs, applied to the CPAS for payment of minimex, a minimum subsistence allowance paid in Belgium. This would enable him to complete his university studies. CPAS granted Grzelczyk the minimex. However, when the CPAS applied to the Belgian state authorities for reimbursement of the payments, the application was declined on the grounds that Grzelczyk was not a Belgian national. Mr Grzelczyk challenged this refusal before a Labour tribunal. A. G. Alber suggested that the student could be seen as a worker and, as such, he would be entitled to minimex under Article 7(2) of Council Regulation 1612/68.[98] But the Court disagreed. Rejecting the minimalist perspective associated with the model of market citizenship (Section 4.1), it stated that 'Union citizenship is destined to be a fundamental status of nationals of the Member States, enabling those who find themselves in the same situation to enjoy the same treatment in law irrespective of their nationality, subject to such exceptions as are expressly

resources required must be higher than the level of the minimum social security pension paid by that state.

[95] Case C-369/90 *Micheletti and Others* v. *Delegacion del Gobierno en Catanbria* [1992] ECR I-2143; Case C-192/99 *R* v. *Secretary of State for the Home Department, ex parte Kaur* [2001] ECR I-1237.

[96] The first declaration was made at the time of the signature of the Treaty of Accession of 22 January 1972. The second declaration was submitted by the United Kingdom in 1982, following the enactment of the 1981 British Nationality Act.

[97] *Kaur* [2001] ECR I-1237, para. 19.

[98] As the work Grzelczyk pursued was sufficiently genuine and effective, he fell within the Community law definition of worker. The interruption of his work did not result in loss of worker status. Compare Case C-413/01 *Franca Ninni-Orasche* v. *Bundesminister fur Wissenschaft, Verkehr und Kunst*, Judgment of the Court of 6 November 2003.

provided for'.[99] Since Union citizens can rely on Article 18 TFEU (formerly Article 12 TEC) in all situations that fall within the material scope of the EC Treaty (*Sala*), Article 18 read in conjunction with Union citizenship led the Court to rule that students studying in another Member State can rely on the non-discrimination clause in claiming social advantages. This ruling overruled *Brown* in so far as the latter judgement was used to exclude students from general social assistance (and not only maintenance grants).[100] Although Directive 93/96 made it clear at that time that students should not be a burden on the social assistance system of the host state (Article 1) and were not entitled to receive maintenance grants (Article 3), the Court observed that the provisions of the Directive do not preclude its beneficiaries from receiving social assistance benefits. Indeed, it can be argued that a certain degree of financial solidarity between nationals of a host Member State and nationals of other Member States must be recognised, particularly in cases of temporary economic difficulties. In such cases, beneficiaries would not be an 'unreasonable' burden on the host Member State.

Grzelczyk gave the Court the opportunity to advance the normative debate on the meaning and implications of Union citizenship. Instead of replicating the established cognitive structures and settled rules, the Court gave a broad and liberal interpretation to the provisions of Directive 93/96, thereby calling into question the link between economic activity and residence in certain circumstances (i.e., temporary economic difficulties). This gave 'a strong appearance of case law moving away from the grant of particular rights to particular groups of (economic) actors and instead embracing a powerful mission of protection of individual rights'.[101] By so doing, it initiated a wider learning process which could not but alter beliefs, perceptions and the behaviour of actors at the national level, since students who face temporary economic difficulties would have to be seen as associates and 'belongers' to the host community, rather than as strangers and a problem. Interestingly, the Court did not extend the application of Article 7(2) of Council Reg. 1612/68 to all Union citizens, irrespective of

[99] *Grzelczyk*, above n 94 at para. 31. Under the Commission's proposed directive, on completion of a four-year educational course in a Member State, the self-sufficiency conditions attached on the residence of students would cease to apply, thereby enabling former students to stay on in the host state and to receive social security entitlements on the same basis as nationals (Articles 7 and 8(4)).

[100] Case C-197/86 *Brown v. Secretary of State for Scotland* [1988] 3 CMLR 403.

[101] Stephen Weatherill, *Cases and Materials on EU Law* (Oxford: Oxford University Press, 2003), p. 490.

their worker status. Nor did it disentangle residence from economic status by deriving a directly effective right from Article 21 TFEU – an approach that the Court followed in *Baumbast* (see below). Rather, it transformed Union citizenship into a building block of the evolving EU legal order, by giving prominence to the principle of equal treatment that strikes at its heart.

D'Hoop gave the Court the opportunity to rule that Belgian legislation granting tide-over allowances to Belgian nationals, who have completed their secondary education in Belgian establishments, contravened Articles 18 and 21(1) TFEU.[102] Ms D'Hoop, a Belgian graduate who had obtained a baccalaureate in France, was denied a tide-over allowance from the Belgian National Employment Office (ONEM) under the Royal Decree of 25 November 1991. The tide-over allowance targeted young graduates by giving them access to special employment programmes. Although Ms D'Hoop's situation was governed by the provisions concerning free movement of workers, her status of a citizen of the Union gave her a right to equal treatment in all situations which fall within the scope ratione materiae of the Treaty. And although D'Hoop was claiming rights against her home state, the link with Community law and the cross border element were evident owing to her completion of secondary education in France. D'Hoop's differential treatment thus came close to discrimination based on nationality, since her situation 'may be assimilated to that of any other person enjoying the rights and liberties guaranteed by the Treaty'.[103] It would contravene EU law if a citizen received in her own Member State treatment less favourable than that she would otherwise enjoy had she not availed herself of the right to free movement. Using the deterrence argument used in *Singh*, the Court ruled that Community nationals might be deterred from leaving their country of origin in order to take advantage of the opportunities offered by the Treaty.[104] The Court proceeded to argue that the differential treatment was not objectively justified and went beyond what was necessary to attain the objective pursued.

A truly innovative approach was followed in *Carpenter*. In this case, the principle of respect for family life was elevated at the expense of national migration laws and the settled jurisdictional distinction between purely

[102] Case C-224/98 *Marie-Nathalie D'Hoop* v. *Office national de l'emploi*, Judgement of the Court of 11 July 2002.

[103] Case C-115/78 *Knoors* v. *Secretary of State for Economic Affairs* [1979] ECR 399, [1979] 2 CMLR 357 at para. 24.

[104] Case C-370/90 *R* v. *Immigration Appeal Tribunal and Surinder Singh, ex parte Secretary of State for the Home Department* [1992] ECR I-4265, [1992] 3 CMLR 358.

internal, on the one hand, and Community law governed situations, on the other. In establishing such an interpretive hierarchy, the Court was attuned to debates about the legal status of the Charter of Fundamental Rights of the EU and the possibility of accession to the ECHR by the Union. Mrs Carpenter, a national of the Philippines and the spouse of a UK national, challenged the deportation order issued by the Home Secretary. She claimed a right of residence in the United Kingdom on the grounds that her deportation would impede her husband's right to provide and receive services in other Member States, since she was looking after his children from his first marriage. The UK authorities maintained that, since Mr Carpenter was a national of the United Kingdom living in the United Kingdom, the cross-border dimension required under Community law was absent. Both the Advocate General and the Court did not agree with the UK Government's submission, albeit following different lines of reasoning.[105] Whereas Advocate General Stix-Hackl read Directive 73/148 through the lens of the right to respect for family life, and interpreted it as allowing a right of residence for Mrs Carpenter, the Court stated that Directive 73/148/EC applied only to cases where a Community national and the members of his/her family leave the state of origin and reside abroad for the period stipulated in the Directive. But the Court went on to rule that the right of residence of Mrs Carpenter might be inferred from other principles or rules of Community law. Since Mr Carpenter was carrying out a significant proportion of his business abroad, he had activated his right to provide services which 'could not be fully effective if Mr Carpenter were to be deterred from exercising it by obstacles raised in his country of origin relating to the entry and residence of his spouse'.[106] Article 56 TFEU (formerly Article 49 TEC) read in light of the principle of respect for family life, which is recognised by Community law,[107] must thus be interpreted as precluding Carpenter's deportation.[108]

Carpenter is a remarkable case of judicial activism; a derivative right of residence has been implied from a Treaty article (Article 49 TEC), thereby overriding restrictive national immigration rules.[109] In light of *Carpenter*, possible extension of residence rights to service recipients and other third country family members of the service provider, such as relatives on

[105] Case C-60/00 *M. Carpenter*, Judgment of the Court of 11 July 2002, paras. 28–30.

[106] Ibid., at para. 39.

[107] On this, see the provisions of the Council Regulations and directives on the free movement of employed and self-employed persons as well as Article 8 ECHR.

[108] Carpenter's deportation could not be justified on public order or safety grounds.

[109] Gavin Barret, 'Family Matters: European Community Law and Third Country Family Members', 40 *Common Market Law Review* (2003), pp. 369–421, 406.

the ascending line, cannot be ruled out. By emphasising the principle of respect for family life, the Court established a hierarchy that can influence and guide future interpretive choices and the behaviour of actors. More importantly, it did so on the basis of a constructive interpretation of the situation rather than by purely instrumental calculations. Arguably, critics might point out that the link between Carpenter's right of residence and the perceived impediment to trade is inexact. But the crux of the matter is that the Court used the interpretive process in order to reach a solution, which intuitively appears to be the right one, thereby constructing a new institutional reality.

On 25 July 2002, the Court had another opportunity to rule on the legality of restrictive measures on the movement and residence of third country national spouses of Community nationals. These issues had been raised in proceedings between the Movement Against Racism, Anti-Semitism and Xenophobia ASBL (Mouvement contre le racism, l'antisemitisme et la xenophobie ASBL (MRAX)) and the Belgian State. More specifically, MRAX challenged the legality of a Circular of the Ministers for the Interior and Justice of 28 August 1997 on the grounds that it contravened the Community directives on the movement and residence and the principle of respect for family life, which is protected by Community law. Drawing on *Carpenter*, it emphasised the importance of ensuring protection of the family life of Community nationals. It ruled that while the Member States may demand an entry visa or equivalent documents from family members of a Community national, who are third country nationals, Article 3(2) of Directive 68/360 and Article 3(2) of Directive 73/148 stated that such persons must be given every facility for obtaining the necessary visas and that this meant that a visa must be issued without delay.[110]

Accordingly, the Court ruled that the national practice of sending back to the border third country national spouses of Community nationals who did not possess the necessary entry documents (i.e., an identity document or visa) was disproportionate and unlawful under Community law. Since the residence rights of such persons do not derive from states' authorisation of their entry, but are based on their family ties, spouses who are able to prove these ties and their identity, and do not represent a risk to the requirements of public policy, public security or public health should not be sent back to the border. Similarly, Member States cannot deny a residence permit or order an expulsion order against such persons solely on

[110] Case C-459/99, Judgment of the Court of 25 July 2002.

the grounds that they had entered their territory unlawfully (Article 4 of Directive 68/360 and Article 6 of Directive 73/148). Such measures would not only hinder the right of residence of third country national spouses of Community nationals, which is directly conferred by Community law, but they would also be manifestly disproportionate to the gravity of the breach of national migration laws.[111]

In addition, should third country national spouses overstay their visa, the issue of a residence permit to them cannot be made subject to the condition that their visa has not expired, under Articles 3 and 4(3) of Directive 68/360 and Articles 3 and 6 of Directive 73/148. Nor could they be expelled. It is interesting that following the Court's ruling in *MRAX*, and the EP's recommendation, the Commission amended Article 9(2) of the Draft Directive by stating that 'family members may not be refused a residence card solely on the grounds that they have no visa or that their visa has expired prior to submission of the application for a residence card'.[112] Finally, the Court held that the procedural guarantees of Article 9(2) of Directive 64/221 applied to third country national spouses 'who have been refused a first residence permit or issued with an expulsion order before the issue of a permit, even if they are not in possession of an identity document or, requiring a visa, they have entered the territory of a Member State without one or have remained there after its expiry'.[113]

The Court's stance on the mobility rights of third country national family members of Union citizens shows that European judges do not faithfully serve the interests of the Member States, as Garrett had argued.[114] Nor would it be correct to say that its strategic interventions were confined to policy areas that have low costs for the Member States. The cases examined above show the Court did not hesitate to initiate institutional change in key areas of 'high politics' drawing on the normative dimensions of Union citizenship and a favourable organisational climate. Its activist stance reflects its interest and capacity to provide principled solutions

[111] See Case 48/75 *Royer* [1976], Case 159/79 *R* v. *Pieck* [1980] 3 CMLR 220 and Case C-363/89 *Roux* [1991] ECR 273, [1993] 1 CMLR 3, para. 12. The ECJ's ruling reflects Article 6(4) of the Commission's draft directive (COM (2001) 257 final; 2001/0111 (COD) Brussels 23.5.2001), which states that 'Where a Union citizen or family member does not have the necessary travel documents or, if required, the necessary visas, the Member State concerned shall, before turning them back, give such persons every opportunity to obtain the necessary documents or have them brought to them or to corroborate or prove by other means that they are covered by the right to freedom of movement'.

[112] Article 9(2a) of the draft Directive, COM (2003) 199 final, 15.4.2003.

[113] *MRAX*, n 110 above.

[114] Garrett, 'International Cooperation and Institutional Choice'.

to problems, thereby advancing a constructive understanding of Union citizenship.[115]

This, of course, does not mean that change should come at the expense of national security. On 26 November 2002, the Court ruled that administrative police measures limiting Mr Olazabal's right of residence to a particular department of the French territory were not precluded by Community law in so far as they are justified on public order or public security grounds, as defined by Community law and Court's case law.[116] In particular, they must relate to individual conduct, which represents a genuine and sufficiently serious threat to public order or security, and must meet the test of proportionality.[117]

In *Baumbast*, the Court went beyond the predictive confines of settled law in order to realise the promise inherent in Union citizenship and to bring about institutional change. It did not only derive a new right of residence for a third country national family member from Article 12 of Council Regulation 1612/68, but it also ruled that Article 21(1) TFEU has created directly effective rights enforceable in national courts. Mrs Baumbast, a Colombian national, married Mr Baumbast, a German national, in 1990 in the United Kingdom. The family had two daughters – Mrs Baumbast's natural daughter who had Colombian nationality and a younger daughter who had both Colombian and German nationality. Having worked in the United Kingdom for several years, Mr Baumbast was working for German companies in China and Lesotho. Following Mrs Baumbast's application for indefinite leave to remain in the United Kingdom for herself and her family in 1995, the Secretary of State refused to renew Mr Baumbast's residence permit and the residence documents of Mrs Baumbast and her children. Mr Baumbast challenged this refusal before the Immigration Adjudicator. Although the Adjudicator noted that Mr Baumbast was neither a worker nor a person having a general right of residence under Directive 90/364, he ruled that the children had a right of residence under Article 12 of Council Regulation 1612/68 and that Mrs Baumbast enjoyed a right of residence for the period of her children's studies. Following Mr Baumbast's appeal and the Secretary of State's cross-appeal

[115] Compare here Pollack's view that the ECJ's activism is a function of the efficacy and the credibility of control mechanisms possessed by the Member States; Mark Pollack, 'International Relations Theory and European Integration', 39(2) *Journal of Common Market Studies* (2001), pp. 241–4, 229.

[116] Case C-100/01 *Ministre de l'Interieur* v. *Aitor Oteiza Olazabal*, Judgement of the Court of 26 November 2002.

[117] On the ECJ's jurisprudence concerning the public policy, public security and public health derogations, see Paul Craig and Grainne de Burca, *EU Law* (Oxford: Oxford University Press, 1998).

to the Immigration Appeal Tribunal, the case reached the Court. Drawing on the normative principles underpinning Council Regulation 1612/68 and its purpose of facilitating the integration of the Community worker's family in the society of the host MS,[118] the ECJ ruled that Mrs Baumbast's daughters have the right to pursue their studies under Articles 10 and 12 of Council Regulation 1612/68. Accordingly, denying permission to remain in the host Member State to a parent who is the primary carer of the child would infringe the migrant child's right to education.[119]

The *Baumbast* ruling mirrored the Commission's suggestion that the children of Union citizens, who are studying in the host Member State and are integrated in its education system, have a right of residence which may be limited to the duration of their studies, irrespective of nationality.[120] Additionally, under Article 13(2)(b) of the Commission's draft directive a third country national spouse of the Union citizen would retain their right of residence in the event of divorce or annulment of marriage if 'by agreement between the spouses or by court order, the spouse, has custody of the EU citizen's children'.[121] Influenced by the opportunity for strategic change contained in the Commission's proposal, the Court interpreted Council Regulation 1612/68 in an expansive way in order to reach an equitable solution that respects family life and human dignity. As the Court put it, 'Article 12 (now 18 TFEU) cannot be interpreted restrictively and must not, under any circumstances, be rendered ineffective'. The Commission, in turn, responded to the Court's ruling in *Baumbast* by amending Article 12(3) of the draft directive:

> The Union citizen's departure from the host Member State shall not entail loss of the right of residence of his/her children or of the parent who has actual custody of the children, irrespective of nationality, if the children reside in the host Member State and are enrolled at an educational establishment, at secondary or post-secondary level, for the purpose of studying there, until the completion of their studies.[122]

118 Case C-413/99 *Baumbast, R* v. *Secretary of State for the Home Department*, Judgement of the Court of 17 September 2002, para. 58.

119 Similarly, R's children also had a right of residence and the right to pursue their education under the same conditions as nationals of the host Member State. The fact that the children of R's first husband did not live permanently with him does not affect the rights they derive from Articles 10 and 12 of Council Regulation 1612/68.

120 Article 12(3) 2001/0111(COD) 2001.

121 If the Commission's draft Directive had been adopted, Mrs Baumbast would have probably enjoyed a right of permanent residence since she had met the qualifying residence period of four years in the UK required under Article 14(2).

122 2001/0111 (COD) 2001.

The third and final question that was referred to the Court concerned the direct effect of Article 21 TFEU. Could Mr Baumbast as a citizen of the European Union enjoy a right of residence in the United Kingdom by direct application of Article 21(1) TFEU? Although the German and UK Governments submitted that the latter Article was not intended to be a free-standing provision, the Court relied on the normative weight of Union citizenship and ruled that:

> The Treaty on European Union does not require that citizens of the Union pursue a professional or trade activity, whether as an employed or self-employed person, in order to enjoy the rights provided in Part Two of the Treaty, on citizenship of the Union. Furthermore, there is nothing in the text of that Treaty to permit the conclusion that citizens of the Union who have established themselves in another Member State in order to carry on an activity as an employed person there are deprived, where that activity comes to an end, of the rights which are conferred on them by the Treaty by virtue of that citizenship. As regards, in particular, the right to reside within the territory of the Member States under Article 18(1) EC, that right is conferred directly on every citizen of the Union by a clear and precise provision of the EC Treaty. Purely as a national of a Member State, and consequently as a citizen of the Union, Mr Baumbast therefore has the right to rely on Article 18(1) EC.

In this respect, any limitations and conditions imposed on that right are subject to judicial review and thus 'do not prevent the provisions of Article 18(1) TEC (now 21(1) TFEU) from conferring on individuals rights which are enforceable by them and which the national courts must protect'.[123] Such an interpretation further weakened the link between economic status and the right to free movement and reflected broader normative aspirations for a constructive understanding of European citizenship that eventually found their way into juridicopolitical reform ten years after the establishment of this institution. As an institutional designer in a complex environment, the Court of Justice believed in the coherence and viability of the constructive meaning of Union citizenship. By so doing, it paved the way for what would follow.[124]

[123] See, to that effect, Case 41/74 *Van Duyn* [1974], paragraph 7. Compare also Advocate General L. A. Geelhoed's statement that '... these conditions and limitations may not result in the citizen's right being robbed of substantive content'; Opinion delivered on 5 July 2001. Some commentators, however, believe that the court did not confer direct effect on Article 18(1); it merely used the principle of proportionality to strengthen citizenship rights related to free movement.

[124] See European Parliament and Council Directive 2004/38/EC below.

In 2003 the Court continued to utilise Union citizenship in a radical way.[125] In *Garcia Avello*, a refusal of the Belgian authorities to register a child of dual nationality with the surname of both parents, following the Spanish pattern of entering the mother's maiden name in addition to the patronymic surname of the father, constituted discrimination on the grounds of nationality prohibited under the Treaty.[126] And although the Belgian Government submitted that the immutability of surnames is conducive to the social order and integration of non-Belgian nationals into the Belgian society, the Court dismissed this argument, by stating that the children, who enjoyed the status of EU citizens, should not suffer discrimination in respect of their surname and that the Belgian practice was neither necessary nor appropriate for promoting the integration of non-Belgian nationals.

Akrich gave the opportunity to the Court to address the Member States' sensitivities about possible abuses of Community law by Union citizens.[127] It ruled that Article 10 of Council Regulation 1612/68 applied only to freedom of movement within the Community, and the spouse of an EU citizen can benefit from it, if (s)he is lawfully resident in a Member state when (s)he moves to another Member State to which the citizen of the Union is migrating or has migrated. In this case, a British citizen, married to a Moroccan national who had been deported to Algeria and whose application for the revocation of the deportation order and for entry clearance to the United Kingdom had been refused, moved to Ireland to take up employment as an employed person. When they sought to return to the United Kingdom, the Secretary of State considered that the worker and her spouse had misused Community law in order to circumvent national migration law. While acknowledging national competence in the design and enforceability of migration laws, the Advocate General stated that 'the intentions of the worker and his spouse in making use of the rights conferred on them by Community law are immaterial'.[128] The Court stated that Community law would be abused

[125] Other cases in the area of free movement of persons, which have been decided on the basis of existing jurisprudence, include: Case C-405/01 *Colegio de Oficiales de la Marina Mercante Espanola* v. *Administracion del Estado*, 30 September 2003; Case C-47/02 *Albert Anker, Klaas Ras, Albertus Snoek* v. *Bundesrepublic Deutschland*, 30 September 2003. See also Case C-428/01 *Orfanopoulos and Others*, Opinion of the Advocate General – No. 72/2003, 11 September 2003.

[126] Case C-148/02 *Garcia Avello* v. *Etat Belge*, Opinion of the Advocate General Jacobs delivered on 22 May 2003, and Judgement of the Court of 2 October 2003.

[127] Case C-109/01 *Secretary of State for the Home Department* v. *Hacene Akrich*, Advocate General's Opinion on 27 February 2003.

[128] Case C-109/01 *Akrich*, Judgement of the Court of 23 September 2003, Proceedings of the European Court of Justice, No. 7/03 at 35.

if individuals who had entered into marriages of convenience in order to circumvent national migration laws invoked Article 10 of Council Regulation 1612/68. Conversely, in genuine marriages, the fact that the spouses installed themselves in another Member State in order to obtain the benefits conferred by Community law on their return to the Union citizen's state of origin is not relevant to an assessment of their legal situation by the competent authorities of the latter state. Given that Akrich's marriage was genuine and that Article 10 of Council Regulation 1612/68 could not be relied upon by virtue of the fact that the spouse was not lawfully resident on the territory of a Member State, the Court stated that his removal from Britain would infringe Article 8(1) of the ECHR (i.e., respect for family life) which is protected in the Community legal order according to the Court's case law.[129]

Drawing in this ruling, the UK Home Office distinguished between the intra-Community movement of lawfully resident family members of Community nationals, which allegedly falls within the ambit of Community law, and the entry of such persons from outside the Community which is seen to fall within the sovereign prerogative of the United Kingdom.[130] Accordingly, the *Immigration (European Community Area) Regulations 2006* stated that third country national dependent relatives or members of a household of a Community national seeking to exercise rights of free movement in the United Kingdom must have previous lawful residence in another Member State in order to be eligible for a resident permit. Denmark, Finland and Ireland also required prior lawful residence in another Member State.[131] The Court took issue with this interpretation of EU law in *Jia*. By distinguishing *Akrich* and *Jia*, it ruled that Community law does not require a prior lawful residence in a Member State for the grant of a permanent residence permit to a family member of a Community national who has exercised her right to free movement.[132] And in *Metock and Others*[133] it outlawed national legislation making the

[129] Ibid.

[130] See the reply of Baroness Scotland of Asthal to the question by Lord Tebbit on 17 November 2003, HL Deb 17 November 2003 Vol 654 cc 252-3WA.

[131] But following the Court's ruling in *Metock and Others*, which is discussed later, national regulations had to be amended, notwithstanding delays and legal challenges in some Member States. See, for example, *R. on the application of Yaw Owusu* v. *Secretary of State for the Home Department* (21 January 2009) [2009] EWHC 593 (Admin).

[132] C-1/05 *Jia* v. *Migrationsverket* [2007] ECR I-1. See also the Commission's 5th Report on Citizenship of the Union, 15.2.2008, which mention's the need to interpret the right to free movement in the light of fundamental rights and in particular the right to respect for family life and the principle of proportionality.

[133] Case C-127/08, Judgement of the Court of 25 July 2008.

right of residence of family members subject to prior lawful residence in another Member State. Although the ruling was consistent with the ECJ's case law prior to *Akrich* and the secondary legislation adopted in the 1960s and 1970s, it was, nevertheless, viewed by Ireland and Denmark as an illegitimate judicial interference with national policies designed to combat undocumented migration and 'marriages of convenience'.

In *Pusa*, Advocate General Jacobs stated that, far from being limited to a prohibition of direct or indirect discrimination, Article 21 TFEU applies to non-discriminatory restrictions.[134] And building on its case law (i.e., *Kraus*, *Gebhard* and *Sager*), the Court stated that

> national legislation which places at a disadvantage certain of its nationals simply because they have exercised their freedom to move and to reside in another Member State would give rise to inequality of treatment, contrary to the principles which underpin the status of citizen of the Union, that is, the guarantee of the same treatment in law in the exercise of the citizen's freedom to move (*D'Hoop*, paragraphs 34 and 35). Such legislation could be justified only if it were based on objective considerations independent of the nationality of the persons concerned and proportionate to the legitimate aim of the national provisions.[135]

On the same day that the Court delivered its judgment, the Directive *on the Right of Citizens and their Family Members to move and reside freely within the territory of the Member States* was adopted.[136] The Directive remedied the sector-by-sector, piecemeal approach to free movement rights by incorporating and revising the existing Directives[137] and amending Council Regulation 1612/68.[138] Building on the rights-based approach characterising the rights of free movement and enhancing it by giving concrete form to the principle that residence generates entitlements, the Directive gave further substance to Union citizenship by establishing an unconditional right of permanent residence for Union citizens and their families[139] who have resided in the host Member State for a continuous

[134] Case C-224/02 *Heikki Antero Pusa* v. *Osuuspankkien Keskinainen Vakuutusythio*, AG's Opinion of 20 November 2003, paras 18–22. See also the Judgment of the Court of 29 April 2004.

[135] Ibid., para. 20.

[136] European Parliament and Council Directive 2004/38/EC, OJ 2004 L 158/77.

[137] Directives 68/360, 73/148, 72/194, 75/34, 75/35, 90/364, 90/365, 93/96 and 64/221 are repealed with effect from 30 April 2006.

[138] Articles 10 and 11 of Council Reg. 1612/68 are repealed with effect from 30 April 2006.

[139] The definition of a 'family member' includes a registered partner if the legislation of the host Member State treats registered partnership as equivalent to marriage.

period of five years. The right of permanent residence entails a right of equal treatment with nationals in areas covered by the Treaty which will be extended to family members who are not nationals of a Member State and who have the right of residence or permanent residence. In light of the typology of residence rights established by the Directive, shorter periods of residence exceeding three months entail a right of residence for Union citizens and their family members if they: (a) engage in economic activity; (b) have sufficient resources and comprehensive sickness insurance cover in the host Member States as non-active economic actors and (c) are enrolled at a private or public establishment, have comprehensive sickness insurance cover and are self-sufficient in order to avoid becoming a burden on the social assistance system of the host Member State. More importantly, a novel provision of the Directive provided that as long as the beneficiaries of the right of residence do not become an unreasonable burden on the social assistance system of the host Member State they should not be expelled, thereby incorporating the ECJ's ruling in *Grzelczyk*.[140] This provision displayed Union citizenship's capacity to change our understanding of community membership and to prompt a rethinking of the meaning citizenship itself with a view to creating more inclusive forms of political association. Finally, for short periods of residence of up to three months, Union citizens shall have the right of residence without any conditions or any formalities other than the requirement to hold a valid identity card or passport. In sum, the Directive created the institutional preconditions for a constructive approach to citizenship, which is more respectful of 'difference' and more inclusive than nationality-based models of citizenship, be they of either liberal or republican or of a deliberative nature.[141]

The Lisbon Treaty, which entered into force on 1 December 2009, enhanced the deliberative and participatory aspects of Union citizenship. The provisions on democratic principles (Title II, TEU) refer to the principle of equality of EU citizens and their right to receive equal attention from the Union's institutions, bodies, offices and agencies. This is further reinforced by Article 10(3) TEU which states that 'every citizen shall have the right to participate in the democratic life of the Union' and Article 10(4) which provides that 'European political parties at European level contribute to forming European political awareness and to expressing the will of Union citizens'. Likewise, the principle of participatory

[140] Ibid., Article 14.

[141] However, egalitarian processes co-exist with the practice of exclusion of long-term resident third country nationals from the personal scope of Union citizenship.

democracy underpins the need for a more inclusive dialogue with, and input from, citizens and representative associations in policies that affect them. But in contrast to the republican model of citizenship outlined in Section 4.1, participation is confined to: (a) the opportunity for citizens and representative institutions (not voluntary associations) to make known and publicly exchange their views on all areas of Union action (Article 11(1)); (b) the maintenance of open, transparent and regular dialogue between the Union institutions and representative institutions and civil society (Article 11(2)); (c) broad consultations to be carried by the Commission[142] (Article 11(3)); and (d) the citizens' initiative of inviting the Commission to submit a legislative proposal (Article 11(4)). Having said this, however, it should be noted here that the updated provisions concerning the transparency of the proceedings of the Union's institutions and providing greater access to documents enhance citizen participation and promote a more deliberative model of European citizenship (Section 4.1).

4.4 Implications and Concluding Remarks

The foregoing discussion has demonstrated that European Union citizenship was built within a complex environment. The existing templates did not capture its transformative potential. Actors looked beyond the immediate imperatives to a unique vision of the future notwithstanding opposition from the Member States (Section 4.1). As institutional designers and agents of change, the Court of Justice and the Commission succeeded in institutionalising it, in giving meaning, specificity and value to it, thereby establishing new institutional norms which will impact on and modify national legal cultures. In this way, European citizenship developed into a project to be realised as the 'grand conversation' about the political restructuring of Europe continues (Section 4.1). In the subsequent chapter, we shall see in more detail how national authorities participated in its co-creation and the role of nested institutional settings. It is true that the Court's rulings in the third phase sit uncomfortably with Garrett's account of the Court as an agent of Member States, which reflects the rational preferences of the most powerful states.[143] Nor can they be explained on the basis of the Court's institutional interest in increasing its institutional

[142] Compare here the Commission's Communication on *Towards a reinforced culture of consultation and dialogue*, COM (2002) 704.

[143] Garrett, n 86.

power and prestige.[144] Such approaches tend to sidestep the impact of ideas and norms on actors' self-awareness and the role of institutional actors in processes of concept-formation, meaning-making and norm-extension. An institutional constructivist perspective can thus go some way towards unravelling the normative and interpretive frames that provide templates which guide actors' behaviour and the role of institutional actors in constructing and altering beliefs, norms and understandings via discursive practices and strategies, as earlier discussed.

Along this line, I have argued that institutional change in the field of Union citizenship was not a consequence of institutional crises and 'critical junctures', where one set of institutional ideas replaces another (see Chapter 3). Rather, it occurred in a fluid, quiet, non-linear and transformative manner. The market citizenship template has been superseded by a constructive understanding of Union citizenship which makes the status of European citizenship – and not economic activity – the core of the new European citizenship policy framework (Section 4.1). This finding is at variance with the institutionalist literature which privileges stability and continuity over change, innovation and risk. It also confirms my argument that institutional change is a much more complex phenomenon than is generally portrayed in the literature (Chapter 3). Without doubt, the study of European integration would benefit from the articulation of more rigorous theoretical frameworks of institutional change that transcend the contours of old debates and schools of thought and embrace actor-initiated institutional change.

In opposition to existing paradigms, which have been shaped by a 'quest for simplicity', that is, a quest for a single, overriding variable, Figure 4.1 captures the multiple factors that influence and shape the European judicial process of bringing about incremental, transformative institutional change. Believing that 'Union citizenship is destined to be a fundamental status of the nationals of the Member States' (constructive European citizenship), and in keeping with the norms of European integration,[145] European judges have made principled decisions in dialogue with the Commission and by taking into account the wider organisational climate. Besides normative reasoning and the influence exerted by the constructive template for Union citizenship, the discussion has

[144] Damian Chalmers, 'Judicial Preferences and the Community Legal Order', 60(2) *Modern Law Review* (1997), pp. 164–99.

[145] Concerning the ECJ's pro-integrationist interest, see Stone Sweet and Brunell, 'Constructing a Supranational Constitution'.

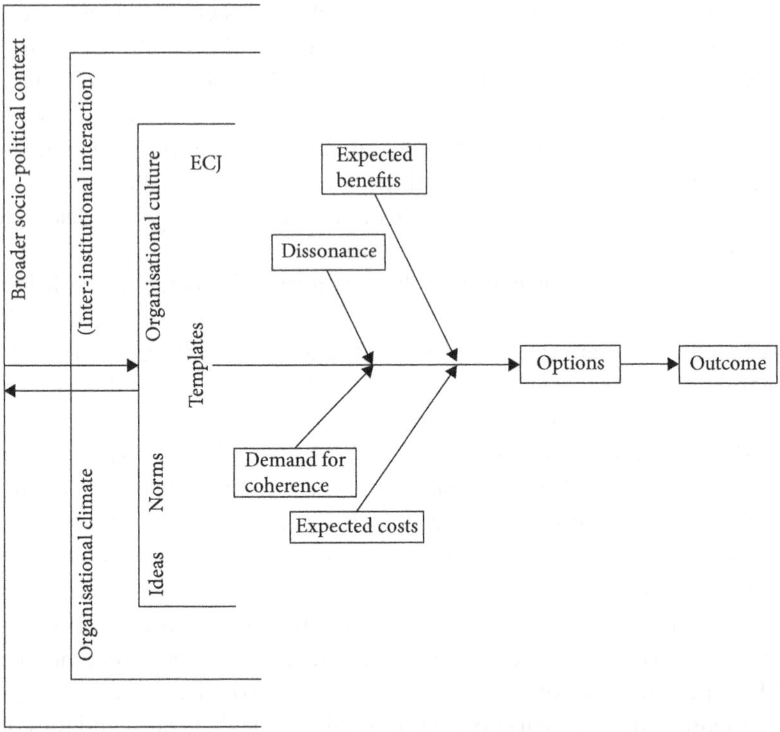

Figure 4.1 The anatomy of the judicial institutionalisation of European Union citizenship

highlighted the effects of institutional interaction, dialogue, and competition, and the impact of the general organisational climate and critical events, such as the adoption of the EU Charter of Fundamental Rights, on judicial decision-making.

This shows that the Court is not a unit surrounded by a faceless environment, but that instead it operates within a cluster of polymorphous relations. Through flows, meaningful and routinised exchanges and interactions with the broader socio-political structures and other institutions, the Court takes part in what may be termed 'a reflexive European circuit' (see also Chapter 2). In this circuit, normative frames, ideas and information about the positioning of other institutions circulate and crosscut organisational boundaries. Although it is difficult to depict the matrix of relationships, the arrows in Figure 4.1 show that connecting lines among the broader socio-political context, the organisational climate and the Court are indispensable.

In the first phase the organisational climate prevented change, as European judges were aware of intergovernmental opposition to it. In contrast, in the second and, even more so, the third phases the organisational climate permitted change. Capitalising upon a favourable climate, in the final phase European judges looked beside the immediate impediments to a unique vision of the future. Existing case law and the demand for coherence could not of itself provide adequate answers to the lacunae of law that confronted them. Unlike *Skanavi*, *Stober and Pereira* and *Kremzow* which could be adjudicated by drawing on existing Community law and reproducing the established cognitive frames, 'staying on track' was no longer an option in cases such as *Sala*, *Grzelczyk*, *Carpenter*, *MRAX* and *Baumbast*, which revealed the mismatch between European citizenship norms and reality (Figure 4.1, dissonance). Hence, they proceeded to make brave decisions that adjusted the dissonance between European citizenship's constitutional design and reality, thereby realising the transformative possibilities of European citizenship in the process of interim integration as shown in Figure 4.2, which maps the process of change in a schematic way.

To be sure, judicial incrementalism in the field of Union citizenship has been both evolutionary and fragmented. The Court did not embark upon a linear, strategic action based upon its interest in inscribing European citizenship into reality. A comparative examination of the three phases of judicial decision-making, as captured by Figure 4.2, reveals the existence of contradictions and tensions among them and in each of them. More importantly, given the background normative frame of European citizenship (i.e., European citizenship as a fundamental status), the foregoing discussion sought to answer the question as to why European citizenship norms were not as consequential in the first two phases as they were in the third phase. The model outlined in Figure 4.1, in my view, has the distinct advantage of helping us to grasp more clearly why European judges failed to embark upon an innovative legal interpretation of European citizenship in the first and, to some extent, the second phases. For as much as it is true that the Court is an autonomous institution,[146] it is important that we are

[146] Compare here Burley-Slaughter and Mattli's (1993) neo-functionalist account of the ECJ, 'Europe before the Court'. See also Karen Alter, *Establishing the Supremacy of European Law: The Making of an International Rule of Law in Europe* (Oxford: Oxford University Press, 2001). Martin Shapiro has stated that: 'because courts must engage in law making in order to do conflict resolution, and because they must be partially independent in order to do conflict resolution, it follows that no matter what the framers' initial intentions or the subsequent preferences of the other power holders, the court created will yield a certain degree of independent law-making authority'; (Winter 2000) *ECSA Review* 3.

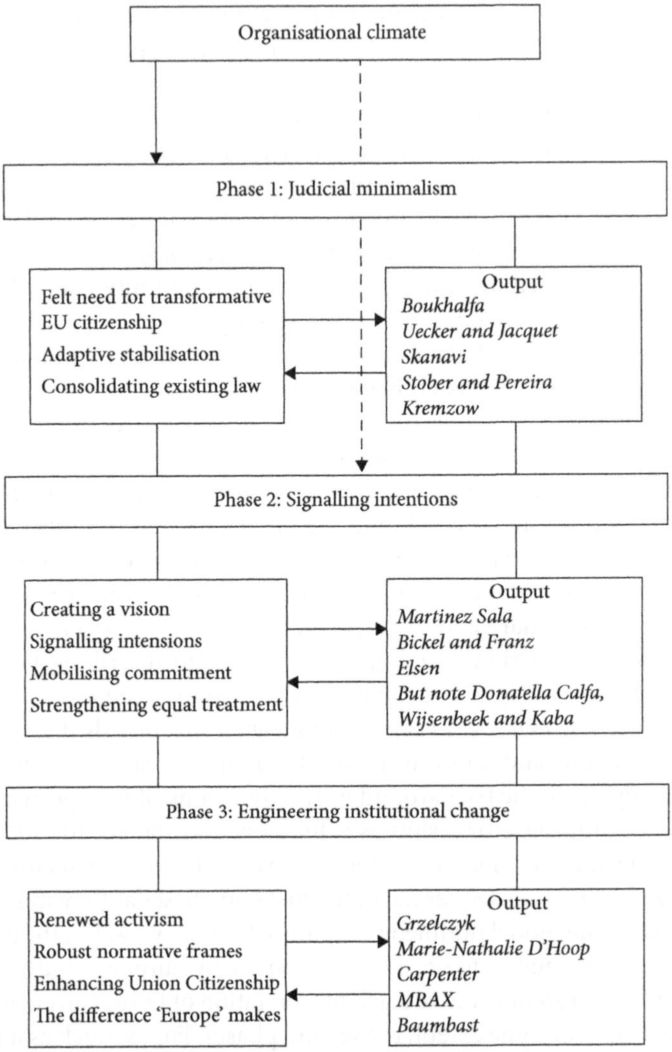

Figure 4.2 Mapping the process of institutional change

in a position to uncover both the decisional complexity and the weight of the specific factors affecting the Court's institutional autonomy to develop and extend European citizenship norms and to contribute to the development of the European polity.

The judicial institutionalisation of European citizenship induced further institutional change in law and the wider political environment, as attested by the Commission's legislative initiatives. The Court's rulings in *Carpenter*, *Baumbast*, and *MRAX* gradually found their way into the legislative and policy-making framework in Member States, as the discussion in the subsequent chapter will show. As such, they provide the impetus for vertical normative socialisation and social learning. In this respect, scholars and policy-makers alike were not justified to be either pessimistic or ambivalent about the promise of the institution of Union citizenship. The Court has carried through on this promise, despite the prevailing understanding of European citizenship as a purely symbolic institution in the 1990s. By adopting a norm-perspective and a phased approach 'in-between' Treaty amendments, the Court enhanced the constitutional importance and substance of Union citizenship in the evolving Community legal order.

5

Co-creating European Union Citizenship: Institutional Process and Crescive Norms

5.1 Introduction

In the previous chapter, the application of institutional constructivism to European Union citizenship shed light on its transformation into a 'fundamental status of the nationals of the Member States',[1] and the reasoning of the Court of Justice of the European Union (hereinafter 'the Court') before and after *Grzelczyk*. We saw that the Court's rulings in a number of important cases have swung the pendulum away from the market bias that characterised most, but not all, of the literature for nearly two decades and have endowed EU citizenship with a normative vision.[2] Of course, this process has generated a debate about the legitimacy of the Court's interventions. Participants in this debate have observed that

This chapter originated as a paper presented at Manchester University, Conference on 'The Human Face of the Union' (20 July 2012), the UACES 42nd Annual Conference, Old Borders, New Frontiers, University of Passau, 3–5 September 2012 and at the Centre for European Legal Studies, Cambridge University (23 January 2013). I would like to thank all the participants for questions and comments. It also formed the basis of a presentation at the conference on 'EU Citizenship and the Market' at the European Institute, UCL on 17 June 2011, and I am grateful to all the participants there for their observations. It was published in the *Cambridge Yearbook of European Legal Studies*, Vol. 15, 2012–3 (Oxford: Hart Publishing, 2013), pp. 255–82 and has been revised here.

1 Case C-184/99 *Grzelczyk* v. *Centre Public d'Aide Sociale d'Ottignies-Louvain-la-Neuve* [2001] ECR I-6193 [31].

2 See, *inter alia*, Dimitry Kochenov and Richard Plender, 'EU Citizenship: From an Incipient Form to an Incipient Substance?', 37 *European Law Review* (2012), p. 369; Ferdinand Wollenschlager, 'A New Fundamental Freedom beyond Market Integration: Union Citizenship and Its Dynamics for Shifting the Economic Paradigm of European Integration', 17(1) *European Law Journal* (2011), p. 1; Josephine Shaw, 'Citizenship: Contrasting Dynamics at the Interface of Integration and Constitutionalism', in P. Craig and G. de Búrca (eds.), *The Evolution of European Union Law* (Oxford: Oxford University Press, 2011); Niamh Nic Shuibhne, 'The Resilience of EU Market Citizenship', 47 *CML Rev* (2010), p. 1597; Willem Maas, 'Unrespected, Unequal, Hollow? Contingent Citizenship

legal interpretation is arbitrary and that judicial decision making undermines democratic processes by subverting the legislature's mandate and function.[3] This reasoning features centrally in the debates surrounding Brexit, which is the subject matter of the subsequent chapter.

Although this debate is not confined to EU citizenship and EU law and politics, in general, one can easily discern that in these discussions important issues surrounding the origin, evolution and content of EU citizenship and the role of law as interpretation are often sidestepped. By resting on a series of oppositional logics, such as the individual versus society, the Member States versus supra-national institutional actors, freedom of movement of persons versus the sociality it involves, the economic versus the socio-political, and law as enacted versus law as interpretation, scholars and policy practitioners fail to capture the complexity and multi-dimensionality of EU citizenship. And as I argued above, in reality, none of these dimensions can have a definite meaning or effect independently from the others.

More specifically, the free movement of persons has strong socio-political dimensions which market-based perspectives underscore. Individuals are almost never solely economic agents; they are also social actors and moral agents, and to insist on prioritising the former over the latter results in positing fragmentary selves which bear little resemblance to real human beings (Chapter 1). Similarly, EU citizens are not, and have never been, 'consumers' of lifestyle choices provided for by EU integration.[4] For the term 'consumer' captures neither their membership

and Reversible Rights in the European Union', 15(2) *Columbia Journal of European Law* (2009), p. 265; Everson, 'The Legacy of the Market Citizen', pp. 73–90. Compare also Ettore Recchi, 'Cross-State Mobility in the EU', 10(2) *European Societies* (2008), p. 197; Dora Kostakopoulou, 'European Union Citizenship: The Journey Goes On', in A. Ott and E. Vos (eds.), *50 Years of European Integration: Foundations and Perspectives* (The Hague: TMC Asser Press, 2009), pp. 270–90; 'EU Citizenship: Writing the Future', 13(5) *European Law Journal* (2007), p. 623; F. Jacobs, 'Citizenship of the European Union – A Legal Analysis', 13(5) *European Law Journal* (2007), p. 591; M. Elmore and P. Starup, 'Union Citizenship – Background, Jurisprudence and Perspective: The Past, Present and Future of Law and Policy', 26 *Yearbook of European Law* (2007), p. 57.

[3] For a recent overview, see Bruno de Witte and Hans-W. Micklitz (eds.), *The European Court of Justice and the Autonomy of the Member States* (Leiden: Intersentia, 2012). But compare Alec Stone-Sweet, *Governing with Judges: Constitutional Politics in Europe* (Oxford: Oxford University Press, 2000).

[4] See Chapter 3. Compare, here, Favell's notion of 'Eurostars': Adrian Favell, 'Immigration, Migration, and Free Movement in the Making of Europe', in J. T. Checkel and P. J. Katzenstein (eds.), *European Identity* (New York: Cambridge University Press, 2009), pp. 167–89.

status and their concrete life experiences nor the complexity of the social and political relations that envelop them and are, in turn, created by their actions and multifarious practices. Living, working and engaging with the world go beyond the individualised consumption of 'choices', goods and services. The content and actual exercise of EU citizenship rights, on the other hand, depend on the Member States' decisive input and their role in implementing treaty provisions, the secondary legislation and the Court's rulings. And, finally, law as interpretation plays a very important role in realising legal provisions. Without the former, legal rules are not 'living' prescriptions and their relevance to individuals appears to be limited. In other words, the antithetical logic characterising the above debates conceals both correlational realities and social and institutional processes.

In all institutions, and in the process of European integration itself, the economic and the socio-political are closely intertwined and nothing happens disconnectedly. In addition, institutions are not monolithic creations obeying a singular logic.[5] They are situated in time and space, and are multi-layered constructions that are subject to ongoing change (Chapter 2). As noted in Chapter 3, from moment to moment, from past to present to future, various institutional dimensions, be they essential or non-essential, mutate, expand or just become replaced by others. Moreover, the valuations, objectives, functions and principles animating them are themselves products of socio-political processes. In what follows, I build on these reflections and argue that the correlational thinking and the processual approach underpinning the *connexio rerum* framework enable us to see EU citizenship as a complex whole, to understand its evolution over time and to produce more nuanced accounts of the recent case law and its transformative potential.

By making both process and institutional change the foci of inquiry, EU citizenship emerges as a co-created institution.[6] By the latter I mean that it is the product of institutional design and co-creation by actors at all levels of governance and is shaped by multilogues at the 'top' and 'bottom' as well as 'sideways', and by citizens' formal and informal actions. A co-creation

[5] I adhere to a broad definition of institutions, as noted in Part 1 of the book.

[6] The co-creation or co-construction of reality was the subject matter of Berger and Luckmann's book entitled *The Social Construction of Reality*. In it, they sought to develop a theory of society as a dialectical process between objective and subjective realities. They referred to the existence of multiple realities and the process of weaving a coherent sense of meaning among them. Their thoughtful comments and observations unravel the activist, in the sense of participatory as well as activity-based (that is, practice-oriented), construction of all institutional realities.

perspective leads us to reconsider state-centred assumptions about which form of citizenship should be predominant and the dualism of centralism (supra-nationalism) versus 'home-rule' (intergovernmentalism).[7] This perspective is not premised on the existence of pre-established ideas about the primacy of one level of governance or of certain institutional actors. Nor does it rely on preconceived notions about where or how co-creation should take place. Instead, it welcomes the co-involvement of actors, both individual and collective, the combination of old and new ideas and law and policy experimentation with a view to upgrading rights' protection, tackling policy gaps, providing more enriched life horizons for citizens and reducing the structural and ideological barriers to their self-realisation.

The subsequent discussion is structured as follows. In Section 5.2, I unravel the main dimensions of the co-creation of EU citizenship, while Section 5.3 examines EU citizenship's evolution and the double movement of co-creation. In Section 5.4, I discuss in more detail the unfolding logic of co-creation and the Court's contribution to refining, and redefining, EU citizenship by aligning judicial output during the period 2010–15 to institutional change. The concluding remarks are contained in the last section.

5.2 Dimensions of Co-creation

One might identify three important dimensions in the co-creation of EU citizenship. First, EU citizenship is not the product of mimesis;[8] it is a construct and the product of human imagination (see Chapter 2, Section 2.2). Lacking clearly defined and well-functioning predecessors, this form of citizenship beyond the nation state did not have to exist. Its juridical roots lie in the free movement of workers provisions of the Treaties of Paris and Rome, which Walter Hallstein, the first President of the Commission (1958–69), saw as the foundation of a 'European Economic and Social Community'.[9] Since the very beginning, labour mobility was thus tangled with a broader normative vision, that is, of establishing a European citizenship. This is how Lionello Levi Sandri, the Vice-President of the Commission, imagined the future.[10] The Preamble to Council Regulation

[7] Dora Kostakopoulou, 'The European Court of Justice, Member State Autonomy and European Union Citizenship: Conjunctions and Disjunctions', in de Witte and Micklitz (eds.), *The European Court of Justice and the Autonomy of the Member States*, pp. 202–3.

[8] Aristotle, *Poetics*, 1448b.

[9] Walter Hallstein, *Europe in the Making* (London: Allen & Unwin, 1972 [1969]), pp. 173–4.

[10] The Free Movement of Workers in the Countries of the European Economic Community, Bull EC 6/61, 5–10, 6.

1612/68 explicitly referred to 'the fundamental right of workers to improve their standard of living which must be exercised in freedom and dignity'.[11] And as workers could invoke and exercise their free movement rights without the unnecessary interference and approval of the host Member States, it has been convincingly argued that the EEC Treaty established an incipient form of EU citizenship for certain classes of persons, that is, workers, professionals, service providers and their families.[12]

In addition to its construction *ex nihilo*, it has undergone, and is still undergoing, change due to the simultaneous interaction, and sometimes collision, of four spheres; namely, the European Union one, national-statist orders, exogenous developments of a more global nature, and actors' normative expectations and claims. The system comprising these four spheres is thus neither closed nor open; neither structured nor structureless; rather, it is in constant flux (Chapter 2). All of them are changing, thereby triggering changes and mutations to one another. In the late 1990s, I used the term 'nested EU and national citizenships' in order to study the mutual interactions and the Europeanisation of national citizenship.[13] But nestedness also implies nestedness within a bigger setting, that is, within the world, as well as within a network of micro-actions by agents who activate processes of systemic change. Rules are located within the context, which, in turn, is nested within a larger context and this, in turn, is nested within a larger environment. All of them are interlinked and are capable of triggering ripples of change in time t. In this sense, context does not merely point to entailment, detail and causation, but also reveals constraints as well as possibilities and openings, as discussed in Chapter 3 on institutional change above.

Historically, it is not difficult to trace the mutating and enriching nature of EU citizenship. In the early 1970s, the Member States manifested their determination to build 'a Community of law and democracy which measures up to the needs of the individual and preserves the rich variety of national cultures by adopting the Declaration on European Identity'.[14] Leo Tindemans, the Belgian Prime Minister, who was instructed by the Paris conference to articulate concrete proposals for strengthening citizens'

[11] European Council, Regulation 1612/68 of 15 October 1968 on freedom of movement for workers within the Community, OJ Special Edition 475, [1968] OJ L257/2.

[12] Richard Plender, 'An Incipient Form of European Citizenship', in F. Jacobs (ed.), *European Law and the Individual* (Amsterdam: North Holland, 1976).

[13] Kostakopoulou, 'Nested "Old" and "New" Citizenships in the European Union', p. 389. See also Kostakopoulou, *Citizenship, Identity and Immigration in the European Union*.

[14] European Commission, '7th General Report EC' (1973) annex 2, ch. II.

rights, produced a report which advocated the protection of fundamental rights in the EU, consumer rights for European citizens and the protection of the environment.[15] The establishment of common European rights was envisaged to bring 'Europe close to its citizens', create a feeling of identification with the EU as a whole and to make a 'people's Europe' a reality. In this respect, Tindemans' report on the EU contained a number of recommendations for the creation of a 'Europe of citizens' anchored on solidarity.

Further reforms at the turn of that decade, such as the first direct elections to the European Parliament in 1979,[16] the introduction of uniform passport in 1981, the prospect of the abolition of internal frontier controls coupled with the Commission's draft directive on residence of Community nationals in the territory of host Member States in 1979, and its proposal to grant local electoral rights to Community nationals residing in host Member States,[17] gave more impetus to the idea of common European citizenship. In fact, they re-casted established conceptions of community membership and intra-Community migration away from the Member States' classificatory and regulatory matrix.[18] The Member States opposed the relaxation of the national citizenship requirement for franchise in the 1970s, thereby forcing the Commission to shift its attention from political rights to establishing local consultative councils for migrant workers in the host Member States. In the mid-1980s, the Adonnino Report[19] favoured the grant of local electoral rights and voting rights in European Parliament elections in the Member State of residence, and the Draft Treaty on European Union (DTEU) proposed by the European Parliament in 1984 recommended the formal establishment of EU citizenship conditioned on the possession of Member State citizenship. Indeed, the Draft Treaty echoed Spinelli's belief that the Second World War had reduced 'the habitual respect of citizens for their states and their myths and opened the way to the united European transformation'.[20]

[15] For a more detailed exposition, see Wiener, *Building Institutions*; Kostakopoulou, *Citizenship, Identity and Immigration in the European Union*; Willem Maas, *Creating European Citizens* (Lanham, MD: Rowman & Littlefield, 2007).

[16] [1977] OJ 278/1.

[17] (1972) 10 *EC Bull.*

[18] The latter term is borrowed from Rogers Brubaker, 'Migration, Membership and the Modern Nation-State: Internal and External Dimensions of Belonging', XLI(I) *Journal of Interdisciplinary History* (2010), pp. 61, 76.

[19] Pietro Adonnino chaired the ad hoc Committee for a People's Europe in line with the mandate given to it by the Fontainebleau Council in 1984.

[20] A Spinelli, 1966, 7, quoted in Maas, *Creating European Citizens*, p. 120.

Although the Draft Treaty did not have a formal institutional impact in the sense of its provisions finding their way into the concrete articles of the Single European Act, it nevertheless provided important normative and ideational resources which would be utilised at Maastricht and beyond. In fact, it may be argued that the DTEU's provisions on EU citizenship, the Adonnino Committee's work[21] coupled with the Commission's determination to expand the personal scope of free movement beyond active economic actors, which was also reflected in the 1985 Paper on Completing the Internal Market,[22] and the formal adoption of the three 1990 Residence Directives (on students, pensioners and self-sufficient European citizens, provided that they had medical insurance and sufficient means so as to avoid becoming a burden on the welfare system of the host state)[23] led to the constitutional framework on EU citizenship at Maastricht.

The foregoing discussion of the 'generative' citizenship templates during the first decades of European integration exerting a structuring efficacy,[24] which was fully utilised at Maastricht, leads us to the third dimension of a co-created institutional reality: namely, the fact that EU citizenship comes into being by being activated by actors. To put it differently, EU citizenship cannot exist in a meaningful way without EU citizens doing it, that is, actualising it in their everyday lives. True, there exists no compulsion on the part of an EU national to activate it. In fact, one may never activate it and thus may have no clear sense of either its existence or its significance. For until the end of the first decade of the new millennium, it was only by deciding to cross national borders and to enter the territory of another Member State that an EU national became an EU citizen and a bearer of rights which governmental authorities had to respect.[25] EU citizenship was thus not 'given' in a meaningful sense prior to a process of one's participation in border crossings which initiated new experiences, a new form of identification and political negotiations across a whole range of social and political sites.

[21] See Adonnino Committee, 'Second Report', 2(7) *EC Bull Supplement* (1985), pp. 9–14.

[22] European Commission, 'Completing the Internal Market (White Paper)' COM(85) 310.

[23] Directives 90/364, 90/365 and 90/366, which were replaced by Directive 93/96. The European Parliament and Council Directive 2004/38/EC of 29 April 2004 on the right of citizens of the Union and their Family Members to move and reside freely within the territory of the Member States [2004] OJ L158/77, which repeals the above-mentioned Directives, introduces three separate categories of residence rights and establishes an unqualified right of permanent residence after five years of continuous legal residence in the host Member State.

[24] The term is borrowed from Bourdieu, *Outline of a Theory of Practice*, p. 97.

[25] See the discussion in Section 5.4.

This performative dimension inherent in EU citizenship transforms an EU national/EU citizen into a central actor in the overall motion picture. The institutional reality of EU citizenship becomes inseparable from his or her reality[26] and the whole system maintains its equilibrium by internal, agency-related motion. Successive personal 'stages' or 'moments', such as crossing the border without an impediment, residing in another Member State without (unlawful) restrictions, engaging in employment or seeking employment, bringing one's spouse and dependent children to live with him or her, enrolling them in schools, claiming family reduction railcards in order to visit other places during the weekend and so on – in short, the movement from time t to time t + 1 to t + 2, etc. – instantiate EU citizenship. But they may also reveal obstacles to realising it. The expectation of equal treatment which has been nurtured by formal rules may collide with administrative realities, and the experience accumulated between successive moments may lead to future-oriented action and thus to demands for improvement or institutional change. The parameters of what is possible, and what is normatively desirable, become broadened as a result of agents' actions and their claims-making. Having identified the three dimensions of the co-created reality of EU citizenship, namely: (a) institutional design and construction without precedent; (b) the presence of dynamic and restless change on multiple levels; and (c) the involvement of a *social self in action*,[27] it is important to examine how co-creation works before investigating the evolutionary dynamics of this institution.

5.3 How Co-creation Works: Crescive Norms and the Double Movement of Co-creation

When ideas become translated into policy prescriptions and legal regulatory templates, it is only natural that they take a concrete, sedimented form which appears to be divorced from their previous penumbrae. By the latter, I mean the meanings, conceptions, norms, notions, conditions, facts, programmatic statements and so on that surrounded them. Crystallisation invariably freezes a fluid context and institutional

[26] Compare, here, the wonderful discussion on social reality by Alfred Schutz; Maurice Natanson (ed.), *Collected Papers I: The Problem of Social Reality* (The Hague: Martinus Nijfoff, 1962), pp. 3–47.

[27] Compare here Dewey's understanding of society and agents as forming a restless and fully integrated system. Indeed, according to Dewey, we are parts of a moving, dynamic, interactive system: 'we, who are also parts of the moving present, create ourselves as we create an unknown future': Dewey, *Individualism Old and New*, p. 83.

crystallisation constitutes no exception. What existed before, and was intimately connected with the chosen form or rule, becomes forgotten and previously strong connecting links become fragmentary, isolated and discrepant. The pre-existing ideas and notions also lack coherence and their often floating meanings circulate around the chosen law or policy, but have not yet found their appropriate place.

Painstaking archival work and the personal accounts of the actors who sat at the negotiating table and took part in the discussions which culminated in the adoption of the final legal text often shed light onto the penumbra of law. Other (activist) actors seeking to make a claim for the development or revision of law or policy will often find the unchosen 'might have beens', give them recognition and will incorporate them into their agendas. And, eventually, changed conditions and the requisite need to respond to them might resurrect them, thereby inaugurating processes of extending and thus transforming the form, scope and value of the institution. The history of the present (the past of the present) affirms itself and both present and past are altered by the present circumstances, which inevitably bring the future within the present.[28] The future more often than not is in the past in the same way that if one starts peeling off layers of the present, one uncovers the traces of the past. In a slightly different way, Thelen has discussed the 'layering process of institutional change, whereby certain elements of a given set of institutions are renegotiated whereas others are left in place'.[29] This is one way of orchestrating the co-creation of institutional realities.

Instead of focusing directly on the penumbra of a policy, legal rule or norm, another, but not necessarily unrelated, way of understanding co-creation would be to put the emphasis on their core and to amplify the normative or cognitive depth of the idea or principle underpinning them. This amplification happens as a result of the 'collision' of the idea or principle with empirical reality or the raw data. The latter constantly reveal openings which could have been anticipated. This sparks a double movement from the ideational or the principled template to partial (and often confused) observations and raw facts and from the latter back to the former. This back-and-forth movement from the abstract to the particular connects the idea, principle or norm with the actual data or need, thereby expanding the former's application and possible meanings. New operations of the same principle or modifications of the principle emerge.

[28] Compare Mead, *The Philosophy of the Present*.

[29] Kathleen Thelen, 'How Institutions Evolve: Insights from Comparative-Historical Analysis', in J. Mahoney and D. Rueschemeyer (eds.), *Comparative Historical Analysis in the Social Sciences* (Cambridge: Cambridge University Press, 2003), p. 225.

The new circumstances become premises of reasoning and opportunities for experimentation which impact upon the abstract whole. General principles thus convert isolated particulars on the one hand, and particulars refine, extend and revise general principles on the other. This working back and forth flows in a way that is almost impossible to stop; it is an ongoing relational process that is bound to remain incomplete, always flowing like a stream and craving for more inclusive and far-reaching meanings, and for a better reciprocal adjustment between the ideational and the real.[30]

Institutional development and change are thus intrinsic parts of the process – and not epiphenomena of critical junctures, as the institutionalist literature has indicated.[31] The double movement described earlier can occur in a more or less regulated manner as well as at random. Certainly, it is likely to be more successful if the surrounding environment is congenial, but even an uncongenial environment cannot thwart change; it merely affects its rate and amplitude. The adoption of the Citizenship Directive (2004/38)[32] is a manifestation of the former process, while the unpredictability of cases on EU citizenship reaching the Court and of adjudication are manifestations of the latter. Notwithstanding their differences, however, both processes fill existing breaches, bridge gaps in coherence, bring previously unconnected facts together under the ambit of a norm, extend the norm by linking it to other adjacent norms, jump from one consideration to another and discover new connections between principles and pragmatic considerations in the light of new environmental exigencies and the facts at hand. The process is quite complex and multi-dimensional.

[30] As Dewey has observed,

> in every judgement some meaning is employed as a basis for estimating and interpreting some fact; by this application the meaning is itself enlarged and tested. When the general meaning is regarded as complete in itself, application is treated as an external, non-intellectual use to which for practical purposes alone it is advisable to put the meaning. The principle is one self-contained thing; its use is another and independent thing. When this divorce occurs, principles become fossilised and rigid; they lose their inherent vitality, their self-impelling power ... A true conception is a moving idea

Dewey, *How We Think*, p. 59.

[31] See North, *Institutions, Institutional Change and Economic Performance*; Thelen and Longstreth (eds.), *Structuring Politics*. But compare Pierson, 'The Limits of Design'.

[32] Directive 2004/38/EC of 29 April 2004 on the right of citizens of the Union and their family members to move and reside freely within the territory of the Member States amending Regulation (EEC) No. 1612/68 and repealing Directives 64/221/EEC, 68/360/EEC, 72/194/EEC, 73/148/EEC, 75/34/EEC, 75/35/EEC, 90/364/EEC, 90/365/EEC and 93/96/EEC [2004] OJ L158/77 (Citizenship Directive).

In the unfolding process of co-creating EU citizenship in the 1990s, the Court played a key role. In the previous chapter, it was shown how it began to display an innovative reasoning in the *Martinez Sala* case by planting the seeds for a shift from protecting the rights of active economic actors to affirming the equal treatment of all EU citizens irrespective of their nationality.[33] Soon afterwards, it stated that 'Union citizenship is destined to be a fundamental status of nationals of the Member States, enabling those who find themselves in the same situation to enjoy the same treatment in law irrespective of their nationality'.[34] In that case, EU national students studying in another Member State and facing temporary economic difficulties could rely on the non-discrimination clause in claiming social advantages, provided that they did not place an unreasonable burden on the welfare system of the host Member State. More frequent judicial interventions in the new millennium made EU citizenship more loosely connected with economic and migration status and more closely aligned with 'a powerful mission of protection of individual rights'.[35]

Accordingly, it comes as no surprise that in *Baumbast* the Court explicitly recognised that Article 21(1) of the Treaty on the Functioning of the European Union (TFEU) (formerly 18(1) TEC) is directly effective, that is, it confers rights on individuals which are enforceable before national courts.[36] Since *Baumbast*, the Court has almost re-defined EU citizenship: besides direct and indirect discrimination, it has outlawed non-discriminatory restrictions that hinder or make the former less attractive by posing 'unjustified burdens'[37] and 'serious inconveniences',[38] and

[33] Case C-85/96 *Maria Martinez Sala* v. *Freistaat Bayern* [1998] ECR I-2691.

[34] *Grzelczyk* (n 1) [31].

[35] Weatherill, *Cases and Materials on EU Law*, p. 490; Peter Van Der Mei, *Free Movement of Persons within the European Community* (Oxford: Hart Publishing, 2003); Kostakopoulou, 'Ideas, Norms and European Citizenship', pp. 233–267; Norbert Reich, 'The Constitutional Relevance of Citizenship and Free Movement in an Enlarged Union', 11 *European Law Journal* (2005), p. 675; Michael Dougan, 'The Constitutional Dimension of the Case Law on Union Citizenship', 31 *European Law Review* (2006), p. 613; Albertina Albors-Llorens, 'A Broader Construction of the EC Treaty Provisions on Citizenship', 57 *CLJ* (1998), p. 461.

[36] Case C-413/99 *Baumbast and R* v. *Secretary of State for the Home Department* [2002] ECR I-7091.

[37] Case C-224/02 *Heikki Antero Pusa* v. *Osuuspankkien Keskinainen Vakuutusythio* [2004] ECR I-5763; Case C-406/04 *G De Cuyper* v. *Office national de l'emploi* [2006] ECR I-06947; Case C-192/05 *K Tas-Hagen and RA Tas* v. *Raadskamer WUBO van de Pensioen – en Uitkeringsraad* [2006] ECR I-10451; Joined Cases C-11/06 and C-12/06 *Rhiannon Morgan* v. *Bezirksregierung Köln and Iris Bucher* v. *Landrat des Kreises Düren* [2007] ECR I-9161.

[38] See Case C-391/00 *Runevic-Vardyn* (ECJ, 12 May 2011); Case C-208/09 *Ilonka Sayn-Wittgenstein* v. *Landeshauptmann von Wien* [2010] ECR I-13693.

has made denationalisation (and naturalisation) decisions taken by the Member States subject to judicial review and subject to a proportionality test,[39] thereby intruding into what was previously thought to be the Member States' core preserve of sovereign jurisdiction.[40]

Although the Court's rulings have not escaped criticism in some quarters, it would nevertheless be problematic to ignore the arrow of time[41] and to disregard the relation between seemingly momentary and fragmentary factual details and binding principles or rules. EU citizenship has assumed central constitutional importance and this paradigmatic change, which the Court has effectuated, has taken place in a coherent as well as a reflexive way. Coherence captures to a greater extent the unfolding logic of realising equal treatment irrespective of nationality, which is the normative premise of EU citizenship, and less pleas for predictability and smooth outcomes, while reflexivity, on the other hand, points to the construction of a paradigm that discourages neither criticism nor modifications. The latter is a characteristic of the tradition of constructivism (Chapter 2). True, our lives would be easier if we were confronted with certainties, but we all know that the predominant trend is change and evolution. The latter unfold with little regard to predictive rules and linear determinism, and the abovementioned cases show how the 'new', which does not fit into the established grid, prompts modifications and extensions of the EU citizenship template. Norms are crescive, that is, evolving and growing, and the general process of institutional change brought about by actors exhibits a clear direction.

5.4 Co-creation's Ways

The process of co-creation outlined in the preceding sections presupposes neither the existence of a determinate agenda nor the presence of a given and closed universe of meaning whereby change will be activated by the existence of a lack, or a fault, or, indeed, a weakness and therefore concomitant attempts to go beyond all of them. As such, it reflects the discussion on the complexity of institutional change in Chapter 3. Co-creation leads us to realise that in all types of institutional decision making and evolution, the index is as important as the agenda, various layers of meaning can be juxtaposed, superimposed or just used to push

[39] Case C-135/08 *Janco Rottmann* v. *Freistaat Bayern* [2010] ECR I-1449. See also Case C-200/02 *Zhu and Chen* v. *Secretary for the Home Department* [2004] ECR I-9925.

[40] Wollenschlager, 'A New Fundamental Freedom beyond Market Integration'.

[41] Paul Pierson, *Politics in Time* (Princeton, NJ: Princeton University Press, 2004).

one another out of the way, and that change can occur without giving prior intimations. In fact, in vast multiverses of meanings, settled interpretations can live for some time or become easily disrupted by sub-universes of meanings which had been previously excluded or left dormant. In brief, history, institutions and politics exist in time, both in the sense of *chronos* and *kairos* (Part I), and time horizons vary.[42]

Although it would be futile to seek to map out such a process so prone to unpredictability and complexity, one can nevertheless discern in both decision making and adjudication some patterns, which are as follows: (a) roundabout moves creating what may be called a pre-pattern; (b) cul-de-sac moves, leaving actors and audiences disappointed and thus occasioning a return to the drawing board; (c) back-and-forth oscillations between new and old meanings; and (d) breaks. The latter can either be a clearly visible derogation from the past (rupture), an enhancement of it (adaptation and acceleration) or an epistrophe to it (regression). In what follows, I elaborate on these patterns by focusing on two areas of EU citizenship case law, namely, family migration and the deportation of long-term resident EU citizens on the grounds of public security. This focus is important not only because of the Court's vital contribution to the co-creation of EU citizenship and to norm-creation, but also because it sheds ample light onto the evolving process of institutional change.

5.4.1 *Step Change*

Although the Court has been influential in the domain of EU citizens' family reunification and has made respect for family life an integral part of the general principles of EU law, thereby causing fictions with national migration laws,[43] it is generally acknowledged that its judgment in *Zambrano*[44]

[42] Ibid.

[43] Case C-60/00 *M. Carpenter* [2002] ECR I-6279; *Baumbast*; Case C-459/99 *MRAX* [2002] ECR I-6591; Case C-540/03 *European Parliament* v. *Council* [2006] ECR I-5769; Case C-127/08 *Metock* [2008] ECR I-6241.

[44] Case C-34/09 *Ruiz Zambrano* v. *Office national de l'emploi (ONEM)* [2011] ECR I-0000. Ruiz Zambrano was a Colombian national who had been residing in Belgium without a residence permit following the rejection of his asylum application, but could not be deported to his country of origin, Colombia, owing to non-refoulement reasons. His wife gave birth to two children, Diego and Jessica, both Belgian nationals and EU citizens since the father failed to register the births with the Colombian embassy. Although Mr Zambrano and his wife could not leave Belgium and were denied work and residence permits, he nevertheless had taken up full-time employment for five years in order to support his family and contributed to the tax and social security burden of the Belgian commonwealth. But when, following his redundancy, he challenged the authorities' refusal to recognise his entitlement to an

is revolutionary.[45] In this case, the Court extended the scope of EU law to a 'wholly internal situation' by ruling that the Colombian parents of two Belgian (and thus EU citizen) children could not be denied residence and work permits if such a denial would result in the children's deprivation 'of the genuine enjoyment of the substance of the rights conferred by virtue of their status as citizens of the Union. A refusal to grant a right of residence to a third-country national with dependent minor children in the Member State where those children are nationals and reside ... has such an effect'.[46] The refusal to grant a right to residence to the parents of the children would thus result in the children's departure from 'the territory of the Union' and the deprivation of the opportunity to exercise their EU citizenship rights.

Prior to *Rottmann*[47] and *Zambrano*, the boundaries between 'wholly internal situations' which are governed by national law, on the one hand, and cross-border activity activating the application of EC/EU law, on the other, had remained settled until the first decade of the new millennium because Justices were unwilling to call them into question.[48] Quite often the boundaries were fuzzy, cases tested them[49] and on several occasions

---

unemployment benefit, he and his family faced the prospect of exclusion from Belgium and thus from the European Union.

45 Sandra Mantu, 'European Union Citizenship anno 2011: Zambrano, McCarthy and Dereci', 26(1) *Journal of Immigration Asylum and Nationality Law* (2012), p. 40; Alicia Hinarejos, 'Citizenship of the EU: Clarifying "Genuine Enjoyment of the Substance" of Citizenship Rights', 71(2) *CLJ* (2012), p. 279; Alina Tryfonidou, 'Redefining the Outer Boundaries of EU Law: The Zambrano, McCarthy and Dereci Trilogy', 18 *European Public Law* (2012), p. 493; Anja Wiesbrock, 'Disentangling the "Union Citizenship Puzzle"? The McCarthy Case', 26 *European Law Review* (2011), p. 861; Kay Hailbronner and Daniel Thym, 'Annotation of Case C-34/09 Ruiz Zambrano', 48 *CML Rev* (2011), p. 1253.

46 *Zambrano* [44]. For commentary, see also Coenraad Lenaerts, '"Civis Europeaus Sum": From the Cross-Border Link to the Status of Citizen of the Union', 2 *Online Journal of Free Movement of Workers within the EU* (2011), p. 12; Dimitry Kochenov, 'A Real European Citizenship: The Court of Justice Opening a New Chapter in the Development of the Union in Europe', 18(1) *Columbia Journal of European Law* (2012), p. 55; Dimitry Kochenov, 'The Essence of EU Citizenship Emerging from the Last Ten Years of Academic Debate: Beyond the Cherry Blossoms and the Moon?', 62(1) *International and Comparative Law Quarterly* (2013), p. 97; Michaela Hailbronner and Sarah Iglesias Sanchez, 'The European Court of Justice and Citizenship of the European Union: New Developments Towards a Truly Fundamental Status', 5 *ICLJ* (2011), p. 498.

47 *Rottmann*.

48 Case 175/78 *R* v. *Saunders* [1979] ECR 1129, [1979] 2 CMLR 216. See also Robin White, 'A Fresh Look at Reverse Discrimination?', 18 *European Law Review* (1993), p. 527.

49 Case 180/83 *Moser* v. *Land Baden-Wurttemberg* [1984] ECR 2539; Case 35–36/82 *Morson and Jhanjan* v. *The Netherlands* [1982] ECR 3723; Case 298/84 *Iorio* v. *Arienda automata delle Ferrovie dello stato* [1986] ECR 257; Cases C-64 and 65/96 *Uecker and Jacquet* v. *Land Nordrhein-Westfalen* [1997] 3 CMLR 963; Joined Cases C-225/95, C-226/95 and C-227/95

the issue surfaced and re-surfaced in judgments and in submissions by the Member States. At this point, one might also argue that the maintenance of these boundaries served the EU integration process by steering an equilibrium between national competences and the evolving Community law. However, as the 'purely internal situations' doctrine has been in itself historically and politically conditioned, it would be a mistake to reify it, that is, to view it as a special kind of doctrine resisting adaptation and critical reflection.

What changed initially in *Rottmann*[50] and subsequently in a clearer way in *Zambrano* was the Court's willingness to address some of the paradoxical results that the wholly internal/EU law dualism had generated, since they did not only appear to contradict the fundamental status of EU citizenship, but they also threatened to make it ephemeral. In this respect, the *Rottmann* and *Zambrano* judgments are seminal as they re-inscribe EU citizenship within a Europolitical frame that cannot tolerate Member States' actions of rendering this status meaningless or completely ineffective.[51] Here, I discern the same rights-based logic that brought about the foundational doctrines of the Community legal order, such as direct effect, supremacy and state liability. This is none other than the need for the intervention of EU law in order to protect individuals in cases of state failure which limits the effectiveness of EU law. This is the moment of co-creation at work – a moment of important institutional change due to the Court's willingness to intervene in extraordinary situations where the EU citizenship status itself is at stake in order to protect the rights of the vulnerable EU citizens. As already argued, *Rottmann* subjects the withdrawal of nationality leading to de facto and de jure statelessness to judicial review and to a proportionality test, while in *Zambrano*, the Court essentially preserves the normative integrity of respect for family life as a fundamental

Anestis Kapasakalis, Dimitris Skiathitis and Antonis Kougiaskas v. *Elliniko Dimosio* [1998] ECR I-4239.

50 In *Rottmann* [42], the Court held that 'by reason of its nature and its consequences, the situation fell within the ambit of European Union law'.

51 Shuibhne does not detect a novel approach in the Court's judgment in *Zambrano* (N. Nic Shuibhne, 'Annotation of Case C-434/09 *McCarthy* and Case C-256/11 *Dereci*', 49 *CML Rev* (2012), p. 349. Kochenov, Hailbronner and Thym see 'the substance of rights' as a judicial innovation: Kay Hailbronner and Daniel Thym, '*Zambrano*', 48 *CML Rev* (2012), p. 1253 (note), 1257; Kochenov, A Real European Citizenship'. Compare also Miguel Poiares Maduro, 'The Scope of European Remedies', in C. Kilpatrick (eds.), *The Future of Remedies in Europe* (Oxford: Hart Publishing, 2000), p. 117, 134–5; Stefan Kadelbach, 'Union Citizenship', in Armin von Bogdandy and Jurgen Bast (eds.), *Principles of European Constitutional Law*, 2nd edn (Munich: CH Beck, 2009), p. 435.

right,[52] which the EU Charter of Fundamental Rights has upgraded to a constitutional guarantee,[53] by precluding the deportation of, and the non-issuing of a work permit to, non-EU national parents of EU citizen children. By so doing, it increased the 'volume' of EU citizenship and extended its 'surface radius' so that it could be invoked by non-mobile children who are EU citizens at home facing departure from the EU.[54]

5.4.2 Back-and-Forth Oscillations between 'The New' and 'The Old' and Change as Direction and Suggestibility

Having stretched the outer limits of EU law in *Zambrano*, the Court decided to circumscribe change in the subsequent case of *McCarthy*[55] by maintaining the cross-border link as the crucial factor for the activation of EU law. But circumscribing change by stressing, for instance, the *exceptionality* of the facts of *Zambrano* does not mean that an institutional actor does not have the conviction to continue on the same path. Nor does it imply that change is stalled. To believe so would be tantamount to viewing institutional change as a continuously upward movement resembling the ascendance of a ladder. But ladder ascendance captures neither the complex process of change nor the multiplicity of the forms it takes, as noted in Chapter 3 on institutional change.

McCarthy, a dual national of British and Irish nationality who wished to secure a right of residence for her spouse, a Jamaican national, by invoking her newly acquired Irish nationality, had not been a worker or a

[52] Advocate General Sharpston, in her Opinion on *Zambrano* of 30 September 2010, highlighted the importance of fundamental rights in the light of the legally binding Charter of Fundamental Rights, but the Court premised its decision on EU citizenship rather than on fundamental rights. Notably, A. G. Sharpston had also stated that 'Article 18 TFEU should be interpreted as prohibiting reverse discrimination caused by the interaction between Article 21 TFEU and national law that entails a violation of a fundamental right protected by EU law, where at least equivalent protection is not available under national law' (point 144).

[53] It would have been impossible for the judiciary, but also for other Community institutions to ignore the Charter's Preamblic reference to '[the Union] places the individual at the heart of its activities, by establishing the citizenship of the Union and by creating an area of freedom, security and justice'. Compare also the British case *ZH (Tanzania)* v. *Secretary of State for the Home Department* [2011] UKSC 4 [30].

[54] Nic Shuibhne, 'Free Movement of Persons and the Wholly Internal Rule', p. 731; Eleanor Spaventa, 'Seeing the Wood Despite the Trees? On the Scope of Union Citizenship and Its Constitutional Effects', 45 *CML Rev* (2008), 13; Alina Tryfonidou, *Reverse Discrimination in EC Law* (Alphen aan den Rijn: Kluwer, 2009).

[55] Case C-434/09 *Shirley McCarthy* v. *Secretary of State for the Home Department* [2011] ECR I-03375.

self-employed person or a self-sufficient person exercising her free movement rights under EU law, and the Court concluded that the UK authorities' refusal to grant a residence permit to her Jamaican husband did not have any impact upon her right to move and reside freely within the EU. The structure of the legal argumentation and decision is premised on a distinction between this case and *Zambrano* in that the restrictive UK migration provisions did not have the effect of necessitating Mrs McCarthy's departure from the territory of the EU[56] and thus did not result in the deprivation of the genuine enjoyment of her rights or impeding the exercising of her freedom to move and reside freely within the territory of the Member States under Article 21 TFEU.[57]

Clearly, this judgment, as well as the subsequent one in *Dereci and others*,[58] represented roundabout moves following the step change brought about by *Zambrano*. Perhaps the Court felt that it had to create a series of buffers that cushioned the impact of *Zambrano*. Alternatively, it might be argued that the Court felt that the time was not right for a total 'rupture', that is, the abolition of the 'purely internal situation' doctrine, since this would trigger an unauthorised upgrading of the EU constitutional settlement. But it would equally be fallacious to view the Court's rulings in post-*Zambrano* cases as simple backward moves (or regress) and thus criticise it for introducing uncertainty, incoherence and ambiguity in EU citizenship-related case law. For it is often the case that radical institutional change, such as the step change in *Zambrano*, is frequently followed by a period of 'back-and-forth oscillations' which prepares the ground for another kind of change, namely adaptive change. In post-*Zambrano* judgments (*Dereci and others*[59] and *Iida*),[60] we thus discern another kind of institutional change, namely, change as direction, a choice and suggestibility.

In *Dereci and others*, the Court distinguished *Dereci* from *Zambrano* by stressing the *exceptionality* of *Zambrano*,[61] that is, its application to an EU citizen's denial of the substance of his or her rights manifested in his or her

56 Ibid. [50].

57 Ibid. [49].

58 Case C-256/11 *Dereci, Heiml, Kokollari, Maduike and Stevic* v. *Bundesministerium fur Inneres* (ECJ, 15 November 2011).

59 According to the Court, third-country national members of the family of EU citizens (in that case, all Austrian nationals) who had never exercised their right to free movement and did not rely on their spouses for their subsistence fell within the ambit of the internal situation doctrine. Accordingly, both the family reunification directive (Article 3(3) 2003/86) and the Citizenship Directive did not apply.

60 Case C-40/11 *Yoshikazu Iida* v. *Stadt Ulm* (ECJ, 8 November 2012).

61 *Dereci* [67].

forced departure from not only the territory of a Member State but also the territory of the EU,[62] thereby compromising the *effet utile* of EU citizenship.[63] It also embarked upon suggestibility, that is, it provided a clear direction that fits into the overall normative context by stating that if the Austrian measures were found by the referring court not to fall within the ambit of the 'deprivation of the substance of the EU citizenship rights doctrine', then 'other criteria, inter alia, by virtue of the right to the protection of family life, a right of residence cannot be refused' may be examined.[64] An 'order of possible options' was thus established:

> Thus, in the present case, if the referring court considers, in the light of the circumstances of the disputes in the main proceedings, that the situation of the applicants in the main proceedings is covered by European Union law, it must examine whether the refusal of their right of residence undermines the right to respect for private and family life provided for in Article 7 of the Charter. On the other hand, if it takes the view that that situation is not covered by European Union law, it must undertake that examination in the light of Article 8(1) of the ECHR.[65]

The activation of the right to respect for private and family life under Article 7 of the EUCFR and Article 8(1) of the European Convention on Human Rights (ECHR), if there exists a connecting link with EU law, thus emerges as an alternative option to mitigate the 'wrongs' resulting from the 'exceptional' applicability of the 'deprivation of the substance of EU citizenship rights' doctrine. In other words, the Court (Grand Chamber) did not wish the novelty of *Zambrano* to melt away and, even though it refrained from commenting on all possible links between Articles 20 and 21 TFEU and fundamental rights,[66] it clearly conveyed the importance of affirming the importance of the right to family life for all EU citizens irrespective of their mobility status, thereby instructing national courts to be circumspect with regard to the application of national migration law to

[62] Ibid. [66].
[63] Ibid. [67].
[64] Ibid. [69].
[65] Ibid. [72].
[66] The association of fundamental rights and EU citizenship was discussed more explicitly in *Yoshikazu Iida* v. *Stadt Ulm*. For the proposal of linking 'the substance of rights' doctrine of EU citizenship with fundamental rights, thereby enabling EU citizens to activate a 'reverse Solange' situation and rebut the presumption that the Member States comply with fundamental rights by relying on Article 20 TFEU before national courts and the Court, see Armin von Bogdandy, Matthias Kottmann, Carlino Antpohler et al., 'Reverse Solange: Protecting the Essence of Fundamental Rights against EU Member States', 49 *CML Review* (2012), p. 489.

the family reunion domain. This was re-affirmed in *Rahman and others*, where the Grand Chamber made it clear that 'other family members' of an EU citizen whose entry and residence in the host Member State must be 'facilitated' under Article 3(2)(a) of the Citizenship Directive are entitled to a judicial review of whether national legislation and its application satisfied the conditions laid down by the Directive.[67] The Grand Chamber reminded national judges of their responsibilities to uphold the fundamental right of respect for family life and to ensure that the Member States fulfil their obligations in this area.

It was not so much in *Iida*, where the Court did not find a connecting link with EU law between a refusal to grant a residence right in Germany to the Japanese father of an EU child residing with her mother in a second Member State and the restriction of the child's free movement rights in order to justify the application of the Charter of Fundamental Rights (Articles 7 and 24(3)) or the ECHR (Article 8),[68] as in *O, S and L*,[69] that this 'instructed normative template' became clearer. These joined cases concerned the derivation of a right of residence for third-country national stepfathers from the EU citizenship of their stepchildren. In *O and S*, a Ghanaian national, who had been married to a Finnish national with whom she had a child of Finnish nationality and had sole custody of the child before and after her divorce, remarried a third-country national (an Ivory Coast national), O, and had another child with him. When O applied for a residence permit, his application was refused on the grounds that he did not have sufficient means of subsistence. The same refusal of a residence permit took place in *L*, where an Algerian national had married another Algerian national following her divorce from a Finnish national with whom she had a child of Finnish nationality who was under her sole custody. The referring Finnish court sought the applicability of the principles of *Zambrano* in the context of a reconstituted family in which the step-parent of an EU citizen child has no parental or financial responsibility over him or her. While the Advocate General was clear about the non-applicability of *Zambrano* on the grounds that, since the EU citizen children were under the exclusive parental and financial responsibility of their mothers, who had a permanent right of residence in Finland, the denial of resident permits to their non-biological and non-custodian fathers could not result in their forced departure from

[67] Case C-83/11 *Secretary of State for the Home Department* v. *Muhammad Sazzadur Rahman, Fazly Rabby Islam, Mohibullah Rahman* (ECJ, 5 September 2012) [25] and [26].

[68] Ibid. See A. G. Trstenjak's Opinion on *Yoshikazu Iida* v. *Stadt Ulm*, which was delivered on 15 May 2012.

[69] Joined Cases C-356/11 and C-357/11 *O, S and L* (ECJ, 6 December 2012).

the territory of the EU,[70] the Court left it to the national court to decide whether the deprivation of 'the genuine enjoyment of the substance of rights' accompanying Article 20 TFEU could take place.[71] But it proceeded to furnish a number of guiding considerations, such as the possibility of depriving the children with all contact with their biological, Finnish fathers if the family had to depart from Finland;[72] the need for the referring court to examine 'all the circumstances of the case';[73] that the *Zambrano* principle is not confined to a blood relationship between a third-country national parent and an EU citizen child;[74] and, finally, that what would compel the child's departure would be the relationship of 'legal, financial or emotional dependence'.[75] And irrespective of the referring court's conclusion on the applicability of the provisions on EU citizenship, the Court, following *Dereci and Others*, proceeded to examine the applicability of the fundamental rights provisions and, in particular, of the right to family life. By so doing, it clearly provided a 'working test of adherence to respect for family life' via either Article 20 TFEU and the 'deprivation of the substance of EU citizenship rights' or the Family Reunification Directive (2003/86)[76] in cases where there exists no cross-border movement to activate the application of the Citizenship Directive (2004/38).

It is in the latter context of the right to family reunification under Directive 2003/86 that the Court gives direction and coherent meaning to its case law and proceeds to make a much stronger claim about the normative authority of this fundamental right and the concomitant obligation of the Member States and national judges to uphold EU law and Charter rights. The third-country national mothers were thus regarded as 'sponsors' of their third-country national husbands within the meaning of Article 2(c) of the Directive and the Member States have 'precise positive obligations with corresponding clearly defined individual rights ... to authorise the family reunification of certain members of the sponsor's family, without being left a margin of appreciation'.[77] Their decision must

[70] Joined Cases C-356/11 and C-357/11 *O, S* v. *Maahanmuuttovirasto and Maahanmuuttovirasto* v. *L*, Opinion of A. G. Bot delivered on 27 September 2012, points 44–6. The Advocate General stressed that such decision would be 'freely' taken by the mother for a reason linked to the preservation of family life.
[71] *O, S and L* [49].
[72] Ibid. [51].
[73] Ibid. [53].
[74] Ibid. [55].
[75] Ibid. [56].
[76] Council Directive 2003/86/EC of 22 September 2003 on the Right to Family Reunification [2003] OJ L251/12.
[77] *O, S and L* [70].

also comply with *Chakroun* ruling on the meaning of the requirement the possession of 'stable and regular resources' by the sponsor under Article 7(1)(c) of the Family Reunification Directive[78] and with the Charter of Fundamental Rights. In particular, Article 7 on the right to respect family life must be read in conjunction with the obligation to take into account the best interests of the child recognised in Article 24(2) and his or her interest to maintain a personal relationship with both parents on a regular basis Article 24(3). As the Court stated:

> The Member States must not only interpret their national law in a manner consistent with European Union law but also make sure that they do not rely on an interpretation of an instrument of secondary legislation which would be in conflict with the fundamental rights protected by the legal order of the European Union.[79]

Without a doubt, promoting family life and taking into account the interests of children are elevated into regulative ideals within the practice of all institutions in the multi-layered legal order, thereby prompting processes of normative socialisation in national legal orders. The obligations of states, migration authorities and national courts have been clearly delineated and the Court provides constraints for the interpretation of either national migration laws or the Family Reunification Directive in ways that do not conform with the shared values of respect for fundamental rights. The general process of change thus exhibits direction and implies normative adjustment tests for the Member States in the interface between EU citizenship and national migration laws.

The Court's judgments examined earlier show that imaginative action and step change, decisive inactions, inconsistent actions, consistent inactions and consistent instructed interpretations are all modes of the incremental co-creation of an institutional reality. In *Zambrano* and *Rottmann*, we discern the development or reconfiguration of EU citizenship as the past becomes unsettled, re-opened and re-read not only in light of a new factual context but also in light of a normative imperative of saying 'yes' to vulnerable individuals who are facing deportation or statelessness. Such facts 'beg' for a response; they have an ethical demand character, as Maslow would argue.[80] The notion of a coherent and easily pigeon-holed

[78] Case C-578/08 *Chakroun* v. *Minister van Buitenlandse Zaken* [2010] ECR I-1839.

[79] *O, S and L* [78].

[80] Indeed, according to Maslow, 'facts are to a certain extent signposts which tell you what to do, which make suggestions to you, which nudge you in one direction or another': Abraham H. Maslow, *The Farther Reaches of Human Nature* (Harmondsworth: Penguin Books, 1971), p. 28.

institutional reality is revealed to be an illusion, since the latter is always susceptible to unpredictable dynamics, chance encounters and visionary projections.

In *McCarthy*, on the other hand, the Court took a step backward. It appeared unwilling to extend the ambit of EU citizenship protection to an adult EU citizen seeking family reunification with her Jamaican spouse who had no leave to remain in the United Kingdom on the ground that the reluctance of the UK authorities to take into account her Irish nationality – the crucial element that would activate the application of EU law – did not interfere with her rights to free movement or 'any other right conferred on her by virtue of her status as a Union citizen'.[81] The Court's decisive inaction (i.e., refraining from extending the 'deprivation of the genuine enjoyment of the substance of rights doctrine') led to an inconsistent action, that is, the differential treatment of an adult EU citizenship who had not exercised her free movement rights, which, in turn, necessitated the explicit differentiation of *Zambrano* from *McCarthy* and *Dereci* by the Court (consistent inaction). Yet, in *Dereci*, the seeds for asserting the normative priority of the right to family reunification of the third-country national spouses of 'static' EU citizens were planted; the non-application of the *Zambrano* test does not rule out the application of the EU law provisions on the protection of fundamental rights (*Iida*; *O, S and L*). And if the Charter cannot apply because the situation is not covered by EU law, then the ECHR is applicable (*Dereci and others*; *Ymeraga*).[82]

Although it is only natural that our attention is fixed on the non-continuation of an evolving logic, co-creating an institutional reality is a multiform process. It is easy to side-step graduated affinities in our quest for clear resemblances among the different moments of a process. But, as argued earlier, it is imprudent to under-estimate the importance of drawing 'available options', modifying interpretations once a 'break' has been made and making fresh 'suggestions for action'. Quite often minor, and thus imperceptible, variations tend to accumulate over time in order to

[81] *McCarthy* [50].

[82] Case C-87/12 *Kreshnik Ymeraga, Kasim Ymeraga, Afijete Ymeraga-Tafarshiku, Kushtrim Ymeraga, Labinot Ymeraga* v. *Ministre du Travail, de l'Emploi et de l'Immigration* (ECJ, 8 May 2013). In this case, a former national of Kosovo who naturalised in Luxembourg but could not invoke the Citizenship Directive because he had not crossed borders (Directive 2003/86 could not apply because he had become an EU citizen). He could not rely on art 20 TFEU in order to secure a right of residence in Luxembourg for his mother, father and two of his brothers if 'the deprivation of the genuine substance of rights' test was not met.

produce creeping innovations. The importance of choice in legal grounds for reaching the 'right' solution, suggestibility and the call for normative adjustment processes on the part of Member States' authorities emerge clearly in *O, S and L*.

Although national executives may complain about the Court's intrusions into their regulatory powers in the fields of nationality and migration, to sidetrack EU citizenship to the task of promoting executive power and restrictive national migration policies would be to miss something important of its range and its vision.[83] In this respect, Lenaerts is correct to state that in light of *Zambrano*, an EU citizen can invoke AG Jacobs' phrase in *Konstadinidis*[84] 'civis Europaeus sum' against all Member States, including his or her own,[85] in order to oppose any deprivation of the genuine enjoyment of the substance of the rights conferred by virtue of EU citizenship.[86] It would also be an error to expect some form of stillness or immutability in EU citizenship's content and personal scope in the new millennium, particularly in the light of developments such as the entry into force of the Lisbon Treaty and the legally binding Charter of Fundamental Rights and the Citizenship Directive (2004/38). In the case of *Reyes*, for instance, the Court ruled that a third country

[83] For if one takes into account its diachronic evolution (see Sections 5.2 and 5.3) and, in particular, the normative ideas surrounding it since the 1970s and the trajectory of the Court's case law in the new millennium, one realises that the Court simply partook of the process of its co-creation by refining it and thus redefining it. In fact, the leap between 'depriving the effective exercise of EU citizenship rights' to 'depriving the genuine enjoyment of the substance of the rights' conferred by EU citizenship is not a big one. Similarly, one can recall the use of the *effet utile* (i.e., the principle of effectiveness of Community law) coupled with the solidarity clause (i.e., the principle of sincere co-operation) by the Court – a line that can be traced back to *Simmenthal* in the early 1970s, in order to pronounce a specific obligation on bodies to provide full and effective protection of Community law rights.

[84] Case C-168/91 *Konstadinidis* [1993] ECR I-1191 [46].

[85] Compare the following recent cases: Case C-359/13, *B. Martens* v. *Minister van Onderwijs, Cultuur en* Wetenschap, Judgment of the Court of 26 February 2015; Case C-650/13 *Thierry Delvigne* v. *Commune de Lesparre-Médoc and Préfet de la Gironde Thierry*, Judgment of the Court of 6 October 2015 and *Case C-583/14 Benjamn David Nagy* v. *Vas Megyei Rendorfokapitanysag*, Judgment of the Court of 29 October 2015.

[86] Lenaerts, 'Civis Europeaus Sum'. Similarly, although Lenaerts has argued that the deprivation effect relates to some and not necessarily to all of the EU citizenship rights and does not require the cross-border element, while the impeding effect refers to the traditional approach of the CJEU to indirect discrimination or non-discriminatory restrictions causing serious inconvenience for EU citizens (compare here Case C-391/09 *Rumenic-Vardyn* [2011] ECR I-03787 and Case 208/09 *Ilonka Sayn-Wittgenstein* v. *Landeshauptmann von Wien* [2010] ECR I-13693), whereby the cross-border link is necessary. In [56] of the *Zambrano* ruling. The CJEU refers to both deprivation and impediment for EU citizens finding themselves in purely internal situations.

national descendant, who is dependent on a Union citizen receiving a steady income, does not have to show that she tried unsuccessfully to find employment in the state of origin in order to obtain a residence permit in Sweden where her mother, an EU national, lived.[87] To impose such a requirement on a dependent family member would contravene the letter (Article 23) and the spirit of Directive 2004/38. And in *O and B* and S and G, the Court held that TCN family members of EU citizens enjoy derived rights of residence when Union citizens return to the Member State of origin following a period of residence in another Member State (*O and B*) as well as when they are travelling to another Member State as frontier workers (*S and G*).[88] All this shows that the world is never closed; mutations happen all the time. In this respect, institutional change, such as the EU citizenship's recent 'high velocity', and evolution are not exceptions in an ever-evolving world, and the intriguing questions concern both the forces that propel such change and its rate, as well as its intended and unintended effects.[89]

But change remains incomplete. The incremental process of institutional co-creation always leaves 'co-creation remainders', that is, unaddressed issues which remain 'in the shadow' because they are denied recognition in time t. These remainders, however, trigger actors' interventions and inspire a search for more comprehensive solutions in the future. The case law discussed earlier shows that children who are EU citizens are no longer appendages of state sovereignty as far as family reunion and their life chances are concerned, and the same applies to adult family members who may be ill and disabled, but adult and fully independent EU citizens are still within the Member States' marked-off enclosure. Migration law has not been 'humanised' yet and the Member States can still envelop peoples' lives into a myriad of oppressive and restrictive provisions which bring about agony and insecurity in their lives. Those who have the resources to cross national borders can find solace in the protective layer of EU legislation, but family reunion has not been recognised as a necessary condition for a stable, peaceful and healthy self, and thus as a good to be shared by all. True, it may well be the case that following the accession of the EU to the ECHR in the future, the two main European legal orders will deliberately converge on an upgraded normative response to the right to family

[87] Case C-423/12 *Flora May Reyes v. Migrationsverket*, Judgment of the Court, 16 January 2014.

[88] Cases C-456/12 and C-457/12, Judgment of the Court (Grand Chamber), 12 March 2014.

[89] These issues are explored in detail in the subsequent chapter.

unity. It should be mentioned, here, that Carlier[90] and Groenendjik[91] have pointed out that the Commission's proposed draft directive on Family Reunification (Dir. 2003/86) included the provision that sedentary Union citizens should be governed by the rules of Community law relating to free movement for the purposes of family reunification. Another possibility might be the future activation of the so-called 'elastic clause' of Article 25 TFEU, resulting in a new explicit template of respect for family life in the TFEU's EU citizenship provisions stating that: The European Union and the Member States shall respect the right of family reunification of all Union citizens.

Critics might argue here that the present environment in Europe is not conducive to enlightened and liberal migration reforms which shift the centre of gravity from state power to liberal norms, and that ultranationalist parties might capitalise on such proposals for reform. Such an observation would undoubtedly be correct. But it will be equally unfortunate if our political life were captured by forces of conservatism. European integration has to make the EU a space conducive to human living. And ordinary human living can only flourish if people are able to experience the care and warmth of their loved ones without the often unnecessary interference of states in their loving relationships.[92]

5.4.3 Cul-de-Sacs

It is certainly counter-intuitive to suggest that institutional change could be associated with decisions that appear to stall it. This is certainly true if one looks at institutional change from a synchronic point of view. In such

[90] Jean-Yves Carlier, 'La libre circulation des personnes dans et vers l'Union europeenne', 4 *Journal de droit europeen* (2013), pp. 103–14.

[91] Kees Groenendijk, 'Reverse Discrimination, Family Reunification and Union Citizens of Immigrant Origin', in E. Guild, C. Gortazar-Rotaeche, and D. Kostakopoulou (eds.), *The Reconceptualisation of EU Citizenship* (Leiden: Brill/Nijhoff, 2014), pp. 169–88.

[92] Compare the International Convention on the Protection of the Rights of All Migrant Workers and Members of their Families adopted by the General Assembly Resolution 45/158 of 18 December 1990. Article 44(2) was phrased rather diplomatically: 'state parties shall take measures that they deem appropriate and that fall within their competence to facilitate the reunification of migrant workers with their "family members"'. For the original text of UN Doc A/C.3/39/WG.1/WP.1 of 14 June 1984, which included a right to family reunification as opposed to recommendation to facilitate family reunification, see Graziano Battistella, 'Migration and Human Rights: The Uneasy but Essential Relationship', in P. de Gichteneire, A. Pecoud and R. Cholewinski (eds.), *Migration and Human Rights: The United Nations Convention on Migrant Workers' Rights* (Cambridge: Cambridge University Press, 2009).

a case, reaching a cul-de-sac is nothing more than a dead end, a limitation. And yet, from a diachronic point of view, a cul-de-sac is also the beginning of change – as is the case in real life, it leads one to reverse and to embark upon a different course of action. It is the decision to 'start afresh', to go back to the 'drawing board' and, with respect to adjudication, to advance a different logic of interpretation that creates the new. In sum, creeping transformations and variations (Sections 5.4.1 and 5.4.2) are also accompanied by deviations in adjacent fields. As Chapter 3 showed more clearly, one must display caution even when revolutionary changes take place or milestone decisions have been made, for institutional realities are complex, that is, non-unified and non-linear.

Distinct and opposing tendencies may occupy the same field and exogenous change or endogenous developments can easily cohabit with endogenous risks. Such contradictions need to be brought out in the open by actors because micro-risks often create macro-limitations[93] and can easily undermine advances that have been made. But at the same time, limitations tend to become stepping-stones for transformations and, as such, they are complementary phases of institutional change. In this section, I wish to highlight this by focusing on the first cases on the application of Article 28(3) of Directive 2004/38 concerning the deportation of long-term residence EU citizens and minors that have reached the Court and the its recent decisions on the grant of social assistance to economically inactive EU citizens.

Although the Member States have always had the power to derogate from the free movement provisions of the Treaty on the grounds of public policy, public security and public health, this power has been circumscribed by the European legislature and the Court.[94] The latter has always insisted on a strict interpretation of the derogations and the full application of the proportionality test. Its preference for a rights-based approach

[93] I have in mind Cover's term 'jurispathic'. According to him, the 'jurisgenerative' is always partnered with the 'jurispathic'; Robert Cover, 'The Supreme Court, 1982 Term – Foreward: Nomos and Narrative', 97(4) *Harvard Law Review* (1983), pp. 4–69.

[94] Council Directive 64/221/EEC on the co-ordination of special measures concerning the movement and residence of foreign nationals which are justified on grounds of public policy, public security or public health [1964] OJ 56 (OJ Special Edition 850/64) 117, which was replaced by the Citizenship Directive. For early accounts, see Durand, 'European Citizenship', p. 3; Evans, 'European Citizenship', p. 674; Ami Barav 'Court Recommendations to Deport and the Free Movement of Workers in EEC Law', 6 *European Law Review* (1981), p. 129; David O'Keeffe, 'Practical Difficulties in the Application of Article 48 of the EEC Treaty', 19 *CML Rev* (1982), p. 35; John Handoll, *Free Movement of Persons in the European Union* (London: John Wiley, 1995), ch. 7.

in this field has precluded the Member States from invoking amorphous threats or abstract risks to public policy or public security,[95] using the expulsion mechanism as a means of deterrence or as a general preventive action,[96] and necessitated concrete verifications that EU citizens pose actual and sufficiently serious threats to the requirements of public policy affecting one of the fundamental interests of society.[97] In this way, it has foiled the 'scapegoating' of EU citizens and the dissemination of xenophobic discourses about 'criminal outsiders'.

The Citizenship Directive (2004/38) has reinforced the system of protection afforded to EU citizens by transplanting aspects of the European Court of Human Rights case law[98] and by establishing a system of graduated protection as regards security of residence. More specifically, permanent residents, that is, those residing for five years in the host Member State, can be deported only 'on serious grounds of public policy or public security' (Article 28(2) of Directive 2004/38), while permanent resident EU citizens for the previous ten years and minors can only be ordered to leave on 'imperative grounds of public policy' (Article 28(3) of Directive 2004/38). The rationale behind this graduated system of protection is that the longer one's residence and thus entanglement with the host society is, the more difficult it becomes to justify forced uprootedness and the ensuing harm caused to him or her and his or her family.

It is true that the terms 'public policy or public security' (Article 28(2)) and 'imperative grounds of public policy' do not have a uniform EU law meaning; they are 'national law concepts' subject 'to some control by the EU institutions'.[99] It is equally true, however, that the Commission has provided guidance on the interpretations of these terms by stating that:

> [T]he Member States need to make a clear distinction between public policy and public security. The latter cannot be covered by the former. Public

[95] Case 36/75 *Rutili* v. *Minister of the Interior* [1975] ECR 1219; Case 30/77 *R* v. *Bouchereau* [1977] ECR 1999.

[96] *Rutili* [29]; Case C-441/02 *Commission* v. *Federal Republic of Germany* [2006] ECR I-3449; Case C-524/06 *Heinz Huber* v. *Bundesrepublik Deutschland* [2008] ECR I-9705. See also Article 27(2) of the Citizenship Directive.

[97] *R* v. *Bouchereau* (Case 30/77) [1977] ECR 1999.

[98] Article 28(1) of the Citizenship Directive).

[99] Case C-268/99 *Aldona Malgorzat Jany* v. *Ministre de l'Interieur* [1975] ECR I-8615; Case C-430/10 *Hristo Gaydarov* (ECJ, 17 November 2011) [32]. I discussed this in 'European Union Citizenship: Enduring Patterns and Evolving Norms' (EUSA 12th Biennial International Conference, Boston, MA, 3–5 March 2011) as well as in 'When EU Citizens become Foreigners' (2nd Jean Monnet Workshop on 'The Reconceptualisation of EU Citizenship', Universidad Pontificia Comillas, Madrid, 7–8 October 2012).

security is generally interpreted to cover both internal and external security along the lines of preserving the integrity of the territory of a Member State and its institutions.[100]

But this guidance has not been followed by the Court in the first two cases on the interpretation of the term 'imperative grounds of public security' under Article 28(3) of the Directive, namely, *Tsakouridis* and *PI*.[101]

Both Tsakouridis and PI, Greek and Italian nationals, respectively, had lived in Germany for more than Twenty years. In fact, Mr Tsakouridis was born in Germany and went to school there. In his mid-twenties, he spent a few months in Greece running a crepe hall in Rhodes where he was eventually arrested for drug dealing as part of a criminal gang. He was transferred to Germany and the Regional Court in Stuttgart sentenced him to imprisonment of six years and six months, while the regional administration threatened him with expulsion to Greece. Mr Tsakouridis challenged this decision and the Administrative Court annulled the expulsion decision because, among other considerations, he had lived to Germany for more than ten years and thus his situation fell within the scope of Article 28(3) and therefore he did not constitute a major threat to the external or internal security of the German state. The Land Baden-Wurttemberg appealed against this decision. When the question concerning the meaning of the notion 'imperative grounds of public security' reached the Court, the latter held that the term does not exclude domestic criminal law matters and that the fight against crime in connection with dealing in narcotics as part of an organised group can fall within the ambit of Article 28(3) of Directive 2004/38.[102]

What is problematic about this judgment is that it renders the distinction between the second and the third paragraphs of Article 28 inexact, as national authorities contemplating expulsion decisions need not be concerned about the fact that public security threats are different from public policy threats or public order disturbances, in that they pose a threat to the existence of a Member State or its institutions, or the survival of the

[100] European Commission, 'On guidance for better transposition and application of Directive 2004/38/EC on the right of citizens of the Union and their family members to move and reside freely within the territory of the Member States (Communication)' COM(2009) 313 final, 10.

[101] Case C-145/09 *Land Baden-Wurttemberg* v. *Panagiotis Tsakouridis* [2010] ECR I-11979; and Case C-348/09 *PI* v. *Oberburgermeisterin der Stadt Remscheid* (ECJ, 22 May 2012).

[102] Compare also A. G. Bot's conclusion of his Opinion on *Tsakouridis* delivered on 8 June 2010 [133].

population is threatened.[103] Instead, any serious form of criminality can lead to the expulsion of EU citizens even though, like Tsakouridis, they may have spent their whole lives on the territory of the Member State concerned. No careful consideration was given to the strong bonds that individuals have formed in the state of residence[104] or to the fact that national criminal justice systems provide ample scope for the punishment of undesirable conduct without the need of transforming EU citizens into criminal aliens who have no right to remain there.[105] After all, the rationale of punishment is to allow individuals to pay their debt to society which has been harmed by their offensive behaviour, not to be extricated from it.

Following *Tsakouridis*, the Court's judgment in *PI* raised similar questions about the security of residence of EU citizens and increased concerns that the status of EU citizenship can become a meaningless normative category in the deportation field. PI had lived in Germany since 1987, and in 2006 he was sentenced to a term of imprisonment of seven years and six months for the sexual abuse, sexual coercion and rape of his fourteen-year-old stepdaughter. He is due to complete his sentence on 9 July 2013, but an immediately enforceable expulsion order was served in May 2008. Advocate General Bot's Opinion referred to what he termed 'genuine integration' considerations and a 'presumption of integration' on the part of EU citizens which is rebuttable.[106] The Court did not follow the 'presumption of integration' argument, but it went on to rule that 'it is open to the Member States to regard certain criminal offences ... [as] posing a direct threat to the calm and physical security of the population' and thus falling within the ambit of Article 28(3), 'as long as the manner in which such offences were committed discloses particularly serious characteristics, which is a matter for the referring court to determine on the basis of an individual examination of a specific case before it'.[107] In other words, in the light of these two judgments, not only does Article 28(3) of Directive 2004/34 become a gradation of Article 28(2) – a development that is not consonant with the intentions of the drafters of the Citizenship Directive and the Commission's written guidance on the proper interpretation of

[103] European Commission, 10.

[104] See recital 24 of the Citizenship Directive. Compare also A. G. Bot's Opinion (n 95) [45].

[105] Kostakopoulou, 'When EU Citizens become Foreigners'.

[106] A. G. Bot, Opinion on Case C-348/09 *PI* v. *Oberburgermeisterin der Stadt Remscheid*, delivered on 6 March 2012. For commentary, see Loic Azoulai and Stephen Coutts, 'Restricting Union Citizens' Residence Rights on Grounds of Public Security. Where Union Citizenship and the AFSJ Meet: PI', 50 *CML Rev* (2013), p. 553.

[107] *PI* [33].

its provisions,[108] but the Member States are given the discretion to place a wide range of criminal offences within the ambit of public security and to defend the seriousness of the characteristics they entail before their national courts. Instead of focusing on the type of security threat itself, they shift the focus on to 'the security constellation' accompanying the offending conduct, thereby being empowered to designate certain crimes as particularly threatening in the light of 'the particular values' of their national legal orders which, according to the Court, cannot be uniform across the EU.[109]

The leeway given to the national authorities in this area undermines the European legislature's intention to guarantee the EU citizens' increased security of residence in the host Member State. In *Onuekwere* and *M. G.*,[110] the Court ruled that periods in prison cannot count towards the acquisition of permanent residence or the enhanced protection of Article 28(3) and that the right to permanent residence could not be based on purely formal considerations such as the time physically spent in a member state's territory, but must also take into account 'qualitative elements, relating to the level of integration in the host member state' (para. 25). In practice, this means that, in the context of that overall assessment, not only should the relevant consideration of one's imprisonment be considered, but national authorities may also take into account other relevant facts relating to the person concerned, such as, for example, that an individual had resided in the host Member State during the ten years prior to imprisonment. Although the Court noted that criminal offences committed by an EU citizen show a lack of respect for 'the values expressed by the society of the host Member State in its criminal law' (para. 26), both decisions are, nonetheless, reflective of the aim underpinning the Citizenship Directive and in line with the Commission's guidance on the implementation of its provisions (European Commission, 2009).

A balance thus needs to be struck between the enhancement of EU citizenship, which is premised on individuals' participation in societal interactions and their living realities, and security. The fundamental status of EU citizenship can easily be undermined by the Member States' attempts to 'securitise' intra-EU mobility and to turn EU citizens into foreigners. In fact, as the landscape is changing in Europe, one cannot discount the

[108] Above n 100.

[109] *PI* [21] and [29].

[110] Case C-378/12, *Onuekwere* [2014] and Case C-400/12, *M. G.* [2014], Judgment of the Court, 16 January 2014.

possibility that the Court might find it more difficult to maintain the fundamental status of EU citizenship and to resist the encroaching of the sociopolitical space that has been created by it by national narratives on migration control and societal security in the future. It remains to be seen how the Court will avoid such a cul-de-sac in this domain and will resist the demotion of EU citizenship from a fundamental status to a mere 'phenomenology' of citizenship.

Another related cul-de-sac concerns the application of the principle of equal treatment to citizens who are economically inactive. Although the mobility of the latter has always been conditioned on the possession of sufficient resources so as 'not to become a burden on the welfare system of the host Member State'[111] and of health insurance, at the turn of the twentieth century the Court attempted to loosen the connection between EU citizenship and socio-economic status. The cases discussed in the previous chapter, including *Grzelczyk*,[112] illustrated its rationale in ruling that a 'certain degree of financial solidarity' might be required among the Member States.[113] But the economic crisis in Europe, coupled with an anti-migrant rhetoric articulated by right-wing parties in several European states and the United Kingdom's explicit commitment to reducing the social benefits granted to EU citizens,[114] led the Court to state unequivocally that Article 24 of Directive 2004/38 does not oblige the Member States to confer social assistance on persons other than those engaged in gainful activity.[115] Ms Dano and her son, both Romanian nationals, had been living in the apartment of Ms Dano's sister who was providing for them materially, but she had never worked in Germany or sought employment there. When she applied for a jobseeker's benefit, a special non-contributory cash benefit, her application was declined by Jobcenter Leipzing. Ms Dano's challenge of this decision before the Socialgericht Leipzing and the referral of preliminary ruling questions to the Court did not yield a positive outcome.

[111] Article 7(1)(b) Directive 2004/38.

[112] Case C-184/99, *Grzelczyk* [2001] ECR I-2691.

[113] Ibid., para. 44.

[114] The former British Prime Minister, Mr Cameron, has explicitly noted his commitment to reducing 'the magnetic pull of the UK benefits system'; 'We are building an immigration system that puts Britain first. We will close bogus colleges, cut benefits to jobless arrivals and stop advertising jobs abroad', *The Telegraph*, 28 July 2014.

[115] Case C-333/13, *Elisabeta Dano and Florin Dano* v. *Jobcenter Leipzing*, Judgment of the Court of 11 November 2014. See Kay Hailbronner, 'Union Citizenship and Access to Social Benefits', 42 *CMLRev* (2005), pp. 1247–58; Daniel Thym, 'The Elusive Limits of Solidarity: Residence Rights of and Social Benefits for Economically Inactive Union Citizens', 52 *CMLRev* (2015), pp. 17–50.

The climate within which the European judiciary operated in 2014 led the Grand Chamber to signal that the EU mobility regime does not condone 'benefit tourism'.[116] On 15 September 2015, the Grand Chamber ruled that Germany lawfully denied certain social assistance benefits to four Swedish nationals, Ms Alimanovic and her three children, who were born in Germany, who had only temporary employment for less than a year and were not looking for employment.[117] The personal circumstances of the family, including the fact that Ms Alimanovic was the primary carer of two minors who had the right to education under Article 10 of Regulation 492/2011, were not addressed by the Court. An awareness of national sensitivities and the political implications of its decision on the availability of welfare assistance to vulnerable citizens of other Member States led it to rule that, following six months of residence as a jobseeker, the Member States could automatically exclude a Union citizen from access to social assistance benefits.[118] On 25 February 2016, the Court reiterated this by ruling that an economically inactive citizen can be automatically excluded from entitlement to social assistance[119] during the first three months of residence in the host Member State.[120] Unlike its previous case law, the Court's formalist reasoning in *Dano*, *Alimanovic* and *Garcia-Nieto* indicated that the new economic and political landscape associated with strong Euroscepticism in the United Kingdom and elsewhere in Europe left little room for the assessment of the personal circumstances of the Union citizen and for the grant of transnational financial solidarity. Once again, the variables of time-space and discourse led the Court to decisions that were out of step with its previous dynamic and rights-enhancing case law.

5.5 Conclusion

By examining the interconnections among agency, institutions and discourse in specific spatio-temporal environments, the foregoing discussion shed light onto the evolving trajectory of EU citizenship and the constraints and possibilities that have accompanied its evolution. In this

116 See paras. 78 and 79, Case C-333/13, *Dano*.

117 Case C-67/14, *Jobcenter Berlin Neukolln v. Nazifa Alimanovic and Others*, Judgment of the Court of 15 September 2015.

118 Ibid., paras. 61 and 62.

119 This includes certain special non-contributory cash benefits within the meaning of Article 70(2) of Regulation No. 883/2004 which also constitute social assistance within the meaning of Article 24(2) of Directive 2004/38.

120 Case C-299/14, *Vestische Arbeit Jobcenter Kreis Recklinghausen v. Jovanna Garcia-Nieto and Others*, Judgment of the Court of 25 February 2016.

non-linear path of connected events, normative aspirations and institutionalised rules, one finds dynamic patterns, complex adaptations, step changes, norm creation and contradictions. There have been no institutional disequilibria. Moving from 'what exists' to 'what may be' and to 'what ought to be', that is, devising legal provisions and institutional openings that make a difference to the concrete lives of people (be they workers, work-seekers, non-active economic actors, EU citizens exercising their mobility rights and, following *Rottmann* and *Zambrano*, non-movers), has essentially been a tektology; a genuine process of institutional co-creation. In this journey of the institutional development of EU citizenship, the combined efforts of so many institutional and ordinary actors have resulted in: (a) positing normative templates; (b) relativising Member States' sovereign prerogatives; (c) generating respect for principles that advance human life and the growth of associated action; and (d) prioritising equal treatment irrespective of nationality in as many spheres of life as possible. True, co-creation's scope, duration and quality are contingent and could thus be reversible. Amidst contingency and indeterminacy, however, we can easily discern the transformation of practices into norms and the growth of EU citizenship. Noticeable too is the existence of an evolution momentum, in the sense of guaranteeing rights, notwithstanding the absence of a clearly defined and finite goal.

However, this does not mean that the evolution momentum cannot be called into question. Institutional evolution does not follow well-defined trajectories. The sovereign debt crisis in the Eurozone has triggered a number of unpredictable developments as well as a search for formulae for macroeconomic stability and for better fiscal regulation. As austerity programmes take hold in several European countries and the disquietness of Europe's populations becomes evident in public arenas, it is only natural that individuals and political actors wonder about the present and future of EU citizenship, particularly since generalised anxiety makes them believe that there are more problems and fewer solutions. Yet, the visible scene cannot subdue our sense of relief since we are not confronted with an historical crisis:[121] our convictions, our principles, our sense of political morality and our desire for common sense solutions to policy dilemmas remain unaffected. So while the debate about how to make undisciplined public expenditures more controllable and sustainable continues in a lively way and the pendulum is swinging towards the direction of a generalised

[121] For the definition of an historical crisis, see Jose Ortega y Gasset, *Man and Crisis* (Ruskin House: George Allen and Unwin Ltd, 1958), pp. 85–6.

reform, the importance of making EU citizenship responsive to citizens' everyday lives remains undiminished.

But this view is no longer universally shared. On 23 June 2016 the outcome of the referendum on the United Kingdom's continued membership and the ensuing activation of Article 50 TFEU by the UK Government on 29 March 2017 brought forth the questioning, and thus, the fragmentation, of the supranational legal and political design. Without warning, EU citizens found themselves in a transition from recognized subjects of EU law to objects of governmental negotiations and discussions between the EU and the UK Government. EU citizens living permanently in the United Kingdom and UK nationals living in the EU risk losing their EU law rights to permanent residence and equal treatment, while UK nationals will lose their EU citizenship status when the United Kingdom's withdrawal agreement enters into force. The latter will be third country nationals while the former will be EU citizens living in a third country, if an EEA or EEA-like agreement is ruled out by the United Kingdom. Clearly, institutional change is not something that simply happens, but, in this case, change takes the form of a regression or the reversal of institutional choice. Agents, or to be more precise, political elites opposing the institutional development of the European Union, are committed to changing institutional realities and, in the light of the earlier discussion on the interconnected spheres, also political and human realities. How the *connexio rerum* model could help us understand Brexit and the unfolding of macro-political institutional change will be explored in the subsequent chapter.

6

From Law, Policies and Norms to European Integration: Supranationalism Contested

In the previous chapter the discussion focused on the establishment and evolution of the EU citizenship norm and its progressive embedment in concrete legal rules and institutions at the European Union and national levels. The Court of Justice's interventions triggered changes in policies and administrative practices which impact on EU citizens' daily lives in the Member States of residence and of origin. These changes transformed EU citizenship into a fundamental status and changed the perceptions, including the self-perceptions, of EU citizens. Institutional change has been incremental, evolutionary and transformative (as discussed in Chapter 3).

In this chapter, I would like to shift the focus from EU citizenship norms, policies and politics to the process of European integration, and to examine fundamental contestations of supranationalism as exemplified by the Brexit outcome of the EU referendum of 23 June 2016 in the United Kingdom. This focus will enable us to examine the opposite direction of institutional change, namely, change as reversal or regression, and the extent to which the institutional constructivist model (Part I) allows us to understand Brexit and the normalisation of a different set of ideas which affirm the primacy of the national and seek to untie the United Kingdom from the entangled European space of government and governance.

Inventiveness in politics is not new,[1] but the Brexit outcome of the referendum on the United Kingdom's continued membership of the EU on the 23 June 2016 made the fragmentation of the EU both thinkable and real. This is an unprecedented development in the process of European

[1] Nikolas Rose, 'Inventiveness in Politics', 28(3) *Economy and Society* (1999), pp. 467–93. Compare, here, the Schuman Declaration (9 May 1950) which gave birth to European integration: 'Europe will not be made all at once, or according to a single plan. It will be built through concrete achievements which first create a de facto solidarity'; The Schuman Declaration, https://europa.eu/european-union/about-eu/symbols/europe.../schuman-declaration_en.

unification; the latter has seen pauses but no retreats.[2] This development tests theories of European integration as well. Premised on an assumed willingness on the part of the Member States to participate in transgovernmental or supranational arrangements, their theoretical repertoire has explained intergovernmental dissent, stagnation, spill backs, incrementalism, differentiated integration and so on. But adjustments are needed in order to account for the British 'no to Europe' and the muscular discourse on the repatriation of powers from the EU to the Member States in the present socio-political and economic conjuncture.

In this chapter, I examine the withdrawal of the United Kingdom from the European Union through the lens of European integration theories and argue that an attention to the interplay of situated agency, discourse, time and space (*Connexio Rerum*) could explain the British project of political fission. By unravelling the origins of the British Eurosceptic opposition to Europe I elaborate on the role of agency-related factors, discourse and time in explaining a fundamental contestation of supranationalism. The concluding remarks are contained in the last section of the chapter.

6.1 Testing, and Stretching, Theorising about European Integration

The previous chapters showed the rich and sophisticated research activity surrounding the study of European integration and EU citizenship.[3] European integration has been one of the most novel and complex political experiments in the world over the last one hundred years and, naturally, the scene of research ideas remains dynamic and constantly enriched.[4] The three 'classical' theories of European integration and their various modulations, namely intergovernmentalism/liberal intergovernmentalism,[5]

[2] Article 50 TEU has never before been activated.

[3] The discussion here is a substantially expanded version of certain arguments I made in 'What Fractures Political Unions? Failed Federations, Brexit and the Importance of Political Commitment', 42(3) *European Law Review* (2017), pp. 339–52.

[4] For an overview of the wide-ranging theoretical perspectives, see Ben Rosamond, *Theories of European Integration* (Houndmills: Palgrave Macmillan, 2000); Mark Pollack, 'Theorising the European Union: International Organisation, Domestic Polity or Experiment in New Governance?', 8 *Annual Review of Political Science* (2005), pp. 357–98; Sabine Saurugger, *Theoretical Approaches to European Integration* (Houndmills: Palgrave Macmillan, 2013).

[5] See Andrew Moravcsik, *The Choice for Europe: Social Purpose and State Power from Messina to Maastricht* (Ithaca, NY: Cornell University Press, 1998).

federalism,[6] functionalism/neofunctionalism,[7] have been complemented by what may be called the 'fourth force' in European integration theorising, that is, the coalescence of various perspectives and approaches that developed mainly in the 1990s, and coincided with the 'political turn' of the EU.[8] These are multilevel governance, comparative politics, policy-making approaches, policy networks and the regulatory paradigm, new institutionalism, constructivism and actor-network and practice theories.[9] More recently, 'new intergovernmentalism' seeks to explain the process of European integration in the post-Maastricht era and argues that the multiplication of agencies since Maastricht coupled with the emphasis on consensus-seeking in the European Council show the demise of supranationalism.[10]

It is true to say that the 'older' theories emerged, and developed, as a result of looking at European integration and the European Community/

[6] Michael Burgess and Alain-G. Gagnon (eds.), *Comparative Federalism and Federation: Competing Traditions and Future Directions* (Hemel Hempstead: Harvester Wheatsheaf, 1993).

[7] David Mitrany, 'The Functional Approach to World Organisation', 24(3) *International Affairs* (1948), pp. 350–63. Neofunctionalism transcended the functionalist distinction between technical and political processes and pioneered the notion of the spill-over effect of integration; Ernst Haas, *The Uniting of Europe: Political, Social and Economic Forces 1950–7* (Stanford, CA: Stanford University Press, 1958). Both Haas and Schmitter enriched the model by developing the concepts of spill-back, spill-around and muddle-about; Philippe C. Schmitter, 'Three Neo-Functional Hypotheses about European Integration', 23(1) *International Organisation* (1969), pp. 161–6.

[8] Rosamond, *Theories of European Integration*, has used the phrase "theorising the 'New Europe'"; see ch. 5 at p. 98.

[9] John Peterson and Elizabeth Bomberg, *Decision-Making in the European Union* (Basingstoke: Macmillan, 1999); Rod Rhodes, 'The New Governance: Governing without Government', 44(4) *Political Studies* (1996), pp. 652–67; Thomas Christiansen, Knud Erik Jorgensen, and Antje Wiener, *The Social Construction of Europe* (London: Sage, 2001); Joseph Jupille, James A. Caporaso, and Jeffrey T. Checkel, 'Integrating Institutions: Rationalism, Constructivism and the Study of the European Union', 36(1) *Comparative Political Studies* (2003), pp. 7–40; Giadomenico Majone, 'The Rise of the Regulatory State in Europe', 17(3) *West European Politics* (1994), pp, 77–101; Christian Bueger and Jan Stockbruegger, 'Actor-Network theory: Objects, Actants, Networks and Narratives', in Daniel R. McCarthy (eds.), *Technology and World Politics: An Introduction* (Abingdon: Routledge, 2016); Rebecca Adler-Nissen and Kristoffer Kropp, 'A Sociology of Knowledge Approach to European Integration: Four Analytical Principles', 37(2) *Journal of European Integration* (2015), pp. 155–73; Adler-Nissen, 'Towards a Practice Turn in EU Studies', pp. 87–103.

[10] Uwe Puetter, 'Europe's Deliberative Intergovernmentalism: The Role of the Council and the European Council in EU Economic Governance', 19(2) *Journal of European Public Policy* (2012), pp. 161–78; Christopher J. Bickerton, Dermot Hodson and Uwe Puetter (eds), *The New Intergovernmentalism: States and Supranational Actors in the Post-Maastricht Era* (Oxford: Oxford University Press, 2015).

the European Union from the outside in. They were keen to depict centres of power, their location and a hierarchy, and focused on what may be called 'two level games'. As a result, they remained much more embedded into the nation-state's vocabulary and assumptions. In comparison, the fourth force developed as a result of looking at the former from the inside out. It sees the EU on more heterarchical and acentric terms and tends to explore multiple and complex games not only vertically, that is between the EU and the member states, but also horizontally at all levels and diagonally. 'New' theorising about the European Union has been more confident in terms of pulling back from statist perspectives.[11] This was due to both the consolidation of globalisation since the late 1980s and the maturation of the EU as a Union and a polity having its own citizenship.

Accordingly, one discerns that 'old' theories commence with the 'vocabulary of the given', that is, a point of departure (their 'alpha') tangled with political commitments and ideological views. Quite often the original presuppositions are concealed or taken as natural and unproblematic assumptions. This cannot but exert a limiting effect on their hypotheses and makes the propositions either selective or not reflexive enough. As a consequence, these approaches are characterised by dichotomic thinking, such as intergovernmentalism versus supranationalism and either/or dilemmas such as 'more' or 'less' 'Europe' and the advantages or disadvantages of competence rebalancing exercises. In contrast, the 'fourth force' appears to be more sceptical about building a theoretical framework on basic presuppositions and is rather hesitant in (or explicitly opposed to) positing an ultimate end. Although scepticism about the latter may not necessarily stem from deep doctrinal objections, it is true that the strands of the 'fourth force' paradigm tend to be less interested in dichotomies and more interested in studying the connectivity among the various layers of governance, synergies, joined up thinking and forms of reflexive governance. This may explain, at least partially, why 'fourth force' scholars are less thrilled by what may be called 'big problems', such as giving a determinate and final answer to questions such as 'who governs in the EU?', 'what is the state of the state?', 'what is the nature of the EU?' or 'to what extent is the EU a mirror image or a positive counter-image of the nation-state?'. Instead of viewing the EU as a monolithic system (as either a tool or an

[11] Kostakopoulou, 'Towards a Theory of Constructive Citizenship in Europe', pp. 337–58; Robert Howse and Kalypso Nicolaidis, 'Democracy without Sovereignty: The Global Vocation of Political Ethics', in T. Broude and Y. Shany (eds.), *The Shifting Allocation of Authority in International Law* (Oxford: Hart, 2008).

agent), they see it as an interconnected network of governance in which distinct centres of power co-exist and antagonise each other.

Finally, the older paradigms tend to view European integration as a process leading to an end state, be this a federal state or a weak confederation providing support to, or re-invigorating, the nation state or a functional bureaucratic organisation meeting peoples' needs. In this respect, the 'unknown future' is not only imagined, but it is also given a concrete institutional form. However, by so doing, that is, by positing an omega, not only is the process of European integration weakly altered by unfolding developments, but it also becomes sandwiched between the two decisive moments, the alpha and the omega (Table 6.1).

The Brexit referendum outcome brought about the reality of a break-up of the European Union. The 'unthinkable' and 'unplanned for' has taken place. Using the existing theoretical lenses in order to account for this unexpected and unprecedented development is a challenging exercise. Intergovernmentalism and liberal intergovernmentalism could accommodate this development within their state-centric and Member State control paradigm, but even these theories are built on the assumption that Member States wish to co-operate and to reduce transaction costs within a broader political framework of conferred (or pooled) powers. New intergovernmentalism, on the other hand, focuses on relations and institutional actors at the EU level thereby leaving out the national level.

Similarly, the new theories of European integration might find it difficult to account for the British 'no to Europe'. They are excellent at highlighting the existence of systems in parallel accomplishing tasks in independent or interdependent jurisdictional areas and the synergy between the EU's constituent units and its institutions. They can account for Europeanisation or 'impact integration', that is the simultaneous changes and transformations at the EU and national levels (Table 6.1), but cannot explain de-Europeanisation easily. It is true that they have been particularly convincing in placing peak events or key moments of integration alongside the ordinary (in between Treaty revisions) process of law and policy-making[12] and judicial adjudication. The advantages of this line of reasoning are evident in studies concerning the Europeanisation of national legislation,

[12] More attention to the micro-level and the everyday experiences of European citizens is paid by recent sociological literature: Adrian Favell and Virgine Guirandon, *Sociology of the European Union* (Houndmills: Palgrave, 2011); Juan Diez Mendrano, 'The Public Sphere and the European Union's Political Identity', in Jeffrey T. Checkel and Peter J. Katzenstein (eds.), *European Identity* (New York: Cambridge University Press, 2009).

Table 6.1. *'Old' and 'New' Theorising about European Integration*

Theories	Lens	'Alpha' (Premise)	'Omega' (End-point)	Institutional change
Inter-governmentalism/liberal inter-governmentalism Federalism Functionalism/neofunctionalism	• Looking at European integration and the EU from the outside in • Hierarchic • Focus on two-level games • State-centric	• The 'vocabulary of the given' • Dichotomous	• Self-unfolding destiny	• Footnote to an overall theoretical blueprint or frame • Focus on outcomes and outputs
The 'fourth force' (multilevel governance, comparative politics, policy-making approaches, policy networks and the regulatory paradigm, new institutionalism and constructivism)	• Looking at EU from the inside out • Heterarchical • Complex games • Pulling back from statist perspectives	• Open, tentative • Reflexive	• Experimental	• Studying 'impact integration': simultaneous changes and transformations at the EU and national levels • Focus on process • Temporal dimension of change

that is, its adaptation to the European Union laws and policies,[13] in reflexive governance approaches associated with policy making in the EU, the emphasis on the constructive effect of EU institutions, policies and norms on national polities,[14] the socialisation of political actors[15] and in research on the formation of elite identities.[16] But the decisive effects of contingent events and happenings, such as Brexit, which may unfold from within the EU, or develop from outside, without any prior warning cannot be neatly mapped onto them.

Politics is marked by uncertainty[17] and time often disrupts efforts to establish a theoretical framework that is geared towards predicting the future and understanding change in the present. Engaging with competence balances, solving problems, filling policy gaps, giving Member States the needed space for adapting to new exigencies and the new environment and for the cultivation of mutual trust and policy experience cannot be understood without a reference to random change, motion and unfixity. In this respect, I believe that *connexio rerum* can offer valuable insights in understanding the recent centrifugalism and fission in the European Union. This is because it provides a more process-oriented and contextual perspective that places actors' concrete endeavours within time and discursive matrixes influencing how and what they decide and do. Let us examine this with respect to the Brexit project.

6.2 The Brexit Process and Project

The absence of a clear political and ideological commitment to the European Union has been an enduring feature of the British Conservative Party's Eurosceptic wing. Nationalism coupled with the belief that the

[13] Tanja A. Börzel and Thomas Risse, 'Conceptualising the Domestic Impact of Europe' in Keith Featherstone and Claudio M. Radaelli (eds.), *The Politics of Europeanisation* (Oxford: Oxford University Press, 2003); Maria Green Cowles, James A. Caporaso, and Thomas Risse-Kappen (eds.), *Transforming Europe: Europeanisation and Domestic Change* (Ithaca, NY: Cornell University Press, 2001).

[14] Ibid.

[15] Christiansen, Jorgensen, and Wiener, *The Social Construction of Europe*.

[16] Liesbet Hooghe, 'Several Roads Lead to International Norms, but Few via International Socialization: A Case Study of the European Commission', 59(4) *International Organization* (2005), pp. 861–98; Jeffrey T. Checkel, *International Institutions and Socialisation in Europe* (Cambridge: Cambridge University Press, 2007).

[17] Kenneth Walthz has observed that theories cannot remove the uncertainty of politics, but only help us to comprehend it; 'Realist Thought and Neorealist Theory', in Charles W. Kegley (ed.), *Controversies in International Relations Theory: Realism and the Neoliberal Challenge* (New York: St Martin's Press, 1995).

'dominocracy' of domestic executives should not be challenged or compromised by political and judicial decision-making above or beyond the nation-state, have characterised its opposition to the European unification project for decades. In the past, these 'winds of doctrine'[18] blew at the fringes of the British political landscape. The demise of the Labour Party's hold on political power opened the way for their influencing of the intellectual temper of the British political scene. And the economic crisis and the austerity policies coupled with increased opposition to migration from the new Eastern European member states facilitated the reception of such ideas by the larger population. In what follows, I wish to shed light onto the roots of the 'Let's take back control' opposition to Europe. The ideational anchoring of British Euroscepticism shows the persisting absence of a political commitment to the vision of an integrated Europe.

As the 1991 Intergovernmental Conference was negotiating the Treaty on European Union (in force on 1 November 1993), Conservative Eurosceptics felt compelled to defend British national sovereignty against a possible federal scenario. They argued that the morphing of the European Community into a European Union was based on the false assumption that the nation-state had no future in Europe. They believed that both the state, as a primary organisational concept, and British sovereignty were at risk and thus had to be defended. These beliefs were mandated by a particular way of viewing developments in Europe.

In fact, Baroness Thatcher's successor, Sir John Major, did not preside over a united Conservative party.[19] The entry into force of the Treaty on European Union (the so-called Maastricht Treaty) was fuelling anxieties about the future of statehood in an integrated Europe. In late 1994, nine Conservative backbenchers defied Sir Major's policy on fishing rights in the House of Commons and eight of them were deprived of the party whip in January 1995. Refusing to accept this predicament, the Euro-rebels produced an eight-point policy paper that called for the renegotiation of Britain's relationship with the European Union. In interviews and the media, they argued that further European integration threatened the 'survival' of the United Kingdom and that a different relationship with the EU based on free trade and friendship was needed.

Their ideology was distinctly nationalist and intergovernmentalist. The limitations imposed on 'national sovereignty' by the EU were perceived

[18] This term is borrowed from G. Santayana, *Winds of Doctrine: Studies in Contemporary Opinion* (New York: Charles Scribner's Sons, 1913).

[19] The discussion here draws on a Lecture I delivered at Durham University in February 2015.

to result in the weakening of the national community of belonging and identity. The whipless Euro-rebels thus articulated a manifesto which demanded a reduced role for Britain in Europe. In the four page document they produced, they demanded the end of the Common Agricultural and Fisheries policies, the end to the Court of Justice's activism, a right to ban the export of live animals, an issue that was topical at that time, the UK's opt out from the European Monetary Union and the Common Foreign and Security policies and the abolition of the directly elected European Parliament. In its place, they suggested an assembly consisting of members of national parliaments nominated by the Member States. They also demanded the curtailment of the EU budget.

Although Sir Teddy Taylor, the most senior of the rebels, was insisting that their manifesto was not a direct challenge to the Government's policy on Europe, in reality their discourse was procuring a schism in the Conservative Party.[20] Their 'mission statement' to 'defend a sense of country' and their calls for the repatriation of decision-making from 'unaccountable and undemocratic foreign institutions' were influencing moderate Conservatives and public opinion. In its Editorial, *The Guardian* criticised those statements: 'These policies are not Euroscepticism. They are Europhobia. They are anti-Europe in every way. They remove any meaning or substance from membership of the European Union'. And it continued: 'An old-fashioned anti-European agenda like this ought not to be serious politics in the 1990s ... The Europhobes have succeeded and are succeeding in dragging the Prime Minister, his party and thus the country even further off base'.[21]

The Prime Minister could not ignore the Euro-rebels' discourse. Their arguments and strategies were creating new inter-subjectively shared meanings about the EU's domination of the United Kingdom. Their call for the 'restoration' of British sovereignty by loosening the ties with the European Union, in effect, implied the questioning of the European Union acquis and the dissolution of the UK's legal and political obligations. In such a discourse there was little appreciation for the institutional layering and the legal and procedural interweaving that had taken place during the European integration process. Preparations for the 1996 Intergovernmental Conference, which culminated in the Treaty of Amsterdam (in force on 1 May 1999), had commenced and, in an attempt to appease the Euro-rebels

[20] Hugo Young, 'Grey Clouds Lift to Reveal Major's Bleak Euro-Vision', *The Guardian*, 19 January 1995.

[21] *The Guardian*, Editorial, 20 January 1995.

and to foreclose the possibility of a referendum on EU membership, he declared publicly that the United Kingdom would not join the single currency and that he would not agree to any further extension of qualified majority voting in the Council of Ministers. His Defence Secretary, Sir Malcolm Rifkind, delivered a speech in Brussels emphasising that the Union is a Union of nation-states, while Sir Major was stating internally that there was no need for a referendum because he would not accept any 'constitutional changes' during the negotiations for the amendment of the Treaties. Pro-European members of the Cabinet were marginalised and Lord Douglas Hurd, who had produced a paper on the 1996 IGC and had criticised the Euro-rebels' manifesto, was eventually forced to retire from the Cabinet in the summer. All this did not prevent Sir James Goldsmith to launch a new party, the Referendum Party. The Party had a single aim, namely, the enactment of a Referendum Bill. Sir Goldsmith stated that as soon as the Bill was enacted, the members would resign their seat and the party would dissolve itself.

The Euro-rebels and Sir James Goldsmith continued to call for an EU membership referendum in subsequent years. The same pressures that John Major encountered in 1995, Mr Cameron encountered a decade later. Unable to appease his Euro-sceptic backbenchers, Mr Cameron entertained the idea of an EU membership referendum in 2010. In January 2013, he pledged a referendum on the United Kingdom's continued membership of the EU if the Conservatives won the 2015 election. He subsequently sought a 'New Deal for the UK', which resembled the Euro-rebels' 1995 manifesto. The only major difference was the replacement of the dissatisfaction with the Common Agricultural Policies with the EU free movement regime.

In his letter to the President of the European Council (10 November 2015), Mr Donald Tusk, Mr Cameron outlined the British demands for a renegotiated EU membership.[22] Free movement rules and the Court's judicial activism remained key concerns for the Government, in addition to affirming the UK's opt-out from the Eurozone and enhancing competitiveness. The United Kingdom also sought the amendment of the Treaty's reference to 'an ever closer Union', an enhanced role for national parliaments which would involve a collective national parliamentary veto of EU legislative proposals, less 'Europe' in line with the principle of subsidiarity and the continuation of the UK's opt-outs from justice and home affair issues. Concerning the free movement of EU citizens (it is noteworthy that the title used

[22] The British Prime Minister's letter to the President of the European Council, Mr Donald Tusk, 10 November 2015; www.gov.uk/government/publications/eu-reform-pms-letter-to-president-of-the-european-council-donald-tusk, accessed on 18 March 2016.

was not 'internal mobility', but 'immigration'), Mr Cameron requested extended transitional arrangements for future participating countries, tackling the alleged abuse of free movement provisions and taming the activism of the Court of Justice in this policy area. The most controversial proposal was the postponement of the application of the principle of non-discrimination on the grounds of nationality as regards the EU citizens' entitlement to in-work benefits and social housing. In this respect, Mr Cameron suggested a four-year residency criterion and envisaged that all these proposals would form the content of an agreement which would eventually morph into a legally binding protocol which would be attached to the Treaties.

Although Mr Cameron wished for the United Kingdom to remain within the European Union, his commitment to the European Union project was not wholehearted. He had already succumbed to the pressure exerted by the Eurosceptic wing of his party and had pledged a referendum in 2010. Self-serving political ambition triumphed over political conviction and a commitment to 'the good' for the whole of Europe. In 2015, the same pressure led him to question fundamental, overarching principles of the European Union legal and political framework which had been settled since the late 1950s and the early 1960s, such as the role and powers of the Court of Justice of the European Union and the fundamental freedom of free movement and residence, one of the four pillars of the single market. Instead of leading both his party and the country, he allowed nationalist centrifugalism to dictate a new generative perspective which, unavoidably, weakened the 'case for Europe'[23] in the United Kingdom.

The similarities between the Euro-rebels' manifesto in 1995 and Mr Cameron's proposals two decades later are striking. Both reflected a call for the emasculation of state elites and the worshipping of a rather illusionary notion of state sovereignty.[24] In both cases, agency-related factors, discourse and their entanglement with broader temporal and spatial dynamics played an important role. Owing to their attention on actors' perceptions, beliefs, political and ideological commitments, strands of constructivism

[23] This is borrowed from Philippe de Schoutheete, *The Case for Europe; Unity, Diversity, and Democracy in the European Union* (Boulder: Lynne Rienner, 2000).

[24] See H. J. Laski, *Studies in the Problem of Sovereignty* (New Haven, CT: Yale University Press, 1917); N. G. Onuf, 'Sovereignty: Outline of a Conceptual History', 16 *Alternatives* (1991), pp. 425–46; N. MacCormick, 'Liberalism, Nationalism and the Post-Sovereign State', 44(3) *Political Studies* (1996), pp. 553–67; 'Beyond the Sovereign State', 56(1) *Modern Law Review* (1993), pp. 1–18; Dora Kostakopoulou, 'Floating Sovereignty: A Pathology or a Necessary Means of State Evolution?', 22(1) *Oxford Journal of Legal Studies* (2002), pp. 135–56; Neil Walker, *Intimations of Global Law* (Cambridge: Cambridge University Press, 2014).

and discursive institutionalism could accommodate this.[25] However, more emphasis on actor-based non-linear change and the institutional and temporal conditions for its embedment are needed. The Eurosceptic wing of the British Conservative Party maintained the same discursive claims about Europe for two decades, undid stable systems, created new narratives and new inter-subjectively shared meanings about the United Kingdom being dominated by 'Brussels' and 'under siege' by 'EU migrants' and refugees. In addition to 'path-dependent' and 'path-shaping' dynamics, to use the terms of the variant of historical institutionalism articulated by Hay[26] and of Schmidt's discursive institutionalism,[27] we saw the importance of the cumulative evolution of the British Eurosceptic discourse, the continuous political pressure actors exerted since the 1990s, misjudgements, defective leadership and the presence of politicians, such as Mr Farage, Mr Gove and Mr Johnson, the leaders of the Brexit campaign, who made such views appealing and legitimate.[28]

Mr Boris Johnson, a protagonist of the 'Vote Leave' campaign in the United Kingdom, delivered a personal message to the readers of a newspaper on the eve of the referendum. He wrote:

> tomorrow the people of this great country face a once-in-a-lifetime choice: ever closer political union inside a failing and anti-democratic EU, or freedom ... The EU is undemocratic, bureaucratic and unrepentant for its failings. Tomorrow you have an once-in-a-lifetime opportunity to take back control. To lift our eyes beyond the strangulation of the EU, to co-operate and trade not just across the European continent but with the rest of the world.[29]

[25] Colin Hay, 'Constructivist Institutionalism', in R. A. W. Rhodes et al. (eds.), *The Oxford Handbook of Political Institutions* (Oxford: Oxford University Press, 2006), pp. 56–74; Vivien Schmidt, 'Institutionalism', in Colin Hay, Michael Lister, and David Marsh (eds.), *The State: Theories and Issues* (Houndmills: Palgrave, 2006); 'Taking Ideas and Discourse Seriously: Explaining Change through Discursive Institutionalism as the Fourth New Institutionalism', 2 *European Political Science Review* (2010), pp. 1–25.

[26] Hay, 'Constructivist Institutionalism'.

[27] Schmidt, 'Institutionalism'; 'Taking Ideas and Discourse Seriously'.

[28] This differentiates my perspective from discoursive institutionalism and its conception of policy change as punctuated evolution. Generally speaking, discoursive institutionalists link institutional change to perceptions of institutional crisis coupled with the presence of alternative discourses providing solutions to perceived problems. For a critique and a defence of an agent-centred historical institutionalism; see Stephen Bell, 'Do We Really Need a New "Constructivist Institutionalism" to Explain Institutional Change?', 41(4) *British Journal of Political Science* (2011), pp. 883–906.

[29] Published in METRO, Wednesday 22 June 2016 at p. 5.

The view that EU is an undemocratic and bureaucratic organisation was not an invention of the 'Vote Leave' campaign in 2016; this line of reasoning was being disseminated in the public arena by the Right in the United Kingdom since the early 1990s.

In all this, timing is crucial. Strong path-dependencies can explain Mr Cameron's proposals as well as the 'sovereignty' maintenance preference of Eurosceptic MPs in the United Kingdom. But they cannot explain the popular appeal of this agenda among citizens disadvantaged by austerity and by other regional economic dislocations. Nor can they explain the circulation and reception for almost fifteen years of the 'no to Europe' ideas which had not been embedded within the formal institutional setting and did not resonate with long-standing institutional frames and policies.[30] Hence unanticipated developments, such as the Brexit vote in June 2016, which require adjusted theoretical frames.

Space and time thus intersect and impact on the (re-)production of discourses and their reception by the population. Pre-existing knowledge, personal ambitions, political commitments and ideology all play a role in the formation of actors' perceptions of the surrounding environment, their belief systems[31] and choice of actions in a specific setting.[32] This by no means rules out crucial errors, the adoption of flawed strategies, and the promotion of fictional goals. Error, confusion, irrational expectations and illusion are normal features of the human experience. But different ways of seeing things, pursuing interests and effecting changes in policy and politics are the by-product of the co-presence, co-dependence and co-implication of situated agency, institutions, discourse and space-time (*connexio rerum*). By maintaining the connectivity and interlocking of all these variables we can better understand the British Eurosceptic contestation of European supranationalism.

[30] My argument differs here from the premises of discursive institutionalism which looks at ideational variables in the context of institutional and/or interest-based variables; Vivien A. Schmidt and Claudio M. Radaelli, 'Policy Change and Discourse in Europe: Conceptual and Methodological Issues', 27(2) *West European Politics* (2004), pp. 183–210.

[31] Archer has outlined the mutually constitutive relation among structures, institutions and agency, but she also hesitates to imbue agents with a radically creative role; *Realist Social Theory: The Morphogenetic Approach.*

[32] Vivien Schmidt, 'Discoursive Institutionalism: The Explanatory Power of Ideas and Discourse', 11(1) *Annual Review of Political Science* (2008), pp. 303–26.

6.3 Conclusion

The foregoing discussion on the Brexit campaign showed that personal factors, deep-rooted attitudes of nationalism and insularism need to be considered alongside discourse and space-time. Following the result of the referendum held under the European Union (Referendum) Act 2015, the Prime Minister, Mr David Cameron, resigned, and Mrs Theresa May was selected by the Conservative Party as his successor. Although during the referendum campaign Mrs May campaigned for the Remain cause, she announced that her Government would ensure that the United Kingdom leaves the EU because 'Brexit means Brexit'. Her intention was to Activate Article 50 TEU, the Treaty's withdrawal clause, without seeking the UK Parliament's consent. The Miller litigation frustrated,[33] but did not abort, this intention. Article 50 TEU was triggered by Mrs May on 29 March 2017 thereby confirming, once again, the vital role of agency and the other integrated *connexio rerum* dimensions in procuring institutional and political change and the anticipated transition from supranationalism to some form of intergovernmentalism outside the Union.

[33] *Miller and Others* v. *Secretary of State for Exiting the European Union* [2016] EWHC 10 and [2017] UKSC 5.

Conclusion: Time and Understanding in Socio-Legal Research

Much of the research conducted in social sciences examines the multifarious activities of individuals and collectivities, their vulnerabilities as well as the role of institutions in the socio-political world. Although there exist many vantage points from which one can weave an understanding of how agents act, interact, bear, adapt to and shape the world, in the epistemology of social sciences monism and dualism have been seen to be convincing models.[1] In this book I called this assumption into question. I argued that neither monism nor dualism can provide convincing pathways for our quest for knowledge. This is partly because they cannot capture the complexity of our micro-, meso- and macro-worlds.

Seeking to address this lacuna, I outlined a *connexio rerum* model, based on the interrelations of agency, institutions, discourse and space-time (Chapter 1). I termed this institutional constructivism and showed that it enables multiple 'loops' among the above-mentioned variables. Agency, institutions, discourse and space-time all interact in the production of social phenomena, but they do not become fused (Chapter 2). They remain distinguished within a unitary structural inter-relation and are conjointly present. There is thus no absorption and no negation of any of these variables within the overall explanatory framework. It would not be correct to characterise institutional constructivism as either agency-centred or institution-centred or as discourse-centred. Instead of emphasising a 'variable-centeredness' and one-link conceptualisations, it is premised on connectionalism. In other words, it highlights the importance of an awareness of the correlation of time(s), space(s), institutions(s), discourse(s)

[1] Compare Stephen Toulmin, 'From Form to Function: Philosophy and History of Science in the 1950s and Now', 106(3) *Daedalus* (1977), pp. 143–62. Toulmin notes the changes that triggered intellectual and conceptual innovation and seeks to understand 'how historical changes give authority to new concepts, new theories, even new methods of thought, inquiry and argument'; Ibid., at p. 148. See also Arthur L. Stinchcombe, *Constructing Social Theories*, (New York: Harcourt, Brace and World, Inc., 1968); Russell Ackoff, *The Design of Social Research* (Chicago, IL: Chicago University Press, 1953).

and agency in seeking to account for phenomena, human conduct, policy outputs, institutional designs, crises and changes (Chapter 3).

I then sought to apply the model to aspects of EU law and policy which I have theorised and examined for more than twenty years and to the contemporary contestation of supranationalism in the United Kingdom. This application revealed that institutional constructivism discourages quests for premature ultimates and for quick answers by definition. It calls for circumspection, and for the careful examination of the variables and their co-implication. Lifting one variable out of their interacted play and privileging it would involve a serious risk of over-simplification. For in reality, everything is tangled within a reflexive circuit.

In this respect, institutional constructivism aids social scientific enquiries by reminding – not prescribing. It reminds researchers that the interactions among the variables and their manifestations, be they clearly visible or less so, have no beginning and no end. They merge in different ways, enfold and unfold in a cyclical and dynamic pattern. It is as if we are observing an unfolding scroll or a motion-picture. But the interactions are also bound to remain incomplete for the knower (the GIT variable discussed in Chapters 1 and 2). As noted earlier, when the focus of scientific attention is a concrete and particular *x*, be this either a phenomenon or an event or a policy or an institution, we often tend to adopt an instantaneous view. We forget that *x* took place within a certain spatio-temporal matrix and that it has had its own time (both past and future) and its own context that, in fact, may no longer exist. And if *x*'s time no longer exists and the wider context within which *x* needs to be understood may have been phased out, it becomes difficult to place it within them. We might seek deeper explanations of its content, estimate the motives and analyse the decisions of the parties involved, and ask a plethora of questions. Does *x* exemplify a deeper trend? Or was it triggered by *y* alone or *y* and *z*? Should it have been predictable on the basis of our knowledge of our practices or circumstances? But, naturally, our questions and answers cannot eliminate uncertainty and ambiguity.

The ambiguity that accompanies social scientific enquiries is doubled, if one switches the lens from *x* to the observer and the knower. It is always possible that when we are looking at *x* in time *t*, we do not see all there is to see. We may have a partial view; we only observe one aspect of it and disregard others. It could also mean that we focus on its beginning, because we are interested in establishing a causation and not in examining outcomes or implications. By so doing, we bracket the process of its unfolding. Or we might focus on the outcome and follow a reverse causation process in an attempt to figure out actors' interests and preferences. More often than not we also dissect it into small pieces or choose to look at one side of a prism thereby imposing our own boundaries on a complex and multidimensional reality in motion. By so doing, we reduce the variety and variability that surround realities. Our observations thus have their own temporal, spatial and substantive limits.

In fact, even when we intend to capture *x*'s duration, we tend to give it a beginning, a middle point and an end. In other words, we freeze it in time in order to be able to examine it. Its dynamic reality is unavoidably reduced consciously or unconsciously. Its wholeness could also become fragmented because what is to be known or what is of interest is determined by the observer who will then utilise their (imperfect) knowledge to decipher it.[2] In this way, several dimensions of *x* might be omitted because we cannot (due to bounded rationality, limited knowledge) or will not (due to misleading premises and flawed lenses) or choose not to (due to ideological reasons or other cognitive bias) include them. In an attempt to avoid staticity, fragmentation and partiality, the *connexio rerum* approach brings forth an interactive multivariable and yet integrated alternative.

This epistemological perspective stands in contrast to linear models, consisting of straight lines between A and B, one link causation patterns and ideas of progressive development and of life evolving in an upward dimension. Those who believe that humankind is progressively moving towards more advanced and liberated states of existence and in upward development might discern that there is nothing remotely teleological in this model. Constructivism furnishes connections, potentialities and possibilities; it does not delineate finalities or destinations. This is how it contributes to knowledge.

Readers might wonder, here, whether my alternative could succeed in eliminating what Kahneman and Tversky have called the 'anchoring' of the past on the present or the base present.[3] This is a significant problem in social research. The problem is that, in such cases, our 'optikon', that is, the observation standpoint, often determines how we look at the past, what we see in it and how we assess it. We may select elements of the past which fit nicely with the information we hold in the present or which may reflect

[2] Compare Alain Badiou's argument that 'the event appears as an interruption of existing order, the supplement that is knowable and accounted for' in *The Theory of the Subject* (Bloomsbury Academic: London, 2009), p. 270. See also, Sheldon Wolin, 'What Time Is It?', 1 *Theory and Event* (1997), p. 1; K. Hutchings, *Time and World Politics: Thinking the Present* (Manchester: Manchester University Press, 2008).

[3] Kahneman, *Thinking Fast and Slow*, ch. 11.

the valuations we hold in the present. In other words, from an optikon, the observer has one view and this is also a view from above. Understandably, this has implications. As Mead noted: 'the past, which must then be looked at from the standpoint of the emergent, becomes a different past'.[4] In responding to this concern, I would argue that neither institutional constructivism nor any other epistemological model could eliminate fully the problem of 'anchoring' or the retroactive action of the present on the past. In mathematics, researchers refer to a Markov chain in order to show that what happens next depends on what has just happened. Although indeterminism in social science research would not accommodate Markov chains perfectly, it is, nevertheless, true that we are embedded within a present and that all we can do is to be aware of the fact that the past is the locus of another reality which is parallel to our realities. Starting from the latter, researchers thus have to travel into the past thereby modifying, adjusting and eventually changing the lens. Social scientific enquiries therefore cannot but be hermeneutical[5] and full of turns and zig-zags.

Herein lies an additional difficulty: would the application of institutional constructivism lead to authoritatively correct explanations of social scientific phenomena? I must confess that this is a very hard question to answer. Answering it in the affirmative would lead me to impose an inappropriate, and thus arbitrary, closure on the past. The future is radically open, but I would have to assume that the past is not and thus an inquiry would yield the 'correct' or 'authoritative' narrative of it. I am rather reluctant to do so. This is not because I believe that the past can be re-written; clearly, it cannot: past decisions cannot be unmade, events cannot be undone and courses of actions cannot be reversed retrospectively. But, they can be reinterpreted, 're-presented', and aspects of them could be seen in a new light or be assessed on the basis of new realisations. Knowers could commence their observations from different premises, or be situated within different frames of reference which may influence, or, sometimes, even command the dimensions of the past they select or the relevance they attribute to it or to the conditions of it for present purposes. In other words, the past is encased within an open circle, and, when we investigate it, we bring it into a free and dynamic relation with the present and our present reality. It becomes assimilated and this sustains its openness. No investigation, no social scientific inquiry is possible with reference solely to the past and

[4] Mead, *The Philosophy of the Present*, p. 2.

[5] Hans Georg Gadamer, *Truth and Method*, 2nd edn (London: Sheed and Ward, 1979). Compare also E. Bloch, *The Principle of Hope* (Cambridge, MA: MIT Press, 1986).

without this double movement between the present and the past. Both are intertwined and this means that the past never assumes an authoritative 'final' shape. It cannot become ossified. It is thus quite likely that both Researcher A in a spatio-temporal system (st) and Researcher B in another location and ten years later (s2*t*+10) might produce 'correct' accounts of *x* which diverge or converge. But the answers would not be identical. Goethe captured this eloquently: 'one will in the same city hear an important event narrated differently in the morning and in the evening'.[6] It is like the slicing of an orange – the view changes depending on how it is split and sliced. We may have two or more different slices of the same orange or two or more versions of the same story. To return to the question posed at the outset of this paragraph, therefore, institutional constructivism could not lead to convergent stories or to 'authoritatively correct' accounts. But it would lead to more complex and holistic accounts.

The world is changing very fast and it has become increasingly difficult for human beings to keep pace with change and to apprehend it. Yet, the social scientific narratives we produce for a world in change do not reflect this. Instead of accepting the challenge to become more creative and confident problem-solvers, we tend to be either nostalgic about a slower motion of the world or cynical about the present and the future. Both dispositions, however, converge on the inclusion of a bias towards staticity and an (illusionary) preference for certainty. This is due to our need for predictability and our often illusionary quest for certainty. Yet, everything flows and change is everywhere. Heraclitus observed that 'ta panta rei' (all flows) and Whitehead used the phrase 'the flux of things'[7] to describe incessant change.

Is there direction to this change? Do we know where we are heading? Does time have a definite arrow?[8] I am not convinced that it has. Whitehead spoke of supersession, whereby each occasion is superseded by other occasions, but did not incorporate an end point or a climax into his thinking.[9] In fact, he stated explicitly that time requires incompleteness.[10]

6 Cited in Reinhard Koselleck, *Futures Past: On the Semantics of Historical Time* (New York: Columbia University Press, 1979), p. 114.

7 Alfred North Whitehead, *Process and Reality* (New York: Macmillan Co., 1929), ch. 10, part II.

8 See, *inter alia*, H. Reichenbach, *The Direction of Time* (Berkeley: University of California Press, 1956); G. J. Whitrow, *The Natural Philosophy of Time* (London: Nelson: 1961).

9 Alfred North Whitehead, 'Time', in Browning (ed.), *Philosophers of Process*, pp. 313–14. Compare, here, T. S. Eliot's verses: 'Or of a future that is not liable Like the past, to have no destination; 'The Dry Salvages', Eliot, *The Complete Poems and Plays*, p. 186.

10 Whitehead, *Philosophers of Process*, p. 315.

If something were complete, a present without a future, without tomorrow, then one could talk about the freezing of time or the suspension of time. It seems to me that change bears a strong resemblance to the Aboriginal conception of time as an unfolding wave; a wave with ups and downs and curves on which things can move in both directions. The direction of it is instigated by many things, including human actions and reactions. And human actions and reactions entail both beauty and unimaginable destruction, forward and backward motion and upward and downward slopes. There is a line in T. S. Eliot's Choruses From the Rock (1934) which, referring to the unemployed, is quite intriguing:

> But stand with empty hands and palms turned upwards
>
> In an age which advances progressively backwards?[11]

Like the Bergsonian notion of duration,[12] the dimensions of time, past and future, all merge in a present never achieving a completed state but being essentially condemned to a process of ever-changing and ever-becoming. A becoming in time and, simultaneously, making time. This is a becoming without a final shape or a final resting place or even a final destination. Heracletus captured this in Fragment 60: 'The road upward and downward is one and the same' (my translation). This insight should not be absent in social research. For when social scientists examine things a posteriori work in the way that geologists work; they seek to uncover layers of historicity, of decision-making, action, inaction and crisis, each piled on the other. They look for, and ascribe, serialities and causations. There is nothing fundamentally wrong with this in so far as it is acknowledged that such 'sociogeochronology' is just one dimension. Everything is complex and enquiries about the object-to-subject-to-object, the self-to-other-to-self, here-and-now to there-and-then to here-and-now bring forth the possibility of a knowledge of the dynamic interdependence of agency, institutions, discourse and space-time. The latter can only be understood in their necessary correlation.

If one pauses for a moment to appreciate the creativity involved in theoretical frameworks and models, one will realise that the ultimate source of our conceptual categories and systems of thought is socio-political life itself. And even though it is often understood in retrospect and explained

[11] Eliot, *The Complete Poems and Plays*, p. 161.

[12] It is important to mention here that Bergson did not split 'duree' into before and after; he maintained the fusion of past, present and past; Henri Bergson, *Time and Free Will* (New York: Macmillan, 1910).

in partial ways, it is lived and relived in all its diversity, multi-layered quality and ambiguity. The point of any scientific inquiry is not to reduce this diversity and complexity by embracing monism or dualism, but to capture them as fully as possible. This is what I endeavoured to do in this book. As Cooley beautifully remarked a hundred years ago, 'any real study of society must be first, last, and nearly all the time a study of process.'[13]

[13] Cooley, *Social Process*, p. 396.

INDEX